2019

Pause you who read this, and think for a moment of the long chain of iron or gold, of thorns or flowers, that would never have bound you but for the formation of the first link on one memorable day.

— Charles Dickens, *Great Expectations*

PRAISE FOR *THE PRINCE AND THE ASSASSIN*

It illuminates a fascinating but forgotten milepost in Australian history.
— Professor Geoffrey Blainey, AC

A compelling account of one of the most controversial political crimes in Australian history, it shows how religious zealotry, bigotry and political over-reaction can bring a community to the brink of disorder...

All contemporary politicians and community leaders dealing with the continuing fallout from 9/11 should read it.
— Professor Greg Woods QC, legal historian.

Marvellous...A truly gripping tale, wonderfully researched.
— Jane Ridley, Author, Broadcaster and Professor of Modern History, University of Buckingham, United Kingdom

A gripping tale of royal debauchery, abandoned priesthood, mental infirmity and Irish rebellion, leading to the attempted assassination of Queen Victoria's favourite son... This book has the excitement of a racy political crime thriller, backed by the most sound historical research. It gives the impression of an account written by an eyewitness. There are lessons for us today from the politicians' overreaction to what was mistakenly viewed as an existential threat to Australian society.
— Mark Tedeschi, AM, QC Senior Crown Prosecutor, NSW

...One and half centuries later, in an era of fresh anxiety about terrorism, Australia is again facing a test of character. This time it is Muslim Australians who bear the brunt of prejudice, suspicion and guilt by association. Harris's book, a fascinating read at multiple levels, helps frame current anxieties in a deeper context.
— Professor Greg Barton, Research Professor in Global Islamic Politics, Alfred Deakin Institute (ADI), Co-Editor, *Islam Christian Muslim Relations*, Senior Fellow, Hedayah, Abu Dhabi

Harris aims to be more than simply a teller of history. He also wants us to learn from history and uses many quotes from the archives that are remarkably similar in tone and temper to the anti-foreigner, anti-Muslim language of today.
— John Algate, *The Weekend Australian*

Steve Harris's book The Prince and the Assassin *has excavated from the past a little remembered incident that had huge implications at the time and still resonates to this day.*
— Ronan McGreevy, *The Irish Times*

For the golden chain that
has been my mother and father.

THE LOST BOYS OF MR DICKENS

Published by Melbourne Books
Level 9, 100 Collins Street,
Melbourne, VIC 3000
Australia
www.melbournebooks.com.au
info@melbournebooks.com.au

Title: The Lost Boys of Mr Dickens: How the British
Empire turned artful dodgers into child killers
Author: Steve Harris
ISBN: 9781925556988
Cover design: Marianna Berek-Lewis

A catalogue record for this
book is available from the
National Library of Australia

Also by Steve Harris:

*Solomon's Noose: The True Story of Her Majesty's
Hangman of Hobart*

*The Prince and The Assassin: Australia's First Royal
Tour and Portent of World Terror*

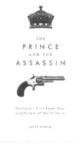

THE
LOST BOYS
OF
MR DICKENS

How the British Empire turned
artful dodgers into child killers

STEVE HARRIS

M
MELBOURNE BOOKS

CONTENTS

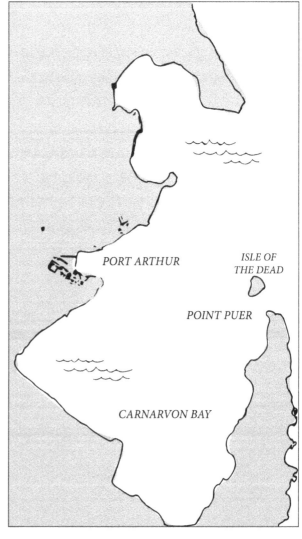

AUTHOR'S NOTE

The Lost Boys of Mr Dickens is non-fictional history, drawing on national and regional archives in Australia and the UK, 19th century British and Australian newspapers, British and Australian court records, British Parliamentary and Colonial Office records, the UNESCO recognised Van Diemen's Land convict records, colonial and convict memoirs and correspondence, academic research, published history, biographies and the reportage of Charles Dickens.

1

A MURDEROUS TYPE

Subdue your appetites, my dears, and you've conquered human nature.
— Charles Dickens, *Nicholas Nickleby*

RUHTRA TROP TA REDRUM.

To an unpractised eye it seemed an obscure Latin phrase, but not to those who spent their days in the alchemy of fonts, picas, stones, quoins and forms that formed a newspaper. The editors, printers and their 'devils', as apprentices were known, knew that only when the reverse type had been compressed, inked, and printed would it reveal to the world its true face.

And its meaning was even better understood by those among them who were amid almost 80,000 men, boys, women and girls born ordinary folk in England, Scotland, Ireland and Wales, whose circumstances and choices in the lottery of life put them on an extraordinary path to the other side of the world. Behind them were lives of impoverishment, abandonment and struggle to survive on the street by picking pockets, robbing orchards, burgling homes or counterfeiting coin, and the prejudice and panic of those who branded them a threat to the cradle of the British Empire. And so they were exiled to the world's newest and most remote settlement 12,000 miles (19,000 km) away, condemned never to return.

Each had endured sentences of seven or fourteen years in this unique place called Van Diemen's Land, where the ancient Aboriginal civilisation had been swept aside to enable, for the first time in the world, a foreign society establishing a new one on the backs of its unwanted. A settlement of conflict between Old and New worlds, man and nature, good and evil, hope and hell.

In a smoky printery, putting the final touches to the July 1843 edition of the *Colonial Times,* their convict irons and manacles were gone but the shadow and stain of convictism were immoveable, their past indelibly inked and readily cited. Their papers showed them to be free men, but they were living in an island run as Her Majesty's gaol. A colonial and penal fiefdom where traditional English rights and liberties were seen as a threat, and colonial officers and convicts were equally familiar with the blurred lines of vice and virtue, and truth and justice — each in the eye of the beholder.

The governor and his loyal faction only wanted their truth and justice to prevail, lest there be any disruption to the dutiful and tyrannical imposition of regulations and punishment. Many under their rule self-servingly or meekly saluted but some resisted and pursued their own voice, marching to the typesetting beat of the *Colonial Times; Hobart Town Advertiser; Courier; Austral-Asiatic Review, Tasmanian and Australian Advertiser; Britannia and Trades Advocate; Hobarton Guardian; Teetotal Advocate; Tasmanian and Austral Asiatic Review; True Colonist; Hobart Town Courier* or *Van Diemen's Land Chronicle.*

Some were founded by those who had been punished but survived and remained resilient enough to take up weapons of ink and paper. Henry Savery, a forger, ignored laws prohibiting convicts from writing to pen satirical newspaper articles and the country's first novel, *Quintus Servinton: A tale founded upon Incidents of Real Occurrence (1831);* Andrew Bent, a convicted burglar, started the colony's first independent newspaper and printed the first literature, *Michael Howe: The last and worst of the Bushrangers of Van Diemen's Land (1818)* by Thomas Wells. Robert Murray, a bigamist, wrote anonymous newspaper letters virulently critical of colonial administration, before turning to journalism and editing. They and their successors were willing to write and publish even under the threat of official closure, commercial and political bastardry, libel writs, damnation or even the challenge of a duel.

The *Colonial Times'* masthead motto steadfastly proclaimed its mission: 'What is it but a map of busy life in its fluctuations and vast concerns'. But one man appreciated, better than most, the enormity and importance of 'mapping' life and its fluctuations of truth and justice, casting his own shadow over Van Diemen's Land without ever setting foot on Australian soil: Charles John Huffam Dickens.

As a boy he had personally lived the perils of severe British punishment and as a young reporter on *The Mirror of Parliament, The True Sun* and covering parliament for *The Morning Chronicle,* he had been appalled by parliamentary and judicial expediency and hypocrisy. He used his newspaper journalism and editing skills to pen powerful social observation and criticism on the journey of boys and men from petty crime to houses of correction, then gaols, prison hulks and convict ships to the colonies of Australia. Then, after his first novel *The Posthumous Papers of the Pickwick Club (1836),* better known as *The Pickwick Papers,* took off, Dickens began to inform and inspire readers around the world, his work translated into French, Italian, Spanish, Turkish, Russian and Chinese. But nowhere did his work resonate more strongly than in faraway Van Diemen's Land: the extreme outcome of the injustices and prejudices he exposed, the fate of those characters transported to Australian colonies in his novels, the real-life world for thousands of 'artful dodgers' like Oliver Twist and Jack Dawkins.

At the human stock exchange that was the Hobart Town docks, the unloading of British or colonial newspapers containing his Boz sketches of life in Britain's streets, courts and gaols were eagerly sought out, as were any crates of his books or complete volumes of magazines containing his serialized work, such as *Master Humphrey's Clock*, the ambitious weekly literary magazine he published himself.

This presence was fully realised in the numerous taverns of Hobart Town, such as the Pickwick Tavern in Liverpool Street. The Pickwick had opened in 1839, capitalising on the popularity of Dickens after a Launceston printer and entrepreneur sensationally published twenty-four serial parts of a pirated copy of *The Posthumous Papers of the Pickwick Club*. It was at places such as the Pickwick where the likes of a coterie, who had traded chains for ink and type, convened to share their passion for the author and his work and bring their own Dickensian dissection to life in a penal colony. Convicts knew better than most about the elusiveness of justice, and convict-turned-newspaper men knew better than most about the elusiveness of truth: sometimes seen and sometimes unseen, or suppressed or dictated or ignored for so long its very meaning became questionable.

For those who had been evicted from life in their homeland to exile at the bottom of the world, Dickens was a welcome voice for those who were long denied one. His own father had been in prison, forcing Dickens to fend for himself, and through his own personal experiences and exposure as a reporter to the trials of the poor and the prejudice and hypocrisy of ruling classes, he became a welcome and influential companion.

Dickens' Fagin, Sikes, Bumble and Dawkins characters were based on what he observed in the streets and courts of London, including some who were transported to Van Diemen's Land such as young Samuel Holmes, thought to be the inspiration for Jack

Early Hobart Town. *Hunters Island, Hobart Town*, illustration, 1829. Image courtesy Libraries Tasmania, NS1013/1/1876.

'the artful dodger' Dawkins. And publicity about the London trial of infamous receiver Isaac 'Ikey' Solomon – who was transported to Port Arthur before running a tobacco shop in Hobart Town and helping the drive to build Australia's first synagogue – was widely thought to have inspired Dickens' pickpocket gang boss Fagin in *Oliver Twist*, the novel whose very name was a Dickens nod to the potential fate of all young criminals: to twist on the end of a hangman's noose.

In February 1843 Hobart Town debated the merits of a 'new domestic drama' based on *Barnaby Rudge 1841*, Dickens' first historical novel, at the Royal Victoria Theatre just down the street from the Campbell Street barracks. Described by the *Courier* 'as amusing as the late favourite *Nicholas Nickleby*',[1] *Barnaby Rudge* touched a nerve with its portraits of ordinary individuals swept up in social crisis amid the contrast of aristocracy and underbelly, revealing how impoverishment and family circumstance could change one's life forever, and how moral pursuits and panic could lead to dangerous and unintended consequences.

These were the underlying themes of the lottery of life and convictism, the basis of many a discussion in taverns like the Pickwick, where more than one observed that law makers and the lawless alike were engaged in the same contests and motivations of power, rivalry, self-interest, deceit and fear. As Dickens observed in 1837 in *Oliver Twist*, there were men who 'acquire peculiar value and dignity' from their cloaks of office, be it the uniform of a governor or soldier, silk gowns of lawyers and judges, or the apron of a bishop, but also that virtue 'shows quite as well in rags and patches as she does in purple and fine linen'.[2] Strip the 'uniform' away, as Dickens asked, 'what are they? Men, mere men'.[3]

Every 'mere man', convict or free, was pursuing his own survival, sense of truth, justice and entitlement. In an article reprinted from *Bentley's Miscellany* on the effects of circumstance on character, the publication's founder Dr William Maginn alluded to Dickens, his first editor, and Shakespeare:

> In the best of us all there are many blots, in the worst many
> traces of goodness. There is no such thing as angels or devils
> in the world….all our virtues close border on vices, and are
> frequently blended…people do not commit wicked actions
> from the mere love of wickedness, there must always be an
> incentive of precisely the same kind as that which stimulates
> the noblest actions – ambition, love of adventure, passion,
> necessity.[4]

No man, woman or child in Van Diemen's Land was born an angel or
devil, but each was uniquely compressed in a place out of sight and
out of mind, each with his or her own ambition, passion or necessity.

This reality was powerfully driven home on a winter's day,
Tuesday 18 July 1843. The *Colonial Times*' publisher, John Macdougall
was transported for life for 'sinking a ship' in a commercial insurance
dispute before being given a pardon after serving fourteen years but
was now a free man and ready to print his latest edition. He called
an end to 'finishing day' and ordered the pumping of the iron press.

His printers and editors probably ended their finishing day's
work by ambling to the Pickwick or their latest tavern of choice
absorb and dissect the freshly printed pages, the paper still slightly
damp but warm, the ink still willing to leave an imprint. Amid the
tightly compressed lines of small type, eyes quickly went to the
Domestic Intelligence column on Page 3. Many sensed these were the
first words of what would be an immediate sensation in the colony,
and perhaps well beyond when the newspaper found its usual way
across the seas to London to the Colonial Office and the Jerusalem
Coffee House subscription room and possibly London's Garrick
Club, where Dickens sojourned with other 'gentlemen of refinement
and education'.

What a printer's devil had typeset as *RUHTRA TROP TA
REDRUM* now revealed its true face: *MURDER AT PORT ARTHUR*.

Then: 'Two youths have been conveyed from Port Arthur to this city, charged with the murder of a free overseer by striking him on the head with a stone hammer.'

Close by was a brief summary of the matters listed for Supreme Court trial that day before his Honour the Chief Justice, eleven cases in total 'including those of two lads for murder at Port Arthur.'[5]

A 'Murder at Port Arthur' headline was nothing remarkable in a colony born of criminality, where reports of violence and manhunts for convict 'bolters' or bushrangers and hangings 'at the usual hour' were part of the everyday, and Port Arthur was frequently painted as a 'Gomorrah — Earthly Hell'[6] of incorrigibles whose repeat crimes meant they had to be isolated even in a land of exile. But a murder involving two lads was not part of the everyday. Young convicts were known to be insolent, profane, thieving and dishonest, but none had been seen as boys capable of murder. Until now.

Those former convicts familiar with settlements of punishment would have quickly sensed the *Colonial Times*' headline was probably not entirely correct: if two lads were involved, then the murder would not have been at Port Arthur, but another place even more isolated, even more extraordinary: Point Puer. A place where some 3000 young boys, real life Oliver Twists, Charles Bates and Jack Dawkins, were exiled between 1834 and 1849 in the British Empire's most desperate and boldest social experiment: to rid the Old World of its unwanted poor and criminal children, be they more victim or villain, by transporting them to the New World.

The proclaimed intent was to suppress what was becoming known as juvenile delinquency, to 'save' boys as young as nine or ten from a lifetime of poverty-induced criminality by transporting them in prison ships to exile on the other side of the world to serve out long sentences under armed guard in the world's first prison created exclusively for boys.

Many convicts first heard it as Point 'Pure', until someone explained Puer was a Latin word for 'boy'. But others knew it as also a term used for the dog faeces collected from the streets and hand-rubbed into hides at the leather tanneries in Bermondsey, or a French word for stink or a Roman term for sex slave. Those who survived Point Puer might have come to their own definition of a place which was portrayed as a chance for a boy to escape an old life, and some did, but others could not see the chance or did not want to take it.

Whatever the true meaning of its name, the story of the juvenile Port Arthur was the stuff of a Dickens novel, a Boys Town created by prejudice and justice at the heart of a rich and mighty Empire, its most remote outpost housing a generation of boys stolen away from whatever passed for their childhood and families. Here they were expediently despatched out of mind and sight to the last inhabited landform before Antarctica where, off-limits to anyone but a few approved visitors, the chain of Her Majesty's justice would employ severe discipline and punishment to perhaps 'save' some and set them on the 'right path'.

The author would have been drawn to the conflict of colonial administrators and their supporters lauding Point Puer as one of humanity's 'most successful and gratifying' experiments, while others boldly denounced it as a cruel and failed expediency. What might he make of this murder story within a bigger convict story which was part of a bigger British society story? Would he see Point Puer boys as cold-hearted killers or as sad victims of a cold-hearted world? How would he judge the world's greatest empire delivering unwanted children to exile on the other side of the world? Where was the true wickedness? Might he paint a picture that, like pieces of printing type, the true face of 'mere men' or 'mere boys' were only ever revealed when they were compressed together?

The judgment of Dickens would never be written, but in the taverns of Hobart Town and the salons of the colony's administrators an unanticipated truth had revealed itself: despite the averred salvation hopes of government and colonial officers in Whitehall and Van Diemen's Land, Her Majesty's Boys Prison at Point Puer had seen the head of an overseer smashed in.

Perhaps this first boys' murder and pending trial was the final chapter of a story that even Dickens himself could not have imagined in the lottery of life's circumstances and choices. But in the days to come, the editors and printers of the *Colonial Times* and other papers in the colony would tell the story of what happened on a murderous day at Point Puer, and whether two boys would soon be hanging by the neck until dead. For now, as an icy air began to drape the Hobart Town darkness, its residents had the same simple question on their minds: How could the lives of two little boys come to this?

2

A LAW UNTO THEMSELVES

There are many pleasant fictions of the law...but there is not one so... practically humorous as that which supposes every man to be of equal value in its impartial eye.
— Charles Dickens, *Nicholas Nickleby*

Experience, newspapers, Boz sketches, and reading of *Oliver Twist, Pickwick Papers, Mr Nickleby, The Old Curiosity Shop and Barnaby Rudge* helped many in Van Diemen's Land piece together some understanding of the causes and circumstances of their lives.

New industrial machines of the 19th century had unleashed power and profit for the cradle of the British Empire, but impoverishment and pain for many. With thousands of poor rural families trying to escape unemployment and poverty by fleeing to larger towns and cities without any promise of work or shelter, and the exodus coming at the same time as the demobbing of the army and navy at the end of the Napoleonic wars, Britain's population almost doubled from about eight million to fifteen million by 1841.

What was harder to understand was that many unemployed, poor and hungry families felt they had no choice but to set their children — nearly forty percent of England's population in the 1830s were aged fourteen and under — on a path of dangerous uncertainty. Thousands, especially boys, were forced to thieve to help sustain a family, or simply abandoned onto the street by impoverished, imprisoned, abusive or drunkard fathers, stepfathers or mothers. Others were orphaned.

The result was a rising tide, estimated at twenty-five percent a year,[1] of youngsters forced to survive by cunning and crime. The outbreak of pickpocketing, theft and house break-ins fuelled a moral panic among middle and ruling classes worried about their personal well-being and property being at risk from immoral and dangerous 'felons' and 'undesirables'. Although when some of the same offences were committed by their own children, they were dismissed as mere 'pranks' or 'frolics', as a Select Committee on Criminal Commitments and Convictions acknowledged:

> Sons of persons of the highest rank in this country… often commit offences out of the exuberance of spirits and activity, which the law, if it visited them at all, must visit by sentences of great severity…(offences) passed over as frolics in the sons of the rich are treated in the children of the poor as crimes of magnitude.[2]

But the pride and prejudice of the 'haves', such as the Lord Chancellor, Lord Eldon, who admitted to his own boyhood poaching and fruit thieving, insisted such offences of the 'have nots' be rigorously pursued. The profane language, gambling and sexual licentiousness of street boys and girls further challenged English morality and stoked fears of a fracturing of the very foundations of English

Depiction of a scene in London's criminal underworld, as illustrated in Charles Dickens' *Oliver Twist*. *Oliver introduced to the Respectable Old Gentleman*, illustration, George Cruikshank, 1837. Image courtesy The Charles Dickens Page website. https://charlesdickenspage.com/illustrations_web/Oliver_Twist/Oliver_Twist_05.jpg

Young children pickpocketing in the streets of England, as illustrated in Charles Dickens' *Oliver Twist*. *Oliver amazed at the Dodger's Mode of 'going to work'*, illustration, George Cruikshank, 1837. Image courtesy The Charles Dickens Page website. https:// charlesdickenspage.com/illustrations_web/Oliver_Twist/Oliver_Twist_06.jpg society, built on obedience to God and law. There were concerns that there would be a replica of the dark moment portrayed by Dickens in *Barnaby Rudge* — the 1780 Gordon riots in London in which the Army killed nearly 300 people protesting on a range of economic, nationalist, social and religious issues — or even of the French Revolution of 1789–1799.

Boy thieves and scavengers were seen to be 'cradled in iniquity',[3] corrupted from birth and dangerous, or perishing under parental neglect, abandonment or tutoring. Living in what was seen as Godless depravity, running wild on the streets, they were variously known as 'street urchins' or 'street arabs' and then 'undesirables' before a new catch-all term emerged: 'delinquent', derived from the Latin for offender.

Within a few years, tens of thousands of delinquents were pressed into court rooms and the harshness of correction houses or workhouses. Many a boy would, like Oliver Twist, plead 'Please Sir, I want some more', but there was never more food, or sympathy. In the British newspapers some reformers and critics lamented a world where adults created or administered the very environment that forced children into crime, and then exacerbated the problem through legal and judicial zealotry. But the moneyed, pious and powerful reflected an Old Testament view that some, including children, are naturally evil and wicked. Insisting that such depraved, deviant and dangerous street urchins had to be put onto the 'right path' and a higher state of Godly grace, and to preserve and promote the overall 'good' the state had to control and punish any dangerous forces and 'win' the war.

In this climate of impoverishment, fear and loathing, children comprised nearly half the population, but had no laws protecting their childhood. There was nothing to ensure they lived in a proper home or attended school, or were protected from the perils of drinking, gambling or sex. Nothing to stop boys as young as six being used in dangerous work of climbing inside chimneys and scrapping in dirty and dangerous textile mills and factories. They were a generation whose childhood was bereft of family, love, shelter, food, clothing, education and morality, a generation not living as children in heart and mind but not yet adults. Dickens himself had narrowly avoided the same reality: just two days after he turned twelve the author's father was sent to Marshalsea Prison over a debt to a baker. While his mother and younger siblings joined their father in gaol for three months before the debt was paid off, Charles was despatched to Warren's Blacking Factory at Hungerford Stairs on the Thames to paste labels onto blacking pots for ten hours a day, six days a week, for a shilling a day. The Dickens family was relatively fortunate. Other fathers were jailed for petty offences — one was taken from his family for stealing nails to build his son a rabbit hutch — or fined when they clearly had not a penny to their name, and the absence of any household income, legitimate or otherwise, forced wives and children to steal or starve on minimal parish aid.

From 1744, a Vagrancy Act had declared street boys 'rogues' and 'vagabonds' and sentenced them to houses of correction for up to two years, often with a whipping to drive home the message, while others over twelve were effectively dragooned into 'his Majesty's Service, either by sea or land'. But as the criminal tide of 'alien' boys rose, so did the arsenal of severe laws and punishment. The number of crimes for which a person risked a walk to the gallows rose to more than 220 by the early 1800s, not just for murder, treason, rape and counterfeiting, but also for pickpocketing, shoplifting, poaching and burglary — the common purview of children. There was 'probably no other country in the world in which so many and so great a variety of human actions are punishable with the loss of life as in England'.[4]

The 1824 Vagrancy Act made it criminal for boys to even engage in their favourite street pastimes of playing and betting on skittles, coin-tossing, marbles or cards. Hungry boys stealing someone's vegetables or fruit were deemed criminal three years later under a

Malicious Trespass Act — one conservative MP opining that country gentlemen had 'suffered much by the deprivation of our turnips' by young thieves, so 'we have at length determined to put an end to this practice and my good friend the Minister has been so obliging as to make it death'.[5]

In 1829, Sir Robert Peel introduced a full-time professional police force for greater London and new constables enthusiastically pursued the 'enemy', an estimated 50,000 poor and criminal within 5 miles (8 km) of St Paul's Cathedral.[6] New laws allowed police to apprehend, without warrant, anyone they thought to be 'loose, idle and disorderly...or whom he shall have just cause to suspect of any evil designs', or found between sunset and 8am sleeping or loitering outdoors and unable to give 'a satisfactory account of themselves'.[7] A new, tougher Poor Law Act in 1834 disgusted Dickens, and his coverage of it for the *Morning Chronicle* partly inspired *Oliver Twist*. He was outraged that workhouses denied relief for many seeking shelter and food due to poverty, illness, mental or physical disability, or the plight of babies, children, and the aged. The core concern of authority was only whether they were 'deserving' or 'undeserving' poor: those deemed to be at the door from 'idle, disorderly or thriftless habits, have reduced themselves to merited indigence and disgrace', and would find life inside 'harsh, monotonous and characterised by the intent of improving the inmate's moral character'. Such 'improvement' could come through halving of an already miserable diet, time in the 'black hole', or removal to a 'pauper farm' where contractors warehoused the poor even more cheaply.[8]

Some could see the demon of law-making could have unintended consequences, especially when, as Newgate prison schoolmaster Thomas Wontner observed, 'any legal statutes are constructed with no other view than to protect the rich from punishment...protecting the rich...against the poor'.[9] Reforming reporters like Dickens, George Reynolds, Henry Mayhew and John Binny were appalled that boys as young as five and six were being clad in prison dress and branded felons for the 'heinous' offences of throwing stones, knocking on doors and blocking a street passage, the same crimes that, 'if equally visited, would consign almost every child in the kingdom to a jail'.[10]

Convicts well understood the truth spoken by Dickens:

> There are many pleasant fictions of the law in constant operation, but there is not one so pleasant or practically humorous as that which supposes every man to be of equal value in its impartial eye, and the benefits of all laws to be equally attainable by all men, without the smallest reference to the furniture of their pockets.[11]

Many convicts had spent time at Newgate prison, as Dickens had as a visitor, where its schoolmaster could see that neither the law, nor the world, was any friend of the juvenile with 'no parent, or those of such habits and temper as would have rendered orphan-ship a blessing, and that in all probability, most of them…never had a kind or affectionate sentiment imparted to or drawn out of them, by any human being they could look to as a friend'.[12] Wontner and Dickens were asking the timeless question: 'If a country does nothing for a man, what shall allure him to obedience to its laws?'[13] And so 'delinquent' boys had 'been driven to take up arms against society, meeting, from their earliest recollections, with nothing but an enemy in man'.[14]

To survive the enemy, boys honed their skills, attitudes and codes on the streets and in flash houses run by Fagin characters where magistrates reported children as young as eight being 'initiated into the trade of picking pockets'[15] and seeing their peers and other criminals 'sitting and drinking together on terms of good fellowship, inculcating a view that they could continue to rob without fear of punishment'.[16]

For many boys, life on the streets was safer than their home life and more exciting and rewarding. One magistrate, William Miles, said, 'these urchins are taught to look upon the world as a fisherman views the waters: all that can be obtained…depends upon the skill or luck, or in the terms of the common adage, 'all is fish that comes to their nets'.[17] Pickpocketing and thieving realised enough to eat and sleep under a roof, and garnered the badges of manhood such as alcohol, tobacco and female company. The *London Metropolitan Conservative Journal* described how the 'abandoned of both sexes… after prowling for their prey, return to their lairs either moody from disappointment or flushed with gin and success'[18] and magistrate Miles told the House of Lords boys cheerfully told him of spending their criminal gains on 'every pleasure arising from a life of dishonesty', and even those younger than twelve 'revel in the fruits of their plunder and though extremely young, live with girls indulging in every form of debauchery'.[19]

One boy told Miles, 'look ye here Sir, the charm of it is, it comes so easy and it goes just as light, it is better than hard work. It is no wonder boys never reform if they have been in the least successful';[20] for in this 'lottery adventure in each day's life', as Miles described, such 'excitements are attainable at so easy a rate is it strange that these children are fascinated and abandon themselves to crime?'[21]

The prevailing view was, as Miles told the House of Lords, 'among the uneducated the human mind is more prone to evil than virtue'.[22] Dickens had seen it too: 'All people who have led hazardous and forbidden lives are, in a certain sense, imaginative and if their imaginations are not filled with good things they will choke themselves with bad ones.'[23]

The juvenile 'delinquents' were seen as 'a race…different from the rest of Society, not only in thoughts, habits and manners, but even in appearance, possessing, moreover, a language exclusively… their own',[24] a generation living the reality of Fagin that 'every man's his own friend, my dear…he hasn't as good a one as himself anywhere',[25] pitting their cunning and daring against the world and seeing punishment and vice as signs of manhood.

By the early 1800s young delinquents accounted for nearly thirty percent of Britain's committals, but the law allowed no mercy or differentiation for children in the way in which they were charged, the form of trial and punishment, and how and where it was to be enforced. Even young children faced the scaffold: in 1814 five children under fourteen were hanged at the Old Bailey, the youngest just eight, more than 100 children under fourteen were sentenced to death for theft in the thirty-five years leading up to *Oliver Twist*, and the death sentence for those under sixteen would last until 1908.

Notwithstanding all the laws against 'delinquency', some struggled to grasp a long-standing legal principle of *doli incapax* where a child of seven and under was capable of 'mischief' but not criminally punishable because they were deemed too young to know right from wrong, incapable of being sorry and understanding. The 17th century jurist Sir Matthew Hale articulated that, 'an infant of eight years of age, or above, may commit homicide, and shall be hanged for it…if it may appear that he had knowledge of good and evil, and of the peril and danger of that offence.'[26] A century on Sir William Blackstone reinforced Hale but argued that, 'the capability of doing ill…is not so much measured by years and days as by the strength of the delinquent's understanding and judgment.'[27]

The British newspapers reaching Hobart Town reported some magistrates and judges refused to try young children, declaring them 'an infant under the age of discretion'[28] but others, like Sir Joseph Littledale, refused to accept 'that a child of ten years is incapable of committing [a] felony.'[29]

Death sentences for children were mostly commuted, but Britain's ruling classes had long had more taste for punishment than nurture, and what some called the 'demon of obstinancy' meant law-makers, judges and magistrates could not see that unjust laws unjustly enforced 'subvert[ing] the very foundation they would establish.'[30] As the chaplain of Coldbath Fields House of Correction lamented:

When a boy is taken into custody…he loses his character, and it is with the greatest difficulty he can ever come into society again; he then falls into crime as a matter of necessity; he becomes a continual criminal, and we do not lose sight of him until he either dies or commits some crime that will subject him to transportation.[31]

Reformist voices such as Quaker Elizabeth Fry had the same concern, arguing the 'abandoned wickedness' of incarceration meant prisoners were punished but gained 'nothing…but confirmation in the habits of depravity, and afterwards turned out again upon the public, fitted by the punishment of one crime for the perpetration of others. Thus both parties are losers.'[32]

Calls to separate imprisoned juveniles had been advocated since the 1810s, but were not seriously or uniformly trialled. So it remained common in Newgate prison, alongside the Central Criminal Court, to see boys like John Walsby, just eight, among seasoned and often drunken men and women criminals while awaiting trial after 'sneaking' one shilling and one pence from a till so he could buy 'bread, and cakes and fruit'. As *The Times* reported: 'To look at this babe in the gaol of Newgate, under a warrant…which is authority for the detention of the most hardened ruffian, would make many people laugh but many more weep at such a mockery.'[33] Even through to the 1850s, young children could still be found in Houses of Correction: the governor of Westminster Bridewell 'had under his charge one boy not much over five years old and ten more under eight years'.[34] When asked why they had stolen some boots, many an eight-year-old would to reply, 'Cause I haven't got none of my own.'[35]

But time in prison was a badge of honour to some. The Governor of Coldbath said:

The punishment of prison is no punishment to them; I do not mean that they would not rather be out of prison than

in it, but they are so well able to bear the punishment, and
the prison allowance of food is so good, and their spirits so
buoyant, that the consequences are most deplorable.[36]

Some, like the *Metropolitan* journal in London, asked a
deeper question:

Is not prevention better than remedy? Is it not the duty
of a paternal government to put an end to the nursery of
crime? By not interfering with this juvenile delinquency,
they procure a continual supply of subjects for the hulks,
the colonies and the gallows.[37]

But the prevailing answer was an Old Testament belief that 'juvenile
crime is a moral disease'[38] and regardless of age or ignorance those
who made the wrong moral choice deserved to be severely punished
under God's law and man's law.

Some, like magistrate William Miles, gave the House of Lords
another view, that the absence of fear of prison, and easy money
and gratification, gave juvenile boys 'the means to banish thought',[39]
and so:

the listening victim is dazzled and allured on step by step
from the path of virtue, until he reaches that fatal point
where he loses sight for ever of all moral restraint upon
his actions, and the broad and easy road of vice is full
before him.[40]

Was it possible that some young boys might reach this 'fatal point'
of blindness to all moral restraint? To tread a lifepath from playfully
tossing skittles to fatally wielding a stone-hammer?

It now seemed so in Hobart Town, with two boys charged
with the murder of an overseer. Two boys whose names had now
emerged. They were Henry Sparkes and Charles Campbell.

3

A THIEF BY REPUTE

'Stop thief! Stop thief!' There is a passion FOR HUNTING SOMETHING deeply implanted in the human breast. One wretched breathless child, panting with exhaustion; terror in his looks; agony in his eyes.
— Charles Dickens, *Oliver Twist*

The names Henry Sparkes and Charles Campbell meant nothing, just two of thousands of otherwise anonymous and forgettable boys caught up in Britain's passion for hunting, convicting, and transporting its unwanted 'alien vermin' to Van Diemen's Land. But these two would, uniquely, become household names: the only two boys wanted for murder.

Those who loved Dickens' reportage and characterisation of the injustices facing Oliver Twist boys could sense that when the full story of Sparkes and Campbell's lives and their time at Point Puer was revealed, it would be a tale worthy of attention of the great author.

Henry Sparkes was born around 1826 in Nottingham, 120 miles (200 km) north of London. Emerging as a world capital of lace-making, with nearly 200 different manufacturers and 70 hosiery makers, Nottingham had been lauded at the turn of the century for its prettiness but had rapidly become an industrialised and over-crowded home for 50,000. The 'deplorable…defy description' squalid yards and alleys of its lower classes led renowned water and civil engineer Thomas Hawkesley to judge it the worst town in England.[1]

In the squalor many families fell victim to Britain's first outbreak of Asiatic cholera after sailors brought it from Bengal in 1831 to the port of Sunderland, from where it spread across the country and claimed 52,000 lives.[2] In Nottingham the scourge infected those 'Streets and Courts filthy, ill ventilated and crowded with inhabitants too poor, dirty or dissipated to procure necessary food or use the most common means to secure health',[3] and in just a few months more than 300 people died.[4]

Disease and deprivation were a double jeopardy for many families and their children. Small boys like Henry Sparkes were too young to fully understand their circumstances and the consequences of thieving to survive. But Sparkes came to learn the realities of how one's life could quickly change on 31 December 1838. A day that saw the twelve-year-old in a cell, waiting for a bailiff to march him into the Nottingham County Sessions to face Lancelot Rolleston, Esquire and Conservative MP.

At 10am, the clerk of the court commenced the day's sitting by reading a proclamation in the name of the teenage Queen Victoria, crowned at Westminster Abbey just six months earlier. The proclamation discountenanced 'all vice, immorality and impiety', and judges around the country took this as a Royal 'command' to ensure everyone would 'fulfil the duties of religion and support the authority of law' and allow the country to 'resist the machinations and the violence of those who have declared war on this country'.[5]

On this Monday morning, Judge Rolleston told the Grand Jury

he was pleased with 'the lightness of the calendar'[6] but the court would still not rise until 7pm, and Her Majesty's command meant that fifteen boys were not going to get much leniency for stealing clothing and food, even for first-time offences: a fourteen and a sixteen-year-old who stole four fowls were sentenced to a whipping and six months in prison; two boys, aged twelve and fourteen, were sentenced to a week in solitary and a whipping for stealing pork pies; the others, those with prior offences, received transportation for seven or fourteen years.

Henry Sparkes was the last boy to appear, another of the under-sized boys found in inferior districts of towns and cities, with a background heard every day in courts around the country. Just a year or two earlier he had been sentenced to three months in Southwell House of Correction for being found on premises in the night-time, presumably on a thieving foray. Magistrates hoped Houses of Correction — commonly known as Bridewells after the prison and hospital established in the 1500s to punish the disorderly poor and house homeless children in London — would deter young boys from a life of crime by instilling 'habits of working and moral guidance to reform their character'. Magistrates typically declared to boys they had been found guilty of a crime which not long before would have meant forfeiture of their life but hoped that after an initial departure from the path of honesty an escape from hopeless servitude would make them a more worthy member of society. They then gave what was called a nominal punishment of three or four months imprisonment.

But working the treadwheels, known as 'everlasting staircases', and Southwell's moral guidance had not kept Henry Sparkes on a path of honesty. His own father twice charged him with 'robbing him of fifteen shillings, and...again charged by him with stealing other moneys'[7] — although, this was not uncommon and not always the truth. A few fathers and stepfathers might have been genuinely motivated to keep their boy on the 'right' path, but many contrived charges to get rid of children, tiring of a boy thief not delivering enough, or wanting the Houses of Correction to bear the cost of housing, food and clothing. In a report to Lord John Russell, leader of the Whigs, magistrate William Miles explained that:

> [some parents] turn their children out every morning to provide for themselves, not caring by what means they procure a subsistence so that the expense of feeding them does not abstract from their means of procuring gin or beer...other parents require their children to bring home specified sum every night to obtain which they must beg or thieve...others hire out their children to beggars for threepence a day (a cripple is worth sixpence).[8]

The court heard Henry Sparkes had once been charged with stealing a pony but 'on account of his extreme youth he was not prosecuted'[9] but 'extreme' youth was no longer his refuge. He was now charged with the theft of a total of three pence from two women on 21 October:

> Henry Sparkes, late of the parish of Redford in this county, labourer, for feloniously stealing, taking and carrying away one piece of the current copper coin of this realm called a penny and one other piece of the current copper coin of this realm called a halfpenny of the monies of Mary Fletcher, and one other piece of the current copper coin of this realm called a penny and one other piece of the current copper coin of this realm called a halfpenny of the monies of Ann Chambers.[10]

For young thieves, life on the street was one of chance, of always 'calculating all things to a nicety...chances of detection, chances of prosecution and chances of acquittal...'.[11] Having been detected and prosecuted, Sparkes was now taking his chances that he might win some leniency by pleading guilty, but such hope dissipated when the arresting constable who had detained him overnight revealed that 'on bringing him to jail he was found to have taken two pairs of stockings from the constable's house'.[12]

Such a perceived wantonness to ignore magisterial admonitions, and an inability to resist thieving even from an arresting constable, was not going to receive a sympathetic ear from Her Majesty's judges dealing with those who 'declared war on this country'. Courts were tired of such repeat offenders. Magistrates often declared: 'Prisoner, what can we do with you? We have done everything to reclaim you. We have imprisoned you over and over again, and given you frequent floggings, yet all is of no use.'[13] An offence might appear petty, but, as one Middlesex magistrate explained, if they were 'well known to be dangerous characters…you sometimes on account of badness of character sentence them to transportation'.[14]

Tearful pleas and tales of poverty, hunger, abuse and abandonment occasionally pained a judge or magistrate, but often their hearts were, as Dickens termed it, 'water-proof'.[15] A common exchange was that of a ten-year-old boy appearing at Mansion House, London, on a charge of pickpocketing a handkerchief. Asked about his parents, the boy replied 'father lives nowhere's, 'cause he's dead', didn't know where his mother was, and 'I an't got nobody to go to'.[16]

Police said it was evident the youngster 'had no friend in the world' and that bigger boys took advantage of him, leading the alderman hearing the case to declare that: 'from motives of humanity he should be obliged to send the unfortunate boy for trial, in the hope that he would be transported.' When the pickpocket victim asked if he could now withdraw his prosecution against such 'a mere infant', the alderman said: 'You surely wouldn't want to find him starving, and the only way we now have of preventing him is by committing him for trial.'[17]

Henry Sparkes did not have much time to weigh whether he faced transportation as 'a dangerous character' or 'from motives of humanity'. Samuel Fletcher and his daughter Mary quickly outlined the theft of three pence and the jury found he did 'feloniously steal, take and carry away [the money], against the Peace of our said Lady the Queen, her Crown and Dignity',[18] and at the end of what had been a long day, the last in another long criminal year, Judge Rolleston swiftly reached his decision: 'From such a catalogue of crimes, the Court remarked that it was impossible by any imprisonment that he could be reformed.'[19] 'He would therefore be placed in the penitentiary, Millbank'[20] before being 'transported for the term of seven years to such place beyond the seas as Her Majesty by and with the advice of her Council shall direct'.[21]

Four hundred miles (640 km) away, Charles Campbell had been walking the same familiar life path in the north-eastern port town of Aberdeen, where the Dee and Don rivers meet the North Sea. It had grown rapidly on the back of ships, fish and textiles to become one of the biggest provincial towns in Britain. But, like Sparkes' Nottingham, it was struggling in the 1830s with juvenile vagrancy and crime. Barely one in twenty-five children were in school, with hundreds begging and thieving. Some sixty percent of children, according to the inspector of prisons, were orphans or children of convicts, or parents who on entering a second marriage had 'thrown them upon the world without means of support'.[22]

When he was just nine or ten-years-old, Charles Campbell and another boy were found in October 1837 to have stolen clothing, a gold ring and pawn tickets from a woman's house in the Green of Aberdeen. They pleaded guilty and were each sentenced to ten days. At the beginning of 1840, as 'George Hendry Henderson or Campbell' he was found guilty of stealing a cotton shirt and night cap from a house and sentenced to thirty days with hard labour at Aberdeen House of Correction. But he resumed thieving immediately after his release, pleading guilty under the name of 'George Campbell' to stealing clothing from a house in Upperkirkgate. This time he received sixty days with hard labour.[23]

On 23 September 1840, the name Charles Campbell appeared again on the Aberdeen Circuit Court of Justiciary list. After a 'very earnest and impressive prayer', Judges Lord Medwyn and Lord McKenzie and a jury panel began working their way through the thefts, forgery, and house-breaking. One 'little boy', William Mitchell, pleaded not guilty but having the 'habit and repute [of] a thief', was sentenced to eighteen months imprisonment; another boy, William Burnett, only had to wait five minutes for the jury, after 'evidence…tedious and uninteresting', to find him guilty of house-breaking and theft of £17, for which he was sentenced to seven years transportation. Nineteen boys appeared that morning, their guilt and punishment all decided in just two hours, with eight sentenced to be transported for seven or fourteen years.[24]

Even among under-sized boys, Charles Campbell stood out. He was just 4 feet (122 cm) tall with a shock of red hair barely visible behind the dock railing. He was charged with Alexander Boynes of breaking and entering another house, this time in Shiprow, the street running from the harbour to the heart of the town, and stealing three cotton shifts.

Campbell was warned pre-trial that if he confessed, or was found guilty, he 'ought to be punished with the pains of the law to deter others from committing the like crimes'.[25] As Campbell and Boynes could not write, a sheriff prepared a statement on which they put their mark, 'accepting' the charges and pleading guilty that each, 'or one or the other of you', had 'wickedly and feloniously' broken into a widow's room and stolen a cotton shift from her, and two other shifts owned by another woman.[26]

Campbell told the court he believed he was eleven or twelve years old. He was a native of Aberdeen but had been 'absent' for three months, perhaps a sly reference to his time in the House of Correction, and had only been in the city one night, with no place of residence, when arrested. The truth of his birthplace is unclear, but he was later listed in Tasmanian convict records as having been born in Dublin, and been a 'cotton spinner', with a broken finger.[27] Thousands of Irish families and individuals did move to England and Scotland to escape the 1831–32 cholera pandemic or in pursuit of work in cotton mills and textile factories, where boys' small fingers were applied to dangerous machine tasks, 5am to as late as midnight, for perhaps a sixpence or a shilling. Whatever their background, unsurprisingly many boys saw street thieving as safer, more rewarding and exciting.

Witnesses told the court they had seen Campbell and Boynes lingering in the Shiprow building. A Mrs Mitchell said Boynes 'came to my door asking for charity, but got nothing, I desired him to go to work'.[28] She then saw him outside the room of widow Margaret Grant, who had locked her garrett room before returning to find a chair at her door and some boards removed from above the door.

Perhaps in a protective ruse, or mere brazenness, Campbell was also seen going to another room again 'asking for charity', with 'his coat buttoned and something bulky below it…some white cloth sticking out below his coat'.[29]

Out in the street, Campbell's number was up when a sailor overheard him tell Boynes 'I winna tell if you dinna tell', to which Boynes responded 'and I winna tell if you dinna tell'. The sailor could see something stuffed underneath their jackets and enjoined a fellow sailor at Trinity Quay to follow the boys and apprehend them. Spotting the sailors, Campbell 'made off at a quick pace', while Alexander declared 'it was not me who did it but that boy' before running off himself. When Campbell was seized he reciprocated, saying, 'it was not me who stole them, it was that boy running away', pointing to Boyne.[30]

Questioned at Aberdeen police station each boy continued to blame the other. Notwithstanding their 'dinna tell' compact, a sergeant said Boyne told him they 'had been on the outlook all that day in Shiprow to steal something at Campbell's suggestion to enable him to procure pies in the evening'.[31] He maintained Campbell went into the widow's room and emerged with the cotton shifts, giving him one to wear or sell in which case 'he would get a sixpence for it'.[32]

The 'it wasn't me it was him' ploy was oft-used among street-wise juvenile pickpockets and thieves hoping it would help their chances if they could create doubt or convincingly point to the real 'baddin'. But the police were not persuaded by Campbell's efforts to pin the crime on Boynes, or his cunning argument that he had not broken into the garret room because its door was not locked, and knew Campbell 'to be by habit and repute a thief', convicted three times under the names of Charles Campbell, George Hendry Henderson/Campbell, and George Campbell.[33]

When the jury foreman duly announced the charge unanimously found proven, Campbell's final 'chance' rested with Lord Medwyn, a Scottish Episcopalian who had edited a new edition of the catechism: 'Thoughts concerning Man's Condition and Duties in this Life, and his Hopes in the World to Come'.

Medwyn initially said 'in consequence of their youth, [he had] felt inclined to a lenient sentence' but the boys' crime was 'heinous'. He sentenced Alexander Boynes to eighteen months imprisonment, but obviously felt Charles Campbell was the real 'baddin': 'Theft, especially when committed by means of house-breaking and by a person who is by habit [sic] and repute a thief, and who has been previously convicted of theft, is a crime of a heinous nature and severely punishable.'[34]

It was futile to send his like to a prison which turned young petty offenders into 'more expert thieves and more hardened criminals',[35] so he 'could not propose a sentence less severe than transportation'.[36]

A boy of eleven or twelve who wanted to steal some cotton shifts in order to buy a pie was to return to Aberdeen prison, an ancient tower which reformer Elizabeth Fry described as 'a scene of unusual misery',[37] and wait to be 'transported beyond seas for the period of seven years'.

Beyond seas for seven years. This was an unimaginable journey and duration for young boys like Charles Campbell and Henry Sparkes. It had been a punishment since Queen Elizabeth, frustrated at the continued crimes of poor street folk despite whippings and burning of a 1 inch (2.5 cm) hole in their right ear, declared such 'rogues' ought to face death or be transported with the letter 'R' branded on their bodies as 'incorrigible and dangerous rogues' to a colony overseas. Two centuries on and England was still looking to rid itself of 'rogues' through exile, even if they were victims of hunger or homelessness like Charles Campbell and Henry Sparkes.

No amount of tears or fears could elicit any mercy. After hearing one boy's mournful plea — 'I never knew what it was like to have the attentions of a father and mother…I was cast abroad…at a very early age' — and how he would rather die than be transported, a judge sentenced him to be transported 'for the term of your natural life' with a stern warning[38]:

> You speak as if this life were all. Remember, that this life is inconsiderable; it is nothing at all to what is to come after; and if you were to shorten your term of existence by any act of violence, or if you fail to employ the days yet allotted you in penitence for your crimes and preparation for another state, all that you have been suffering for is but nothing as to what you will suffer for eternity.[39]

Lawmakers and judges saw boy thieves like Henry Sparkes and Charles Campbell as criminals unchecked by irresponsible parents, unwilling to stay on a path of honesty, and unable to be 'corrected'. One House of Correction governor, George Chesterton, told a House of Commons select committee reformation was 'utterly hopeless', as 'boys brought up in a low neighbourhood have no chance of being honest, because on leaving a gaol they return to their old haunts and follow the example of parents or associates'[40] who 'wait round a prison gate to hail a companion on the morning of his liberation, and to carry him off to treat him and regale him for the day'.[41] So the judgment was that 'they go to a place where they must suffer disgrace and hardship, and where they must lose that which is the most painful to a human being to lose – all hope of liberty'.[42]

For Sparkes and Campbell, such a place was Van Diemen's Land. After the North American revolution closed Britain's dumping ground across the Atlantic, it scanned its remaining empire and chose the Great Southern Land, formerly 'Terra Australis Incognita' or 'the great unknown land', as its place of exile. Reached only by long and perilous journey and surrounded by ocean at the very bottom of the known world, Van Diemen's Land was its own perfect island for the condemned, and a hitherto untried system of a government transporting convicted men, women and children to seed a new colony.

Henry Sparkes and Charles Campbell had probably never seen a map that showed their destination, as close to the icy edges of Antarctic as London to Rome. They might have heard of it as 'Van Demon's Land', or that it was somewhere near where *Gulliver's Travels' (1726)* author Jonathan Swift had placed Lilliput, his place of greatest imaginable isolation, but leaving the courts of Nottingham and Aberdeen, Sparkes and Campbell could not possibly imagine what lay ahead.

4

A FLOATING BASTILLE

Even if he has been wicked, think how young he is; think that he may never have known a mother's love, or the comfort of a home; that ill-usage and blows, or the want of bread, may have driven him to herd with men who have forced him to guilt. For mercy's sake, think of this before you let them drag this sick child to a prison, which in any case must be the grave of all his chances of amendment.
— Charles Dickens, *Oliver Twist*

Before Henry Sparkes and Charles Campbell could be transported beyond seas they first had to be transported beyond their known world of Aberdeen and Nottingham to Britain's first national prison: Millbank Penitentiary, a yellow brown mass of brickwork on the marshy banks of the Thames between Westminster and Chelsea.

Some boys saw Millbank as an esteemed badge of honour. They

had grown up coming to regard 'pluck' or daring as the greatest virtue in life, their 'trickery or 'artful dodges…the highest possible exercise of the intellect', because honesty was 'monotonous and irksome'.[1] Those who laboured for a living were 'in plain English, fools'[2] when the road of vice was 'full of boundless joy', as the House of Lords was told.[3]

In their own unique code, the greater the risk and crime, the higher the sense of manhood, self-esteem and superiority. Boys like Campbell and Sparkes inhaled their apparent importance and cleverness, pleased with themselves that their court appearances were attended by judges and barristers in wigs and gowns, pressmen taking notes and spectators sometimes paying a shilling. And that, despite their small size, they were held in such dread that society had to place them 'behind huge massive bars which ten elephants couldn't pull down'.[4]

In the fraternity and 'flash patter' of the street, there was a clear hierarchy or aristocracy: at the bottom were the 'pudding snammers', boys who only stole from bakeries to feed their stomachs; 'files' who picked pockets of watches and jewellery were rated higher than those who merely thieved handkerchiefs; 'sneaks' who robbed a shop till; 'snakes' who wriggled their way into small spaces for house burglaries; 'bouncers' who stole while pretending to be bargaining; and the 'swell mob' who dressed respectably to camouflage their criminality. Boys transported for life were of 'greater consequence than the boy who is sentenced to seven years, while the lad whose sentence is a short imprisonment is not deemed worthy to associate or converse with'.[5]

Dickens visited Newgate not long before Sparkes and Campbell arrived in London, and observed of the young pickpocket boys behind bars:

> There was not one redeeming feature among them, not a glance of honesty, not a wink expressive of anything but the gallows and the hulks…as to anything like shame or

contrition, that was out of the question. Every boy…
actually seemed as pleased and important as if he had done
something excessively meritorious in getting there at all…
worth the trouble of looking at.[6]

Even if they were motivated otherwise, it was almost impossible to
avoid old haunts and habits. 'Where else can we go?' one said, 'we
cannot for our 'pals' would torment us to return'.[7] Another said: 'I do
not want to thieve if I can get money honestly, but how am I to get it?
Will you employ me? Will anybody be fool enough to employ me?
Just out of gaol and with no character, just think of that sir, and tell
me if I must not thieve!'[8]

William Miles, who interviewed dozens of boys like Sparkes
and Campbell in prisons and prison hulks as part of a report to the
House of Lords in 1835, concluded: '[They] have no sense of moral
degradation; they are corrupt to the core; they are strangers to virtue
even by name…they are in a state of predatory existence, without
any knowledge of social duty; they may lament detection, because it
is an inconvenience, but they will not repent their crime. In gaol they
will ponder on the past, curse their 'evil stars' and look forward…
to their release, but their minds and habits are not constituted
for repentance.'[9]

Their only 'social duty' was their own 'artful dodge'. Society
had its laws, watchmen and police, but food and thievery trumped
starvation and honesty, and boys marched to a 'we beat you' drum[10]
in a life of taking chances. The chances of finding something to rob,
being seen and detected, being prosecuted, being convicted, and a
modest sentence. Chance was their anthem, with 'every hour of their
freedom…uncertain…in a kind of lottery adventure'.[11]

In this lottery of life it was merely 'evil stars' and bad luck if they
were detected and punished, imprisonment 'merely another step in
the ladder of their sad destiny'.[12] For Sparkes and Campbell their 'evil
stars' saw them moving up the juvenile aristocracy from houses of
correction to Millbank, a premier college of criminality and a rite of

passage for those destined for Van Diemen's Land.

Taking its name from a mill belonging to Westminster Abbey, the prison opened in 1816 as London's largest, a £500,000 English Bastille lauded as the greatest in Europe for its revolutionary panopticon (Greek for all-seeing) design allowing centrally positioned guards to provide constant surveillance over 1500 transportation prisoners in six star shaped blocks.

The sights, sounds and smells of the multi-turreted stone fortress never left convicts who had passed through. Sitting on marshland and surrounded by a stagnant moat, its cold, damp and gloomy passages fuelled cholera, malaria, dysentery and scurvy. The 'revolutionary' Millbank was soon condemned for its design and conditions. The new penal science of dark, silent cells and isolation was, according to some newspapers emerging as a conscience voice, an abomination, an 'unnatural…modern cruelty devised to impair the health, destroy the constitution, and obliterate the mind'.[13] Reforming journalists described Millbank as 'one of the most successful realisations, on a large scale, of the ugly in architecture, being an ungainly combination of the madhouse with the fortress'.[14]

But thousands of small boys endured this madhouse-fortress. Reforming journalist, social researcher and future *Punch* magazine founder, Henry Mayhew lamented 'the little desperate malefactors… many are so young they seem better fitted to be conveyed to the prison in a perambulator than in the lumbering and formidable prison van'.[15] One governor even recalled 'a little boy six and half years old sentenced to transportation'.[16]

The *Morning Chronicle* — the first newspaper to steadily employ Dickens — had earlier declared 'there is but one remedy — to place as much gun powder under the foundation as may suffice to blow the whole fabric into the air'.[17] But sheer numbers of prisoners meant it could not be blown up, nor could little boys who veered from the 'right path' be spared.

Under pressure from reformers, some officials proclaimed they

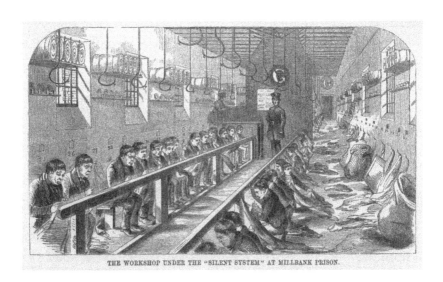

THE WORKSHOP UNDER THE "SILENT SYSTEM" AT MILLBANK PRISON.

Millbank Prison Mayhew. Image courtesy Alamy Stock Photos, A67BWD

were endeavouring to better classify and manage prisoners based on age, criminal record, and behaviour, and take greater account of the capacity of young boys without education or moral guidance to understand the consequences of their thievery or falling under the influence of older boys and men. But the reality was a shadow of any stated intent, and houses of correction and prisons commonly held 'thirty or forty [to] sleep together; and as they are, for young ones, of the very worst description of offenders, the consequence may easily be imagined'.[18]

Millbank was no exception. In between what Dickens described as a 'melancholy waste'[19] of 'making money from old rope' — picking apart thick strands of oakum, the old tarred rope fibres used between planks of a ship and sealed with hot pitch, for the prison to sell for re-use or other hard labour tasks — younger, smaller and weaker boys had to survive the same code of self-interest and self-preservation they had known on the street.

Bigger, more hardened boys, known as nobs, quickly educated or intimidated others to remain silent about their bullying, theft of food, corruption or sexual abuse. Under the code of the nobs, and the ancient code of 'honour among thieves', staying silent offered the best chance of avoiding punishment. Boys also had to obey a strict official code that, by the late 1830s, saw more younger offenders kept in silence and separation to prevent 'contamination' and allow longer periods of 'reflection' in the hope they would become more repentant. Breaking the silence, by word or gesture — even a meaningless smile to a fellow inmate — risked being strait-jacketed or shackled for days; sometimes soaked in water, beaten or whipped; or being 'broken' by spending time in 'solitary confinement like a dog in a kennel'.[20]

Some boys baulked at the two codes of intimidating wardens or fellow boys and the appalling conditions. 'Prisoners showed their resistance in various small ways such as working as slowly as possible, talking during their work, and stealing other prisoner's products and passing them as one's own...prisoners also threatened or bribed guards and other prison workers.'[21] But some were broken: 'Few days passed but some desperate wretch, maddened by silence and solitude, smashed up everything breakable in his cell in a vain rebellion against a system stronger and more merciless than death.'[22]

The 'modern' imposition of 'darkness' was a mental punishment seen to be more painful than the physical, and it would follow convicts all the way to Port Arthur and Point Puer. Dickens was appalled when he witnessed prisoners in America never looking upon a human countenance or hearing a human voice:

> He is a man buried alive, to be dug out in the slow round of years, and in the mean time [sic] dead to everything but torturing anxieties and horrible despair...wasted in that stone coffin...hears spirits tempting him to beat his brains out on the wall.[23]

Dickens condemned it as 'cruel and wrong' and was supported by the *Illustrated London News*, the world's first illustrated weekly news magazine, which called for an end to such 'experiments...[that] degrade the sacred name of justice...make the law monstrous...a disgrace and sin'.[24]

Unlike some, Sparkes and Campbell did not have to endure Millbank's experiments for a long period. Five weeks after his sentence in Nottingham, Sparkes was among those removed by longboat from Millbank to the prison hulk *Euryalus* in February 1839. Campbell followed the next year, two months after his sentence in Aberdeen.

Prison hulks, another penal experiment and expediency, were introduced in 1776 after the American Revolution. The decision was initiated as a 'temporary' two-year utilisation of unseaworthy and de-masted Naval and commercial ships as floating prisons, to help cope with the rising tide of prisoners and overcrowded gaols.

The first prison hulk was the *Justitia*, named for the Roman personification of justice and moral force, widely portrayed as Lady Justice with a blindfold signifying the law being applied with no regard to wealth or power. But few of wealth and power were to be found on the *Justitia* and what became a fleet of hulks at Chatham Thames estuary in north Kent — where Dickens spent some childhood years and incorporated some of his memories into *Great Expectations* — and Sheerness, Deptford, Woolwich, Gosport, Plymouth, Portsmouth and Cork. The 'temporary' hulk fleet lasted eighty years.

Some boys would have anticipated that after stints in Houses of Correction, regional gaols and a few months at Millbank they would soon be leaving such misery behind, about to embark on a voyage to a new and perhaps better opportunity — even an adventure. But their hopes were dashed, Sparkes and Campbell spending seven long months on *Euralyus* at Chatham in conditions that would cause even a resilient and optimistic boy to question his sentence to the other side of the world.

Gloriously launched by the British Navy in 1803, *Euryalus* was named after one of the Argonauts, the mythical Greek band of heroes accompanying Jason in his search for the Golden Fleece. As a 36-gun frigate, the ship had an illustrious naval history in the Napoleonic Wars accompanying Lord Nelson at the 1805 Battle of Trafalgar, and the War of 1812, but there was nothing heroic or golden about it as an aged, de-masted prison hulk.

The outline of dismembered masts in the gloomy Thames mist might have reminded Sparkes and Campbell of the gibbets which horrified boys in Nottingham and Aberdeen. The hulks certainly had their ghosts: death rates had been as high as one in four when the first hulks were employed and were still one in ten by the turn of the 19th century. They were the pits for the unpitied, the physical and psychological conditions so bad some prisoners averred a preference to hang rather than endure what would come to be seen 'of all the places of confinements that British history records…the

Prison-ship in Portsmouth Harbour, convicts going aboard, illustration and etching, Edward William Cooke, 1828. Image courtesy National Library of Australia, nla.obj-135934086.

most brutalising, the most demoralising and the most horrible'.[25]

Sparkes and Campbell were a little more fortunate than their predecessors, who were held in irons alongside older youths and adults before calls for better protection of children led to the *Captivity* becoming the first hulk set aside exclusively for boys in 1823. But it was deemed unsuitable and, after two years, was replaced by the *Euryalus,* a ship which a Select Committee on Gaols and Houses of Correction also recommended in 1835 be abandoned immediately. But authorities did nothing for another seven years, during which another 2500 boys under fourteen, some as young as eight or nine, were hustled aboard.[26]

Regardless of age, such boys were seen by authorities in simple terms: as prisoners who were no longer entitled to walk in the land of their birth and were being banished for the 'good' of the country, and perhaps for themselves.

The conscience of Britain was beginning to be stirred by social reformers like Elizabeth Fry, Quakers like Samuel Hoare, evangelical politicians like Thomas Buxton, lawyer-authors like Thomas Wontner, and reporter-authors like Charles Dickens, Henry Mayhew and George Reynolds. But authorities steadfastly wanted to cleanse themselves of unwanted 'vermin', drain away the 'dregs' and win the war on 'wickedness'.

Young boys on the frontline were not spared, judged more on reputation and looks than the seriousness of their offences and denied benefits of understanding or mercy. So as two casualties of the war, Sparkes and Campbell had to be held in what a Royal Navy captain described as a 'floating Bastille'.[27]

5

A MATTER OF DISPOSAL

By the light of the torches we saw the black hulk laying out a little
way from the mud of the shore, like a wicked Noah's ark. Cribbed and
barred and moored by massive rusty chains the prison ships seemed in
my young eyes to be ironed like the prisoners.
— Charles Dickens, *Great Expectations*

Some boys leaving Millbank feigned illness in the hope of avoiding
the *HMS Euryalus* and transportation. Others feigned good health
in the hope, or chance, that the ultimate destination of Van Diemen's
Land might offer something advantageous. But irrespective of feigns
or fancies, they were all being physically taken off the land of their
childhood, land they would never step foot on again.

Walking up the gangway, Sparkes and Campbell would have
experienced just as Dickens described: 'No one seemed surprised to

see him, or interested in seeing him, or glad to see him, or sorry to see him, or spoke a word, except that somebody in the boat growled at him as if to dogs "give way you!"'[1]

Their initiation to the floating, rotting Bastille was as if authorities wanted to scrub away their 'wickedness'. One prisoner recalled:

> We were stripped to the skin and scrubbed with a hard scrubbing brush, something like a stiff birch broom, and plenty of soft soap, while the hair was clipped from our heads as close as scissors could go. This scrubbing we endured until we looked like boiled lobsters, and the blood was drawn in many places.[2]

And any fellow hulk prisoners offering their friendship or services was, as one convict recalled, only 'with a view to rob me of what little I had, for in this place there is no other motive or subject for ingenuity. All former friendships are dissolved and a man here will rob his best benefactor, or even messmate, of an article worth one halfpenny'.[3]

No friendships but a new number. Henry Sparkes was now recorded as 2434, and Charles Campbell, when he came aboard 1500 boys later, was 4012.[4]

No friends and no comforts. The hulks were wretched, foul-smelling places, with boys sleeping on bare boards, given brackish water and a poor diet with often tainted meat, scant medical care, and little or no religious or moral instruction. Mortality rates had been reduced but there was always on hand a ready supply of empty coffins. Thousands succumbed to typhoid and cholera, or became bearers of disease to Australia.

There were few concerns about numbers squeezed on board — some hulks held as many as 600 to 700 juveniles over three decks 'without overcrowding',[5] at least according to official reports. The *Euryalus* had been home to 264 navy personnel but now it officially housed 400 offenders. Its design and small size — just 49 yards x 12.5 yards (45 m x 11.5 m) — defeated any attempt to adequately classify and separate prisoners. And in any event their age, size and convictions often provided few insights as to true 'badness' and where they ought to be housed: the upper deck designated for first-time offenders, the middle deck for those with more than one offence, and the lowest deck for the 'worst'.

In what reforming journalist Henry Mayhew described as conditions 'very like those found in the zoological gardens,'[6] the first *Euryalus* chaplain, Reverend Thomas Price, presciently said that without greater classification and management based on criminality and behaviour, and adequate separation of the worst from the rest, his task of improving their morals and correcting the 'evil….cannot possibly be accomplished'.[7]

Price was not optimistic about managing poor children 'taken out of our streets, not only deplorably ignorant of all religious knowledge, but with habits opposed to every moral and social restraint'. It had been put to him that 'such was the depravity of the boys that every attempt to moralise them would only terminate in disappointment', and 'I find much reason for the remark'.[8]

Sparkes and Campbell found themselves among boys of all ages, some listed as ten years or older but perhaps as young as eight or nine, and others as old as seventeen or eighteen, divided into small sections and corralled below deck for long periods. Their days were run on a military-like schedule under constant surveillance. Each morning around five, a wake-up call sounded for boys to open their portholes and stow their hammocks. Another signal sent them in small groups to hear prayers in 'chapel'. Mustered on deck they waited in silent ranks for breakfast at about 6am, usually some gruel and a hunk of brown bread, before being ordered to clean the decks and begin their day's labour around 8am, picking oakum or 'tailoring' crude clothing for hulk prisoners.

Groups of boys were monitored by older 'head' boys, chosen

because of perceived 'good conduct' in prison. They were obliged to report any misbehaviour, real or perceived, such as a breach of the 'silent system', insolence, theft, refusing to work or fighting. Summary punishment was quickly decided and delivered. Officially, 'in cases of convicts misbehaviour, mild and persuasive means of correction are first tried'. Such mild and persuasive means might mean reduced food rations, 'confinement in a dark cell with no other food than bread and water, for not more than seven days… or moderate whipping which, in any case, is not allowed to exceed twenty four [sic] stripes.'[9]

Whipping or being 'flogged'[10] on the breech, usually by birch, was not a new punishment for most boys, and confinement in a small cell for up to a week in darkness and silence, with only bread and water as company, was more feared. Authorities saw this black hole as a greater terror for the wicked than the gallows and gibbet, one which might 'break' recalcitrant boys in the hope that solitude and silence would allow a small voice of conscience to be heard. But it could also instil an unbreakable resolve to resist and rebel.

Offences and attitudes were key features of new additions to a boy's penal biography, an incessant and indelible inking of 'badness':

> On board each hulk, a book is kept by the Overseer, in which are entered the names of all convicts; and on the first Sunday of every quarter, they are mustered, and the character of each convict, for the previous three months, is marked against his name, as follows: v.g. (very good); g. (good); in. (indifferent); b. (bad); v.b. (very bad).[11]

At noon the boys were fed more oatmeal gruel or boiled ox-cheek or soup, then allowed to trudge around the deck for an hour of air and exercise 'with the least noise'[12] until 1.20pm when they were again mustered before more labour, or for illiterate boys some basic lessons, until 5pm. After a cursory wash supper was served at 5.30pm, usually a repeat of earlier meals. After another brief stint of silent walking on deck — popular 'games' of cards, dice and marbles were strictly forbidden — and a final muster to ensure they held no weapons or stolen goods, they were ordered to file below to the foul and cramped berths to prepare their hammocks and listen to an evening prayer before a final lock down at 8pm. By 9pm, with 'profound silence' ordered, the ship was 'as quiet as if there was not a soul on board', the eeriness broken only by the lap-lap of the Thames and the strike of the bell and an 'all's well' call by guards every half-hour.[13]

On Saturdays the boys had a weekly wash 'all over in tepid water and soap'.[14] A few had visits from family vainly pleading for their boys to be released, but family was a foreign concept for most.

Authorities budgeted for each boy to have a roughly made shirt, jacket and pair of breeches, but just as police had often confiscated the stolen goods of street boys, hulk officials often pocketed the clothing money. When John Howard, inspirer of the Howard League for Penal Reform, inspected boys on the hulks he found 'many had no shorts, some no waistcoats, some no stockings, and some no shoes'.[15]

As at Millbank, older and more villainous youths formed bullying gangs and implemented their own code of behaviour, often more abusive than overseers. Younger and smaller boys had to sharpen their footwork and harden themselves or accept being victims.

For boys like Sparkes and Campbell, what had passed for childhood had long become the pursuit of 'manhood'. They had been inspired by wondrous tales of 'robbers, pirates and loose women' in the popular penny dreadfuls and colourful street theatre, and street gatherings where boys would 'sit for six or eight hours together, relating and hearing tales of criminal heroes'.[16] And in the flash dens of the Fagins they lived with older and more desperate offenders, and the 'libidinous desires'[17] of puberty became contemporaneous with crime, with the needs and wants of food, shelter, alcohol and sex being met by criminality.

Self-interest, self-preservation and self-esteem was the key to life, one in which the boys' code and hierarchy of conduct and justice saw bigger 'nobs' bully the small and weak to gain 'power', food rations or sexual favours. Those who did not bend to their will, or 'noseys' or 'skunks' who informed against them, risked being the victim of a malicious report and punishment by the hulk commandant or the nobs themselves. Thomas Dexter, a convict assigned as a nurse on a hospital ship serving the *Euryalus*, said the 'nobs' 'have got such an ascendancy' that boys were less fearful of incarceration than of 'ill-treatment of one boy to another'.[18]

> I have known it when three or four have been obliged to be locked up in a cell by themselves in order to shelter them from murder…they were called Noseys, that is those whom they considered had been to the officers to tell them anything that was going on, those who were particularly pointed out by the majority of prisoners on whom to wreak their vengeance.[19]

Bullying led some victims to self-mutilate to gain respite or a fuller meal in a hospital ward. 'I have had patients come into the hospital who have declared that they have not tasted meat for three weeks together, but have been obliged to give their rations to those nobs, and they have fed upon gruel and the parings of potatoes.'[20] Some applied a red hot copper button to their own skin and rubbed the wound with soap until it became septic. Others would claim to have fallen down a ship ladder, but in fact had let 'the edge of the table drop upon [their arms] and break them in two' or had other boys do it for them.[21]

Another put pins in his hand to gain admittance, which further upset the bullies who 'pricked my eyes with needles…and jagged the needle three or four times in each eye.' He knew they would do it, the boy said, 'because they told me overnight they would put my eyes out in the morning…I did not care what had become of me then… because I used to be so ill-used'.[22]

Ill-use included sodomy, the silent currency of the Royal
Navy, prisons and prison hulks. Social reformer and jurist Jeremy
Bentham reported that hulk prisoners were raped as a matter of
course: 'An initiation of this sort stands in the place of garnish and
is exacted with equal rigor.' When the *Euryalus* chaplain complained
that boys ought to be better separated 'for the better ensuring
the improvement of their morals'[23] he was replaced by a more
accommodating chaplain. One hulk convict said sodomy 'rages so
shamefully…that the surgeon and myself have been more than once
threatened with assassination for straining to put a stop to it…[it] is
in no way discountenanced by those in command'.[24] As a dismissive
Sir John Carter, mayor of the convict shipping centre of Portsmouth,
declared: 'such things ever must be.'[25]

The *Euryalus'* management of boy convicts was ripe for
condemnation. Thomas Wontner declared, 'If there be any regular
and established schools for teaching crime, the ship *Euryalus* is
the place,'[26] and William Miles put to Parliament that, 'however
criminal they might have been before their commitments…
previous to their imprisonment in that accursed hulk…they were
comparatively innocent.'[27]

Edward Brenton, a former naval captain turned philanthropist
who wrote the *Naval History of Great Britain*, denounced the *Euryalus*
as 'cruel and vindictive, and I challenge any man to come forward
and justify it'. He described a regime where 'children [are] in iron
cages, who should have been in a nursery garden; children pining
in misery, where the stench was intolerable; where the human mind
is more rapidly brutalized, and where every feeling of humanity
is more speedily destroyed, than could be done by any other
process whatever'.[28]

An MP with a strong interest in crime and punishment reform,
George Holford, who oversaw the design and construction of
Millbank, similarly complained that hulks saw young offenders
listen 'with amazement' to the sins and outrages of others, 'but soon

familiar grows with every crime'. 'Let justice rather strike her victim dead,' he wrote in verse, than send them to a hulk which hardened and corrupted the heart. "t'were better doom him the lion's den than to this curs'd abode of [the] wicked.'[29]

But as with Houses of Correction and Millbank, those in charge of the hulks continued to dutifully, and self-servingly, report complete 'satisfaction' in a chain of superiors all the way to Whitehall. By the time Campbell and Sparkes were leaving the hulk, chaplain Henry John Dawes was pleased to report to John Henry Capper, Esq., the Superintendent in Charge of Ships and Vessels Employed for the Confinement of Offenders under the Sentence of Transportation, that, 'the boys continue to behave remarkably well', lauded their 'orderly conduct and attention in the Chapel' and cited the 'excellent conditions' provided by the ship's commandant. Capper in turn duly reported to his Home Department secretary, Marquess of Normanby Constantine Henry Phipps, that the boys 'have conducted themselves properly and been instructed and employed at those trades as the limited means on board a ship will admit of being put into effect'.[30]

Despite officials' best efforts, the truth of *Euryalus* was becoming clear. It was only teaching boys 'to curse more bitterly that country which gave them birth, and to whose laws they owe their ruin' [31] and when Naval historian Captain Brenton asked those running *Euryalus* whether any boy was likely to be reformed: 'I am told none ever have been, and I infer that none ever will be.'[32]

Hospital nurse Thomas Dexter was unequivocal. Asked whether any boy on *Euryalus* had been reformed, he replied with feeling:

I should most certainly say not; and frequently when I have seen it in a Newspaper that a Judge has sentenced a Boy out of Mercy to him to the Hulks, I have made the Observation that was it a Child of mine I would rather see him dead at my Feet than see him sent to that Place.[33]

Pioneering social and economic reformers Sidney and Beatrice Webb, founders of the London School of Economics and Political Science, described the hulks as 'the most brutalising, the most demoralising, the most horrible' of all places of confinement in British history.[34] Even in Hobart Town, on the other side of the world, convicts' final British 'address' was well known as a 'school of vice and iniquity…an abode of wretchedness' where boys have 'grown and ripened in crime and infamy, and may be truly compared to the fungi of vegetation that grows and flourishes where everything that is beautiful and delicate fades, droops and dies'.[35]

The wretched lives of boys like Sparkes and Campbell were frequently characterised in newspapers and parliamentary debates in education terms: their progress from a 'nursery of crime' on the streets, to the 'preparatory schools' of Houses of Correction, to the 'felony academy' at Millbank Prison and then seven months at the *Euryalus* 'school of vice' or 'college' of crime, as even some of the prisoners called it. Now Sparkes and Campbell were to be sent to the other side of the world to a 'university of the wicked' known as Van Diemen's Land.

Travelling with them was the report card of their lives, just twelve or thirteen years long.

Henry Sparkes, prisoner 2434.	**Charles Campbell**, prisoner 4012.
Crime: Stealing a halfpence, Nottingham.	Crime: House-breaking, Aberdeen.
Convicted: 31 December 1838.	Convicted: 25 September 1840.
Sentence: Seven years.	Sentence: Seven years.
Received Chatham: 6 February 1839.	Received Chatham: 15 November 1840.
Status: Single.	Status: Single.
Read or write: Neither.	Read or write: Neither.
Gaoler's report: Character very bad, thrice in prison, a natural propensity to steal.	Gaoler's report: Convicted before. Character bad. Very bad disposition. Disorderly.
How disposed of: VDL. 28 September 1840.[36]	How disposed of: VDL. 21 June 1841.[37]

The final column spoke a severe truth: Britain's unwanted children were being 'disposed of'. A rich and powerful country with deep-seated traditions of government, religion, charity, education and philosophy had concluded it could do no more than despatch them to an infant colony on the other side of the world. As Archbishop Richard Whatley caustically told the House of Lords, men in power were often 'naturally disposed to…any suggestion or hope that may justify them in withdrawing their attention from an unpleasant subject,'[38] and delinquency was such an unpleasant subject that Prime Minister Lord Melbourne advised young Queen Victoria not to read the serialization of *Oliver Twist* because it was 'all among the workhouses…and pickpockets…I don't like those things; I don't like them in reality and I don't want them represented'.[39]

One of the men in power, Colonial Secretary Lord John Russell, may have been comforted by odious delinquents being rightly removed out of sight and out of mind, but privately discomforted by the boys' fate:

> Is it reasonable that virtuous England should find her vicious
> pollution suddenly transmuted into patterns of virtue and
> innocence the moment they breathe the pure atmosphere of
> Australia? There is no magic in transportation. The vicious
> will remain vicious unless adequate means are provided for
> their reformation.[40]

No magic in transportation, but Henry Sparkes and Charles Campbell were among thousands now being 'disposed of', hustled from the *Euryalus* hulk to a convict ship at Sheerness, in north Kent, for a long and dangerous voyage of more than 14,000 miles (22,000 km) across unfamiliar and perilous seas to an unfamiliar and perilous destination.

6

A BANISHMENT
BEYOND THE SEAS

He lay gasping on a little flock mattress, rather unequally poised between this world and the next, the balance being decidedly in favour of the latter.
— Charles Dickens, *Oliver Twist*

Like 76,000 others who formed Her Majesty's convict cargo bound for Van Diemen's Land, Sparkes and Campbell would not see their homeland again, but the memories of the final moments would take a long time to recede. For Sparkes and Campbell their final impressions of Britain were on the River Medway, a major thoroughfare to the Thames and London, with all the sounds and smells of industrial Britain: shipyards, a large smithery, saw mills, chalk quarries, cement works and flat-bottomed barges ferrying mud and coal to and from the capital.

The Medway was the site of the first major recorded battle of the Roman invasion of Britain in AD43, where Sir Francis Drake learned to sail, and where, soon after the disasters of the Great Plague and Great Fire, London again felt fear in one of its biggest military defeats at the hands of the Dutch in 1667. Now Medway's place in history was as a centrepiece in the battle against delinquency, and Henry Sparkes and Charles Campbell were two of its casualties.

Relieved after seven months to be leaving the ghostly *Euryalus* in the autumn of 1840 and not left behind on Dead Man's Island, the cemetery for convict victims of illness and violence, Sparkes shuffled onto the 424-ton *HMS Hindostan*, an old East Indies trading vessel. Eight months later, in the summer of 1841, Campbell boarded the 360-ton *HMS Lord Goderich*, a former Navy vessel.

Sparkes was one of 143 *Hindostan* boys on a seven-year sentence, while nearly seventy others faced longer sentences of ten, fourteen, fifteen years or life. On the *Lord Goderich*, Campbell was likewise one of 143 boys sentenced to seven years, with forty-three others on longer sentences.

The sentence durations would have meant little to young boys. They could have had no sense of the monumental voyage facing them, facing the longest journey of their lives across seas they had never seen to the far side of the globe. And no notion of where they would next put foot on land. It would be at the very bottom of the maps of the known world, an island born of a Jurassic upheaval, smaller than Ireland, its arrowhead shape like a flint spear aimed at the cold unknown of Antarctica.

And if a boy was to question just how far away was this destination of Van Diemen's Land, he might be told by a sailor that if he knew where the earth ended it was much farther than that, and there was no point thinking of seeing this British land again because it was too far to be coming back.

And they might hear that many did not even survive the journey. A year before Campbell's departure, the *Lord Goderich* was almost lost when it smashed into another convict ship in mountainous seas off the Isle of Wight. England was shocked when 130 passengers, mainly women and children, aboard the *Amphitrite* drowned in the English Channel within sight of Boulogne after the owner-captain spurned rescue attempts because he claimed to not have the authority to land convicts on foreign soil and worried they would escape. Closer to the destination, over thirty children were among more than 200 Irish convicts lost in the *Neva* shipwreck off King Island in Bass Strait. The *George III* was shipwrecked within sight of Hobart Town with 111 convicts lost at sea and others shot to prevent their escape from below deck, and the *Cataraqui* would be lost in Bass Strait with 400 victims.

Fumigation and white-washing did not hide the fact that the convict ships were not built for transporting large numbers of prisoners on long voyages. Sparkes' ship, the *Hindostan*, Persian for the Indian sub-continent where it had traded for the British East India Company before the British Government wanted it for human cargo, had been built twenty years before in Whitby, where Captain James Cook undertook the merchant navy apprenticeship which ultimately led to his historic voyage to the great southern land. Campbell's *Lord Goderich,* named after a former Secretary of State for War and the Colonies who became the shortest-serving Prime Minister of anyone who did not die in office, was one of the smallest convict ships and 'the Dover papers say she is a perfect Noah's ark'.[1]

Now these 'arks' readied to 'save' boys of all ages from around the kingdom, a one-way journey repeated every few months for more than half a century since the First Fleet arrived at Botany Bay and planted a new colony with 586 men and 192 women convicts. Among the 'founders' of Australia were five convict children under sixteen, including a chimney sweep boy convicted at age nine. Since then transportation had grown on an industrial scale. Britain was not the only country to embrace transportation — Italy, Spain, Portugal, Holland Russia also engaged in the trade — but it embraced banishment more enthusiastically. More than 160,000 convicts were ultimately transported to Australian colonies on about 800 ships. As many as 25,000 were under eighteen, with between 10,000 and 13,000 young boys despatched to Van Diemen's Land. By the time transportation ended in 1853, the island colony had received about forty-five percent of all convicts landed in Australia, and nearly twenty percent of all those transported in the British Empire since 1615.[2]

Boys could not fully understand what 'transported across the seas' truly meant, or appreciate the remoteness and isolation 'where the earth ends'. Some 'looked forward to the time of being sent abroad eagerly, for what with close confinement, application to duty, and being closely watched, they are glad to be removed from the (hulk) ship,'[3] and seemed to 'care not for their lives'.[4]

Almost all the boys were undersize in height and weight, reflecting their childhoods of impoverishment, illness, poor diet and incarceration. Superintendent James Baird noted some of his *Lord Goderich* boys 'appeared weakly and pale from confinement'[5] but 'all declared themselves in good health', and those travelling with Charles Campbell were generally 'in good spirits being anxious for the change of life that the voyage promised them'.[6] But Baird knew from experience that some boys feigned good health so they could leave, and one of Campbell's companions 'like all the others reported himself well on coming on board but soon afterwards he was coughing for several days, which he concealed fearing it might cause him to be detained in the hulk…he was in danger of losing his life'.[7]

Others feigned illness in the hope of not being transported. Boys sometimes were carried aboard and 'laid on deck' unconscious or having convulsions 'sometimes hysterical, sometimes…resembling those of epilepsy'.[8] Another superintendent reported 'a number of cases of convulsion…nausea and vomiting'.[9]

Every convict had his or her own tale to tell of their

transportation, but each, if they were honest, felt Dickens' words about the foreboding initiation 'over a boundless sea, with a blood red sky above and the angry waters lashed into fury breath, boiling and eddying up on every side'.[10]

Still, they could have no sense they were on their way to becoming convict slaves. Philanthropist and politician William Wilberforce's campaign against slavery for another twenty years succeeded in 1833, but unwanted convicts and juvenile delinquents would continue to be despatched to Van Diemen's Land in what a British Parliamentary Select Committee described as 'the economical history of a slave colony'.[11] Even hard-lined Van Diemen's Land governor George Arthur and his Attorney-General Alfred Stephen conceded convicts were 'only slaves…transport is truly a condemnation to slavery',[12] while the Archbishop of Dublin, Richard Whatley, went further, telling the House of Lords it was 'worse than negro slavery'.[13]

Sparkes and Campbell were more likely to have heard prison and hulk talk that convict life at least offered regular food and shelter, and a better climate, and they might have heard of convicts bragging to friends they have 'several wives and [life] is filled every day with rum and kangaroo'.[14]

They would not have heard arguments about transportation, which had been raging since Lord Francis Bacon, a former Lord High Chancellor, warned in 1625 of early colonization in North America that 'it is a shameful and unblessed thing to take the scum of the people and wicked condemned men to be the people with whom you plant'.[15] But two-hundred years later, such 'planting of the wicked' continued. Dublin Archbishop Whatley observed that the Government resisted the abandonment of transportation as a convenience borne out of 'despair of finding a substitute',[16] despite it failing the four tests of being a formidable punishment, corrective, humane and cheap: 'To think of diminishing crime by simply removing the criminals without holding out an effectual terror to future offenders is like undertaking to empty a lake by baling [sic] out the water without stopping the river which flows into it.'[17] But Whitehall remained determined that transportation, even of boy convicts, remain as 'an object of real terror to all classes of the community...permanently formidable', and not be diluted by any 'ill-considered compassion for convicts'.[18]

Draining children out of Britain's criminal lake was one thing, but some colonial administrators, reformers, and churchmen were especially horrified that incarceration with older youths and adults risked exposure to 'unnatural crime'. The long-standing abhorrence was rooted in the Biblical story of Sodom and Gomorrah, cities destroyed with fire and brimstone due the wickedness and sin of men who would rather have sex with other men, or boys, than the virginal daughters offered by Lot. A Parliamentary Select Committee declared sodomy in the convict colonies was 'more common than in any part of the civilised world', mostly involving 'the young boys'. It was 'the glory of men convicts to corrupt a boy; in fact they could not live if they resisted' and boys known as 'kitty' or 'nanny' were not particularly detested or abhorred, merely called 'sods'.[19]

With greater concern over sodomy than slavery, and long-standing British Navy laws demanding that 'if any Person in the Fleet shall commit the unnatural and detestable Sin of Buggery or Sodomy with Man or Beast, he shall be punished with Death by the Sentence of a Court-martial'.[20] Sodom and Gomorrah were stains, and strains, too far.

The prospect of boys, even condemned delinquents, being engaged in 'so un-English and unnatural'[21] sin on Her Majesty's convict voyages meant by the time the *Hindostan* drew anchor on 5 October 1840 with Henry Sparkes and 208 other convicts — mostly boys — aboard, and the *Lord Goderich* drew anchor on 29 June 1841, with Charles Campbell and 185 others — a third under sixteen — authorities were making some attempts to separate and protect younger boys. But young boys still mixed with, and were supervised by, older youths and adult convicts in unsuitable ships.

Repeated protests by reformers in London and administrators in Van Diemen's Land did move Colonial Secretary Lord John Russell to finally conclude in 1836 that:

> it appears desirable…that instead of the present practice of sending by each ship…a portion of young criminals, it would be advisable to employ (occasionally) a ship exclusively for that purpose so as to avoid the evil of mixing up that class of offenders with older criminals during the voyage.[22]

The first boys-only *Frances Charlotte* was despatched to favourable reports, but just seven more boys-only ships were sent before economics again prevailed, the desirability of avoiding evil abandoned because separate boys' ships would 'cause increased expense'.[23]

So the likes of Sparkes and Campbell continued to be crowded together, 'the incurably vicious and the novices in guilt'.[24] As one convict recalled: 'Three, four or more are placed in one wooden crib, the seven-year prisoner couched with the convict for life, the thief with the murderer, the simple countryman with the jail-polluted felon and the monster from the hulk'.[25]

Superintendents Andrew Henderson and John Baird could not do much about their ships' inadequate design or resources. They could only resolve to fulfil their duty and receive the reward for each boy landed in Hobart Town by preventing any major illness, mutinous spirit — a fear dating back since the first attempt on the First Fleet — violence or sodomy.

The first preventive measure was to search each boy for any dangerous weapons when they came on board. As one *Hindostan* voyage account emphasised:

> not withstanding every precaution they contrive…to secrete [sic] files, and pieces of metal, which they ingeniously convert to almost any purpose, and constant firmness was absolutely necessary, for too much good nature or leniency… is instantly taken advantage of, and it is surprising how soon they discern the dispositions of those they have to deal with.[26]

Everyone and everything was numbered and monitored. Every boy's name, age, origin, occupation, education, hair and eye colour, physique and distinguishing mark was checked on arrival. They were given berth, mess and division numbers, and were provided with a numbered mattress, blanket and plate.

Such strict discipline and obedience were a way of life for Navy men, but foreign concepts to street boys. They might have heard 'love thy neighbour' in prison hulk religious instruction, but their world was one of 'do to your neighbour what he would do to you'. Their 'treachery toward each other' captivated a London magazine writer:

> They cannot, or will not, be faithful even in the most trifling matters…the itch for thieving among them is wholly unconquerable. They steal from each other, or from anyone else, almost everything they can, without enquiring whether it is worth the trouble, whether they can make use of it, or whether they want it.[27]

Many boys, he observed, 'care not for their lives' and easily became 'sulky, impudent and intractable, insulting those whom they cannot otherwise assail'.[28] The boys' secretive 'flash' language, ever-changing as authorities discovered the true meaning of a word, and the various dialects of townies, yokels, north boys and Dublin boys flummoxed the navy surgeon-superintendents.

But the message was clear from the first muster that while the superintendent would endeavour to make the journey as safe and accommodating as possible, this was a convict voyage, and he was in charge of discipline as much as their well-being. A common message was:

> I have to make a return to the Lieutenant Governor on our arrival at Van Diemen's Land of the good and the bad boys, so you know what you are all to expect. Severe punishment awaits you that behave ill during the voyage, and I shall be most rigid in any punishments on board. Bread and water, solitary confinement is my mode and the cat of nine tails.[29]

They would strive, within the limitations of resources and facilities, to meet Admiralty orders to use 'best endeavours [to]…keep the minds of the people on board convict ships as constantly and usefully employed as possible'.[30]

Naval discipline and penal intolerance meant boys would pay a severe price for any misconduct, insolence, profanity, disobedience and abuse. They faced food and water regimes, black box confinement, leg irons and thrashings. One boy who stole shirts in the hope of selling them on arrival was flogged and made to walk around deck with his bedding on his back and an 'I am a thief' placard.[31] All offences in deed or attitude were more 'bad' citations inked into the black books to be handed to the colonial governor on their arrival.

Sparkes and Campbell found convict ship routine similar to that of the prison hulk. They were roused at dawn each day and mustered on deck to be doused in salt water. After breakfast at 8am the utensils had to be cleaned and decks scrubbed and whitened with a soft sandstone — known as holystone because sailors on hands and knees resembled those performing a devotion — and hammocks stowed. A morning session introduced rudiments of reading and writing, taught by a convict. Then boys received a 'limey' potion: the Admiralty's physician general, William Burnett, having ordered a concoction of lime juice, citric acid and nitrate of potash to help combat scurvy — always a fear on ships unable to carry enough fresh vegetables for so many for so long.

Another lesson followed between lunch and supper — the meals usually a mix of bread, hard tack biscuits, salted beef or pork — after which the boys could, if the superintendent approved, enjoy some exercise or time on deck before being locked up at sunset in the gloom below. This was followed with a final inspection to ensure everyone was in his correct berth. Specific days were set aside each week for washing clothes and hair-cuts, and on Sundays boys were told to assemble 'in a clean and orderly manner' for worship and a hygiene inspection of their eyes, gums, hair, feet and legs — the first time many had experienced even cursory concern for their wellbeing.

Prayers were said at each meal and before lock-down, but prayers were no guarantee Sparkes and Campbell would survive potentially fatal accidents — falling down holds to decks below or being struck by swinging booms — or fire, violence, illness and disease. Waves often washed through the lower decks soaking all the bedding and hampering efforts to quell a bacterial outbreak of erysipelas — known to sailors as St Anthony's fire — which ate into the skin causing painful burning sensations, spasms and seizures. And with only salt water for a weekly wash 'the saline particles allowed to remain day after day on the edge of the eyelids…frequently led to ophthalmia'.[32] The superintendents also dealt with syphilis, gonorrhoea, scrofula (a form of tuberculosis), typhus or 'ship fever', cholera, diarrhoea, dysentery, stomach pains, severe constipation, respiratory issues, anthrax and rheumatism.[33]

Conditions were punishing: casks of fresh water often became slimy and smelly, salted beef and pork often turned putrid, biscuits might have to be tapped first to shake out any weevil grubs, ship rats were common, butter and cheese might be rancid, and peas became as hard as shot. The typical diet alternated between 2 pounds (1 kg) of beef and 1 ¾ pound (800 g) of pork with small rations of flour and peas. Surgeon Henderson admitted the food 'is really horrible; no human stomach could bear it on long voyages'.[34]

Out of concern for 'moral contamination' Superintendent Henderson, a veteran of eight convict voyages, selected forty-eight *Hindostan* boys he felt exhibited 'good conduct' and appointed them as night watchmen. From 6pm to 6am, their duties were to 'preserve order and good behaviour among the boys'. There was to be no 'larking, quarrelling, fighting, swearing, the using of indecent or obscene language and the singing of immoral songs', and Sparkes and others were to be in their allocated berths by 8pm and maintain a strict silence.[35] On the *Lord Goderich*, Superintendent Baird utilised ten adult convicts as supervisors of Campbell and others on his ship.

With seas and juveniles both known for their treachery, the captains of *Hindostan* and *Lord Goderich* forged their way south through the stormy Atlantic as quickly as possible. Their route was to 'cross the line' of the Equator and reach the Cape of Good Hope for some respite and fresh supplies, and then be pushed eastward for about six weeks by the Roaring Forties trade winds, blowing between forty and fifty degrees latitude for 6,000 miles (9,600 km) across the Great Southern Ocean.

The captains well knew it was the longest uninterrupted ocean in the world, but one which could be unpredictably interrupted by hazardous waves and massive icebergs. The *Hindostan* confronted one that was 'grand and imposing…at least 3 miles [5 km] in circumference and 300 feet [91 m] high'. With the ship no more than 'a musket shot' away, Sparkes would have seen 'the highest part had the appearance of an ancient castle in ruins', and 'large pieces of ice fell from its sides into the deep, with an awful splash'.[36]

When ships neared the Great Southern Land and the beginning of Bass's Strait — as the water separating the southern continent from Van Diemen's Land was known — the captains veered southward, following the same land features marked on navigation maps since 1772 when the French broke the isolation which had endured since Dutchman Abel Tasman's voyage of 1642.

The sighting of 'land ahoy' on New Holland, or Australia as it was beginning to be more commonly known, was enthusiastically received. One superintendent described some 'animated eagerness to behold their future country…fun and frolics arise out of the common hilarity'.[37] The end was in sight, although one convict recognised the unknown beginning on the horizon, with much 'conjecture…as to our future destiny…a state of suspense which was to continue for some time'.[38]

After rounding the south-west of Van Diemen's Land, the ships headed north-east toward the mouth of the Derwent, or Riviere du Nord as it was known for thirty years. Their appearance on the horizon would soon be semaphored to authorities in Hobart Town, and a printer at the *Colonial Times* would soon be typesetting details in the shipping intelligence column.

In the ritual of arrival, sailors enjoyed telling the newest convicts that their life trials left behind in Britain were nothing to what they now faced: spear-throwing natives; desperate escaped convicts — christened as 'bolters' or 'bush-rangers' — some familiar with cannibalism; and wild and strange creatures, such as devils, striped tigers, venomous snakes and giant kangaroos. And around the island were wild seas full of sharks and whales.

But no one forewarned wide-eyed young boy convicts of the real trial they faced. One they had to truly understand: that the lottery of life had been transported with them, and the greater the distance from Mother Country the more random the truth and justice. And their destiny.

7

THIS STRANGE LOTTERY

I wear the chain forged in life. I made it link by link and yard by yard;
I girded it of my own free will, and of my own free will I wore it.
— Charles Dickens, *Christmas Carol*

Fourteen thousand miles (22,000 km) from home Henry Sparkes and Charles Campbell now approached the most remote and unforgiving land in the Empire, a Jurassic basalt and granite island born of mother nature's violent smashing of the former super continent of Gondwana and now ruled by unforgiving colonial masters.

Sentries at a string of stations scanned ship flag signals through telescopes and semaphored a ship's imminent arrival up the Derwent River to Mount Nelson, where a 78-foot (24 m) post could raise and lower six arms to communicate over 900,000 separate signals. The most common were a white flag with a red cross signalling a friendly

British ship on Her Majesty's service, and red or blue flags indicating cargoes of male or female convicts. These colours were first raised in 1812 and on another 327 vessels for the next forty years.

From Mount Nelson the messages reached Battery Point, a small hill close to Government House and the heart of Hobart Town, where a Royal Navy gun battery stood ready to resist any French territorial ambitions. As the semaphoring did for the *Hindostan* and *Lord Goderich*, two of sixteen ships which brought 2659 male and 803 female convicts in 1841, one of the busiest years of the island's convict trade, boosted by the cessation of transportation to New South Wales. Except for small numbers despatched to colonies like Bermuda and Gibraltar, virtually all the Empire's 'dregs' were now drained to Van Diemen's Land.

Shipping was also the colony's umbilical cord to the Mother Country and the world, with political, social and economic lives hinging on news, official despatches and cargo. Convicts were the main commodity of the stock exchange that was the docks of Hobart Town. But ships to and from England, France, America and other colonies carried essential supplies and products for the colony's breweries, whale stations, tanneries, timber and flour mills, soap and candle factories, sheep and wheat farms. And also the personal comforts of hats, gloves, tobacco, tea, coffee, casks of rum and wine, snuff, soap, perfumes, furniture, pianos and toys.

A *Ship News* column in January 1841 detailed ten new ships in port, including:

> Jan.19 – Arrived the ship *Hindostan*, 424 tons, Richardson master, from England, with 209 male prisoners; Dr Henderson, RN Superintendent; Lieut. Barclay and a detachment of the 96h Regt.[1]

The True Colonist and *VDL Despatch* further clarified the cargo: 'The *Hindostan*…brings prisoners (boys)'.[2]

And in November the *Colonial Times* reported:

> Nov.18 –Arrived the barque *Lord Goderich*, 362 tons, Miles
> master, from Portsmouth 14th July, with male prisoners (176
> boys and 10 men). The Guard consists of Major Robertson
> and 30 rank and file of the 96h Regt., with 1 woman and
> child. Surgeon Superintendent, Mr John Baird.

And in a separate brief item, 'the prisoners on board the *Lord Goderich* are all boys', and it was hoped 'these boys may be saved and become valuable members of society'.[3]

While Government officers and soldiers waited dockside for convicts, free settlers anxiously sought out anyone who might have news of relatives, friends or home towns, or those who might be a useful maid, cook or farm labourer. Convicts with their 'lynx eyes'[4] scanned for someone who might be an old friend, or perhaps a sibling, or someone best avoided. Newspapers, although three to four months old, were quickly snatched up for Hobart Town editors wanting to hastily reprint the news of Queen Victoria, foreign wars, politics, commerce, crime, colonial appointments and government decisions.

From the *Hindostan* came reports of a nine-day bombardment of 'Beyrout' on the coast of Syria, where 'the English fleet, in concert with Austrian and Turkish forces…reduced it to a heap of ashes… the Egyptians evacuated the town on the night and the allies took possession of it', and the death of Princess Augusta, second daughter of King George III, soon after Queen Victoria's wedding, and 'it is said that the Queen will wear mourning for three months'.[5] From the *Lord Goderich* came news that the 'the Queen and her royal consort are in the best of health and spirits', and of the Tories' electoral victory over the Reformers. A victory, the *Colonial Times* editors caustically commented, which ensured the convict trade would continue for at least another five years, and that the colony would continue to endure 'the hermaphrodite state of powerless legislation, with only the shadow of British rights and British privileges'.[6]

Such news and talk of rights and privileges was foreign and

meaningless to boy convicts. They would have simply wanted to get off the ship and assess this new world and the next chapter of their lives. Like every other convict arriving directly from Britain since the *Indefatigable* twenty-nine years before, Sparkes and Campbell's eyes would have been darting when they arrived, in January and November 1841 respectively. There was much to absorb. The Derwent was bigger than any river they had seen, 2.5 miles (4 km) wide, one of the deepest natural ports in the world and big enough to have white caps and an occasional whale. The sky also seemed so much bigger, the light brighter and the air fresher than any they had breathed. Some things were somewhat familiar: swans swam among more than thirty barques, brigs, brigantines, whalers, schooners and a Royal Navy warship. On shore were busy docks and Salamanca warehouses, and some sandstone buildings, such as Government House, Customs House and Supreme Court, and pubs with names like the Pickwick Tavern, the Cornish, Rose and Crown. There was the clatter of stage-coaches rushing passengers and mail to inland settlements and horse-drawn carriages keeping the well-dressed clear of the dirt and grime, especially around the working-class area of Wapping. Assaulting the crisp air was the whiff of the tanneries, soap and chemical factories, slaughter yards and sewage and waste in the Hobart Rivulet.

Hobart Town, or Hobarton, and its population of 15,000 — second only to Sydney — was not dissimilar to parts of England and Scotland. But beneath the brooding sentinel of Mount Wellington were shadows. This was the world's most unique settlement, the British Empire's most 'peculiar' colony as Lord Bathurst, Secretary of State for War and the Colonies described it,[7] one established with no real view to territorial or commercial advantage, merely a receptacle and symbol of 'considerable terror' for convicts.

This ancient land which had drawn Europeans such as Abel Tasman, Tobias Furneaux, Antoine de Bruni d'Entrecasteaux, and Nicholas Baudin in pursuit of geography and science had been

Salamanca Place in Hobart Town. *Hobart - Salamanca Place*, sketch, 1844.
Image courtesy Libraries Tasmania, PH30-1-447.

recast by the British in the name of punishment. One of the world's oldest indigenous peoples had been pushed aside to accommodate foreign outcasts — rural settlers boasted of how prussic acid, or cyanide, had caused Aboriginals to 'die about the place like rats'[8] — and even free settlers found their Old World liberties subservient to the convicted in this strange New World.

This land was one of conflicts and contests over justice and injustice, bondage and freedom, duty and values, hopes and fears. Half of the 57,000 inhabitants were convict men and women — adults and children — stolen away from all parts of the Empire, not just from England, Scotland and Ireland, but also from Africa, America, Canada, the West Indies, Italy and even Iceland. The other half were soldiers and administrators following orders, and settlers following their dreams.

The conflicts were confronting and often deadly. Sparkes and Campbell would have seen convict men 'manacled by chains' in road labour gangs or pulling carts like bullocks, wearing 'somewhat grotesque' clothing of black and yellow patches which 'remind you of the appearance of a merry clown'.[9] And in the heart of town the neighbouring Supreme Court and gaol, with a scaffold positioned for spectators, where they 'sends a man into eternity every day, at the usual hour, sometimes 10 at a time'.[10]

But penal servitude for Sparkes and Campbell would not be one of 'clown' cloth and manacles, nor would they be under lock and key, unless they re-offended. This was an island prison whose primary walls were those provided by Mother Nature in the form of the notorious ocean waters, a forerunner of infamous island prisons like Devil's Island (French Guiana), Alcatraz (United States) and Britain's recasting of Robben Island (South Africa).

They would also not be part of the 'slave lottery' system under which convicts, including some teenagers, provided enslaved labour for government buildings, roads, bridges and churches, or for settlers in homes, farms and businesses.

And they would not, they were disappointed to discover, even to disembark at Hobart Town, a unique town born of expediency in London. Instead they would be sailed further to a unique settlement born of expediency in Hobart Town — a place called Point Puer.

Since the first twenty-four convicts arrived in the colony from the mainland in 1803, the overall intake steadily grew to about 1200 a year in the 1820s to 2000 a year, then 3000, then 4000, and the juvenile component grew steadily from a handful on a few ships to hundreds on dozens of ships.

Too many boys for the governor Lieutenant Colonel George Arthur. They did not align with his efforts to harness convict labour to develop a sustainable colony, nor his views on discipline, reformation and morality. Forty boys who arrived with 150 men on the *Asia* in 1827 were 'scarcely able to turn their hand to any employment' and as assigned 'slaves' they were 'entirely useless, and generally so mischievous are these corrupt little rogues that they are the dread of every family'.[11] The next year he complained that boys who had been long periods on the hulks to 'inevitably become more vicious' would soon finish their sentences in the colony 'without having felt sufficiently the discipline to which convicts transported to the colony should be subjected'.[12]

When the *Georgiana* arrived in mid-1829, Arthur welcomed a detachment of the 21st Fusiliers and 'a very well selected assortment of fruit trees from the Horticultural Society of London'.[13] But he was disappointed to discover the majority of apple, pear and cherry trees had perished, and more so again to see sixty more boys arriving alongside 120 men. It was dismaying, said the *Hobart Town Courier*, to see so many 'mere boys, on an average not more than 10 or 12 years of age',[14] and one, from Preston, reportedly just seven years-old.[15] When one, about four feet (122 cm) tall and appearing to be ten-years-old was asked by the Principal Convict Superintendent his age, 'the little urchin' replied 'he was so young when he was born that he could not tell'.[16]

The Courier said it was 'distressing' to know 'how to dispose of them'.[17] A few older ones might learn to become bullock drivers or ploughmen, or hut keepers on the stock runs, 'but the majority are, we fear, incapable of even such service' and it could not conceive of a plan worse than keeping them in the Hobart Town Prisoner Barracks where 'the very worst examples must be incessantly before their eyes'.[18] Known as Rat's Castle, the barracks were built by convicts in 1821 to house 640 but had to be progressively extended to squeeze more and more convicts into every inch of available space, including the ceiling cavity. Children were kept alongside older youths and seasoned criminals, including sodomists, rapists and even murderers, and those marked as physically and mentally incapacitated or unsuitable as a 'moral' risk to others.

As the number of boy convicts rose so did an unanticipated truth: they were not wanted, and they could not be protected.

Not wanted, because they were too small and weak to provide the labour to help the government build, mine coal or quarry stone, and too illiterate to provide any clerical assistance. Too profane, dishonest and insolent to be welcomed into settlers' homes, businesses and farms, and not offering enough benefits to justify the cost of their food, clothing and accommodation. Their skills as a textile factory worker, or chimney sweep, poacher or pickpocket were not in demand.

And not protected in barracks where a chaplain wrote of 'twelve hundred men…congregated there like beasts [where] every kind of villainy and wickedness that imagination can invent is planned and carried on'.[19] As a devout Christian and ambitious officer, Arthur well appreciated the 'unspeakable' reality of 'vice Anglais' wherever large numbers of sex-deprived men were held, the 'vice which a Christian is scarcely permitted to name'.[20]

Every 'corrupt little rogue' arriving in Hobart Town was thus both 'useless' and a potential 'stain' on Arthur's administration, and he complained to the Colonial Office that it was not only 'utterly impossible to imagine a more corrupt fraternity of depraved little Felons'[21] but they were 'very young…very depraved and difficult to manage, perhaps more so than grown men'.[22]

On Christmas Eve 1833, Hobart Town was taken aback when the *Isabella* arrived with 'nearly one half of the prisoners, 300…boys from eight to ten years of age'.[23] People lamented 'the appalling sight of a great number of little boys…marched morning and night from and to the Penitentiary to work with the road gangs'[24] guarded by soldiers in Napoleonic war outfits of scarlet jackets, flat-topped hats and muskets. The *Colonial Times* deplored free settlers' children being taught to be familiar with chain gangs:

> The infant looks upon the ironed doubly convicted felon as a being necessary to form part and parcel of the Government. The yellow clothes are looked upon as regimentals, and the nurse takes the child to witness the workings of the chain gangs with much the same feeling as that same nurse would in England take the child to see the soldiers perform their exercise.[25]

Arthur lambasted the *Isabella*'s 'depraved little felons' displaying 'disgraceful levity' instead of 'abject shame and a sense of disgrace attached to banishment'.[26] He delivered his standard address to newly arrived convicts: if they behaved they could eventually look forward to a ticket of leave — perhaps even an appointment in the constabulary (the pay was too low to attract free settlers, and Arthur believed in 'setting a thief to catch a thief') — and 'ultimately emancipation and pardon'. But those whose misconduct:

> subjects him to be repeatedly noted in the black books of the police, whose habits…involve him in a vortex of wickedness, misery and ruin, can look forward to little else than the usual gradation of punishment…namely to labour in the party-coloured garments on the roads, to lashes, the treadmill, chains, a penal settlement and at last, the gallows.[27]

George Arthur, Governor of Tasmania 1824 – 1836, illustration.
Image courtesy Libraries Tasmania, PH30-1-429.

George Arthur had been deemed the 'right sort of chap' for His Majesty's rule of Van Diemen's Land. He had previously commanded a small British settlement in Honduras, where almost 3000 African and native American slaves, accounting for nearly eighty per cent of the population, were harnessed to capitalise on the ready supply of mahogany. While evincing some empathy for any illegal or abused slaves, Arthur built a reputation of taking a hard-line against anyone disobedient or resistant to his authority to the point that the secretary of the British Army Commander in Chief, the Duke of York, criticized his 'most tyrannical, arbitrary and capricious conduct'.[28]

The rising colonial martinet was determined to bring discipline and propriety to the new colony of Van Diemen's Land after his predecessors struggled with its isolation, inadequate supplies, corrupt officers, unhappy military, aboriginal conflict, unskilled convicts, bushrangers, cannibals, shortage of women, criminality and wide-spread drunkenness. Some were also not unfamiliar with 'wickedness': David Collins was criticised by NSW Governor William Bligh for affairs with convict women, Thomas 'Mad Tom' Davey was best known for arriving drunk and inventing the 'Blow My Skull' cocktail, and William Sorell abandoned his wife and seven children in London without financial support and was slated at the Colonial Office for 'living in open adultery' at Government House with the wife of another officer.

By contrast, Arthur arrived with a Bible in one hand and a prim wife, Eliza, on the other. A devout evangelical, he dressed in black, preferred to avoid all public amusements, and refused to patronise activities, such as horse-racing, of which he did not approve.

He was not given a handbook on how to run a penal colony. He would receive few specific instructions, unsurprising given transportation emanated from a House of Commons committee's search for an 'expedient [way] to establish a colony of convicted felons in any distant part of the Globe, from whence escape might be difficult…and…might be enabled to maintain themselves…with little or no aid from the Mother Country'.[29] So he developed his own manual on punishment and management of convicts, but also pursued what he called his 'idol' of promotion and also personal profit by juggling distant superiors and local realities, winning allies and punishing enemies.

Knowing London wanted to put fear back into transportation, his bureaucratic zealotry and the isolation of Van Diemen's Land meant he could, and would, oblige. 'This colony must be considered in the light of an extensive gaol to the empire — the punishment of crimes and reformation of criminals the grand objects,' he declared.[30] His role was to be 'governor of a wretched sequestered lot, peopled by the refuse of Newgate'[31] 'and he described himself as 'little more than a gaoler on an extensive scale'.[32]

British laws of justice and liberty would only prevail when 'the Chief Ruler'[33] and his loyal faction, known as Arthurites, felt it desirable and practical. With the help of an Executive Council — 'the dark enclave'[34] of key officials and the first Supreme Court chief justice — and the loyalty of key appointees, such as the Chief Police Magistrate and Colonial Secretary who had both married into his family, Arthur imposed one of the world's first police states. In a pioneering criminal intelligence system he employed a constable for every ninety people, and brought the zeal of 'the most indefatigable quill driver of his own or any other age',[35] with clerks working fourteen hours a day to maintain volumes of 'black books' recording everything about a convict and his or her identity, movements and behaviour.

And the police state applied to everyone, including free settlers and the press. Arthur told a House of Commons Select Committee that 'Van Diemen's Land being a large gaol, free settlers who had become its willing inmates must abide by the rules of the prison'.[36] Everyone had to 'enjoin the strictest fulfillment of the law upon all convicts sent to this colony, and their punishment should be certain

and severe' and everyone had to 'forbid every species of indulgence…
to every convict'.[37]

Arthur was a classic Dickensian character, espousing Christian
values but delivering a severe and sometimes dark outcome. Arthur's
belief was that all men's hearts were 'desperately wicked' without
salvation, and that convicts were Godless victims of a 'mental
delirium', their moral choice meaning any reformation and penance
could only come from unrelenting hard labour and discipline. Just
as Dickens wrote that the kind of work most abhorred by a thief
or vagrant 'is…sweating profusely at the treadmill or the crank,
extremely galled to know that he is doing nothing all the time but
undergoing punishment',[38] so the Governor demanded convicts be
'kept rigidly at the spade and pick-axe and wheel-barrow…from
morning till night, although the immediate toil of the convicts be
the only beneficial result of their labour'.[39]

If Arthur had to impose harsh labour for no benefit, enforce
'slave' labour, and constantly monitor and punish, he would. If he had
to declare martial law against the rapidly diminishing Aboriginals,
who had declined from perhaps 6000 when the first British arrived
to only a few hundred, so be it. If he had to 'red line' free settlers who
did not follow his 'rules', or they had to endure some of the same
restrictions and punishments as convicts, such as flogging, so be it.
If he felt English liberties of trial by jury and a free press had to be
resisted, so be it.

And if Arthur had to find his own solution to Britain's 'solution'
of exiling boy convicts, so be it. All convicts had to have a complete
absence of 'excitement' and desire, other than for an end to their
punishment, in a regime of 'emancipation or death',[40] whichever
came first. Until emancipation or death. That was the truth of
convictism, even for children.

London did not understand, or want to understand, Arthur's
challenge of child convicts. It turned a deaf ear to his complaints of
'depraved little felons', of boys held for too long in prisons or prison

hulks and being mixed with adults on convict ships. He had tried assigning boy convicts to settlers but too many were condemned as 'useless', untrustworthy and insolent, 'the most miserable of mortals…by far the worst sample of the human kind'.[41] He had even despatched some troublesome boys to remote penal settlements for adult re-offenders at Macquarie Harbour, on the west coast, and Maria Island on the east coast.

But after closing both coastal settlements to cut costs and stop convicts escaping and becoming a new form of criminal, 'the lawless Banditti of Bush-rangers'[42] he instituted a new station on the Tasman Peninsula, less than 30 nautical miles east of Hobart. Accessible only by a narrow strip of land or sea, it was a natural penitentiary 30 miles (48 km) long and 15 miles (24 km) wide offering a cheaper, more easily managed separation from the rest of the world. Known immediately as Port Arthur, and by others as 'worse than Dante's hell'[43] and a 'worse than death abode'[44] the penal timber station quickly grew into the third largest settlement in the colony as Arthur — who envisaged it accommodating up to 25,000 adult prisoners — sought a complex that would be self-funding, even profitable, by harnessing cheap convict labour to extract the ash eucalypt timber, known as stringybark, as well as coal, clay, lime and stone. They were to make all of their convict clothing, boots, and also build small boats.

Arthur sent some boys to Port Arthur in the hope they might 'learn habits of industry and not be spread through the country where they would learn vices and form connections which eventually lead…to their ruin'.[45] Some rudimentary schooling was scheduled in the evening but the Port Arthur commandant conceded that 'after the termination of their daily labour they are somewhat exhausted'.[46]

Port Arthur was not a solution, and the colony could not afford to feed, clothe and house the rising number of juvenile with little prospect of becoming useful labourers or mechanics. Nor could Arthur imagine boys ever moving to the 'right path', or his career path progressing, if a solution wasn't found.

ETABLISSEMENT PENITENTIAIRE DE PORT ARTHUR.

Port Arthur, with Point Puer in the distance. *Etablissement penitentiaire de Port Arthur, Terre de Van-Diemen*, engraving, 1854. Image courtesy National Library of Australia, nla.obj- 135882471.

Something had to be done, but Arthur could not wait for secretaries of state for the colonies and home office to offer something beyond more instructions to save the British Treasury as much as possible. Within a week of *Isabella*'s arrival, with its large number of 'depraved little felons', the Convict Assignment Board, probably prompted by Arthur, met to assess the problem. The board comprised: Matthew Forster, chief police magistrate and husband of Arthur's niece, blind in one eye and with self-interest in the other; Joseph Logan, commander of the 63rd regiment; and Josiah Spode, principal superintendent of convicts, and grandson of the founder of the Staffordshire pottery.

The Board duly concluded there was no prospect of 'getting rid of these boys' or 'turning this labour to advantage'. And no means to avoid 'the evils resulting from allowing these boys to congregate in the Barracks with so great a number of men without classification…much increased by the late arrival of the *Isabella* and her miserable cargo'.[47]

It proposed sending boys to Slopen Main, a flat area behind a long white beach on the Tasman Peninsula, not far from Port Arthur, where the government had 'a barn [which] might be at no great expense converted into a barracks'. It recommended a schoolmaster and medical officer be assigned for 'moral and useful instruction', with the rest of the boys' time devoted to 'manual labour with the spade and the hoe' to generate produce for 'their sustenance'.[48] With some 'severe' discipline administered by those already running Port Arthur 'hopefully' some boys would abandon the habits which had brought them to the colony.[49]

But the administrator of Port Arthur, Commandant Charles O'Hara Booth, felt Slopen was too close to some coal mines where he despatched the worst of his adult convicts, and proposed another site just across a bay from Port Arthur. It was on the end of a point, which would allow 'all the boys [to] be managed much better, more securely, and with less exposure'.[50] Arthur immediately accepted

Booth's recommendation and, without seeking Whitehall's approval, signed an order for the preparation of accommodation for the first intake of boys, despatching sixty older boys to hurriedly erect a 90 foot (27 m) x 80 foot (24 m) rough timber barrack to double as a dormitory, mess, schoolroom and chapel for up to 120 boys.

It was not the first effort to better protect and perhaps reform boy convicts: about one hundred in Sydney had been given a separate dormitory and trade training in 1820 at Carters' Barracks, where adult convict gangs worked in the brick fields. But the Van Diemen's Land initiative to build a juvenile version of Port Arthur would come to be recognised as an extraordinary landmark in the history of juvenile punishment and reformation. The English-speaking world's first state-operated prison built exclusively for juveniles, and the first where emerging penal thinking — segregation based on age and criminality, increased isolation and silence, incentives as well as punishment, trade instruction and classroom education — merged, at least in ambition, into a purpose-built facility, four years before Britain's own move to isolate boy convicts in converted Parkhurst Barracks on the Isle of Wight.

In the most remote part of an Empire, Arthur had been forced to confront the consequences of the lost generation of a Dickensian world, and pursue a solution argued for years in London by reformist organisations such as the London Refuge for the Destitute and Philanthropic Institution and Prison Discipline Society, and individual philosophers, writers, judges, magistrates, church leaders and some politicians. For juvenile criminals to have any hope of reformation, they had to be isolated from adverse influences and moral ruin of parents, peers or older prisoners, and receive adequate moral, education and trade instruction, with reformation utilising incentive and not just punishment.

In this new land of exile where French commentators noted that for the first time in the world 'anyone has dared to fashion a society from all that is wicked in another',[51] Britain's 'wicked children' would be isolated in their own exile.

Within a month of the Convict Assignment Board meeting Commandant Booth told Arthur 'the necessary building for 70 boys, or more if required, is ready for their reception'[52] and reassured him the boys 'will be perfectly safe from any intercourse with the present establishment (Port Arthur),[53] although as an added measure he proposed a security 'wall' of 'a steady sergeant and nine rank and file'[54] on a narrow part of the promontory leading to Port Arthur, and wanted the boys to sleep in hammocks 'as it will conduct in all probability better to their moral habits, cleanliness and regularity'.[55]

Booth celebrated the facility's completion with a New Year's Day boat race and picnic on the site, and put a name to the new juvenile outpost: 'The ladies joined us in a picnic at Point Puer (the new settlement for the Boys) where we spent a very pleasant and social afternoon.'[56] The name Puer perhaps emerged over a convivial glass or two at the picnic: Booth was, like Dickens, fond of language with a hidden or double meaning. And his Port Arthur commissary officer, Thomas Lempriere, the son of a prominent Jersey family, spoke several languages including French. The two may have amused themselves over the clever linguistic use of 'puer' as variously referencing youth, immorality and stench.

Convict superintendent Josiah Spode produced a list of sixty-eight boys 'ready to be forwarded to Port Arthur'[57] but while boys were available, resources were not: Arthur told Booth if he wanted a security wall it would have to come from his own establishment because of the lack of disposable forces and 'only 40 hammocks… can be spared'.[58] And there was no mention of the recommended schoolmaster or medical officer.

On 10 January 1834 Booth reported that after spending two months in the Hobart Barracks the 'miserable cargo' of the *Isabella* had arrived. The sixty-eight 'little transport boys…aged dwarfs',[59] were the first of an estimated 3500 child convicts who London would ultimately 'dispose of' by exile to Van Diemen's Land, and Hobart Town would 'get rid of' by further isolation at Point Puer.

Around Hobart Town, 'the lottery of life is ever thus' was oft-expressed. And the lottery of life's chances involved family circumstance, social, economic and moral forces, prejudice, arbitrary judgment and expediency. And the world's first boys prison in exile was the result of all those chances.

8

AN ABODE OF MISERY

When men...commit or sanction the commission of some injustice, it is not uncommon for them to express pity for the object...and to feel themselves...quite virtuous and moral and immensely superior to those who express no pity at all. This is a kind of upholding of faith above works, and is very comfortable.
— Charles Dickens, *Nicholas Nickleby*

Before Henry Sparkes and Charles Campbell took their final leg to Point Puer, they were kept aboard on the waters of the Derwent while every boy was stripped to the waist and measured, inspected and questioned. Every aspect of their identity was checked and recorded in their introduction to an unprecedented system of surveillance.

In the days before photography and fingerprinting, full records were made of their height, age, complexion, head, hair, facial hair, visage, forehead, eyebrows, eyes, nose, mouth and chin. Any distinguishing features, especially those which could not be disguised, were recorded: deformities, scars from injury or smallpox, speech impediments, birthmarks, pigmented spots. Tattoos, which were favoured by more than a third of male convicts, were particularly noted. Some boys had inked initials of loved ones, and depictions of fish, pistols and hearts were common, as was an anchor for 'I have hope', or inverted for 'heading home'. Campbell was one with a 'pockpitted anchor'[1] on his right arm.

Boys were questioned about their criminal and personal past. Their crime record and behaviour in prison, prison hulks and transport ships were transcribed, along with comments by overseers that they were of 'very bad character'. It was all designed to persuade convicts that everything about them was indelibly in the pages of the black books and escape would be impossible.

Any potential for useful labour was also probed. It wasn't enough to know if convicts had farm labouring experience: could they plough, harrow, sow, mow, milk, thatch, shear, tend or break livestock, castrate? But most of the *Euryalus* boys', as they were known, with no useful skills for government gangs or settler assignment, were simply marked down as 'labourers' and assigned a new convict identity.

Henry Sparkes, hulk prisoner 2434, was now:

Henry Sparkes, convict 2866

Trade: labourer	Nose: medium
Height: 4ft 7 1/2 (141 cm)	Mouth: medium
Age: 14	Chin: medium
Complex: fresh	Read/write: read
Head: round	Native place: Nottingham
Hair : dark brown	Remarks: blue mark inside right
Whiskers: none	arm, top of thumb left hand
Visage: oval	injured, much pock-pitted.
Forehead: rather high	Surgeons report: * (* Appears
Eyebrows: brown	to refer to 'offences' but
Eyes: blue	indecipherable).[2]

Charles Campbell, hulk prisoner 4012, was now:

Charles Campbell 3189

Trade: labourer	Nose: large
Height: 3ft 11in (119 cm)	Mouth: large
Age: 14	Chin: large
Complex: fresh	Read/write: nothing
Head: long	Native place: Dublin
Hair: red	Remarks: pockpitted anchor
Whiskers: none	outside right arm, middle finger
Visage: round	left hand has been broken, cannot
Forehead: low narrow	bend.
Eyebrows: brown	Surgeons report: disorderly,
Eyes: dark hazel	mischievous.[3]

Sparkes was of average height, Campbell one of the smallest. Their Millbank, *Euryalus* and convict transport ship records branded Sparkes a 'very bad' character, and Campbell as having a 'very bad disposition, disorderly and mischievous', although such terms were readily attached. What could not be known or recorded was whether boys like Sparkes and Campbell were mostly villain or victim, or what was in their hearts and minds. For some, Van Diemen's Land offered a real 'change of life opportunity' as Campbell's ship superintendent reported, an escape from hunger and street life, or perhaps from intimidation and abuse. Others had already given up hope, and some of the 'bad' did not care to change.

Whatever their hopes or hearts, the new reality for any boy after a lifetime of 'artful dodges' and 'chance' was contained in the *Colonial Times'* ubiquitous *Hobart Town Police Report*, a roll call of the lottery of life, and punishment, in the colony.

On Sparkes' arrival on the *Hindostan* at the beginning of 1841: two convicts found in a public house after hours sentenced to '14 days solitary', and convicts charged by their masters with insulting them or being lazy respectively given seven days in solitary to 'reflect on the impropriety of such conduct', and '30 lashes'. And even though a court found no legal evidence against a man charged with a shop robbery it could see 'strong moral doubt' and so despatched him to work in chains at Port Arthur for twelve months.[4]

And when Campbell arrived later in the year on the *Lord Goderich*: a convict woman close to receiving her freedom had her sentence extended for two years for having stolen two pairs of boots from her master, a ticket-of-leave prisoner charged with talking to the man in charge at the watch-house 'ordered to the treadwheel for fourteen days', and a man charged with a falsehood about a man visiting a woman while her husband was at church was 'ordered to pass twelve months on the roads' to deter him from such meddling. And a convict servant spurned by his 'fair inamorata' who attempted to enter her lodgings through the chimney but became wedged with a fire burning below, was finally dragged out 'more dead than alive' but still ordered to Port Arthur for twelve months 'to quell his amorous feelings'.[5]

Sir William Molesworth, who headed a House of Commons inquiry into transportation, described Van Diemen's Land as 'this strange lottery' where some gained prizes beyond what they could have honestly gained at home, while others drew 'blanks' and 'suffered severely'.[6]

But this was all for Sparkes and Campbell to grasp. Now as their ships heaved back down the Derwent toward Storm Bay with the Tasman Sea and South Pacific beyond, the bays of the river gave way to a landscape whose sheer physicality reinforced their separation from home and now from Hobart Town. Frenchman Bruni d'Entrecasteaux, who first formulated the view that Van Diemen's Land was an island, wrote in 1793 of 'lying at the world's end, separated as it were from the rest of the universe…twas nature, and nature in her wildest mood'.[7] Antarctic blasts swept through Jurassic pillars of dolerite, the biggest collection of exposed columns in the world thrusting more than 300 yards (274 m) upward, and at the bottom of some of the world's most dangerous waters lay the watery graves of those lost in the previous few years, including the *George III* with 133 convicts aboard, and numerous other wrecks.

The *Hindostan* and *Lord Goderich*, still relying on French navigation maps, passed from Storm Bay by the cliffs of Cape Raoul into Maingon Bay, named in honour of a French Navy officer during Nicolas Baudin's mission for Napoleon Bonaparte to complete the French mapping of Terre Australes. Under the watchful eye of albatross, huge birds with wing spans of more than 6 feet (2 m), and fur seals, the boys' ships headed north between crescent bays to the west and soaring cliffs of Cape Pillar to the east.

Finally after nearly six hours, towards the middle of the bay, arms pointed and eyes turned. 'There's where's yers are goin', a sailor would announce of an isolated finger of land on this isolated island at the bottom of an isolated continent, 'that be yer Point Puer.'

'An' what's on that little island its pointin' toward?' one boy always asked. 'Oh there, you dinna wanna go there me lad', a sailor would always say. 'An why not?' a boy always replied, only to be silenced by being told this small island was Dead Man's Island, the southern bookend of a voyage which began opposite Dead Man's Island in the Medway River in Kent. Over there, was another place they 'dinna wanna go', about a mile (1.6 km) west across the bay: the 'Earthly Hell' of Port Arthur.[8]

Both penal settlements were off-limits to ordinary citizens, a special statute declaring that any unauthorised individuals 'holding intercourse…or anchoring within three miles' (4.8 km) could be arrested and detained without warrant.[9] The few favoured outsiders permitted to visit could not fathom the contrast of nature and man. Readers of a London magazine, *Fraser's*, were told by Scottish-born David Burn of its similarity to the imposing scenery of Loch Linnhe in western Scotland. Burn, writer of 'The Bushrangers', the first Australian drama to be performed on the stage, described Port Arthur and Point Puer as 'a moving panorama of beauty, bight after bight, channel after channel, glen after glen…in all the ethereal loveliness of a spotless empyrean [heaven]'.[10] In the same year of

Sparkes and Campbell's arrival, English novelist Caroline Leakey also saw it as 'a lovely spot but alas it is a penal settlement, where every prospect pleases and only man is vile'.[11]

Amid the loveliness of heaven and the vileness of man, Point Puer was the chosen place for 'the little ones' to be 'saved'.[12] Governor George Arthur declared that all convicts were criminals but 'the object of reform, as well as punishment, must never be lost sight of'.[13] His Christian thinking was that even 'corrupt little rogues' ought to be 'objects of compassion' as they had either been 'thrown on the world totally destitute', or trained in 'a vicious course' by 'dissolute parents [or] dexterous old thieves about London'.[14] Strong discipline, education and moral reform would 'eradicate their corrupt habits'.[15]

Charles O'Hara Booth, who had not long been commandant at Port Arthur, was also confident that 'withdrawing these little urchins from bad company and example will, without any doubt, if proper attention is paid to their morals, be the means of bringing many, if not all, into the right path again'.[16]

Henry Melville, a champion of a free press and individual liberty against Arthur's iron rule, was one of the few brave enough to be sceptical, saying it was dreadful enough to receive boys as young as twelve with the appearance of 'aged dwarfs' but without proper moral instruction in this 'den of wretchedness…they will sink into sullen vice…their minds will become diseased'.[17]

But supporters of the government gushed. 'The experiment… proves one of the most successful and gratifying to humanity of modern times…an invention has been made for eclipsing in our opinion all others in education during the present century', declared the *Hobart Town Courier*,[18] and the satisfaction of boys learning a trade could 'not be surpassed by the Eton boy let loose at his game of cricket or his boat race'.[19] Teacher-journalist James Ross, a strong supporter of Governor Arthur and tutor of his children, declared 'I consider this establishment one of the greatest memorials that Colonel Arthur has left behind him'.[20] And David Burn said Puer's

'full provisions, excellent lodgings and comfortable clothing...
beneficial instruction' would cause England's poor to be 'overjoyed'
and there was much hope and some evidence that 'infamy may be
lost in industry, sin give place to grace, and transportation itself may
through the blessings of God, be the balsam of the reckless' and one
day boys would 'bless the hour'.[21]

Arthur's successor, Arctic explorer Sir John Franklin, continued
the official line, telling Colonial Secretary of State Lord Glenelg
that Point Puer was being run as a 'benevolent experiment' of 'high
national promise'.[22]

When Sparkes and Campbell arrived in 1841, the Empire's
chain of command was still optimistically promoting boys '[to] be
sent to Point Puer to learn useful trades, receive religious instruction
and be taught to read, write and cypher...and if the intention is
properly carried out...may be saved and become valuable members
of society'.[23]

But the truth was somewhat different. It had been thus since
the first *Isabella* boys arrived. When the government brig *Tamar*
delivered them to Point Puer, Commandant Booth was shocked to
discover the boys had 'evinced their dexterity by foraging out in the
hold of the vessel a six dozen case of wine for me,...all but one bottle'
and that the 'brutal' nature of some of the boys 'rather disgusted'.[24]

Booth, who already had his hands full managing hundreds of
men convicts at Port Arthur, gave one adult in the drunken escapade
'half a hundred' lashes and the remainder 'three dozen each'.[25] But
he elected to take 'no harsh measures' against the boys. Instead he
would 'convince them of their error by lecture...my annihilating
countenance...raise my stentorian voice and made them quake'.[26]
He told Arthur he planned to reform boys 'by mild measures if
practicable',[27] as he was optimistic great good could be effected 'by
firmness tempered with kindness and unremitting perseverance'.[28]

But his 'annihilating countenance' did not impress many of the
first boys, and his 'mildness and kindness' was not readily evident.

Charles O'Hara Booth, Port Arthur commandant. *Capt. Chas.
O'Hara Booth of 21st N.B. Fusiliers Commandant of Port Arthur*,
illustration, 1800s. Image courtesy Libraries Tasmania, SD_
ILS:609422.

Thomas Player, sentenced to fourteen years for repeated thefts of handkerchiefs, was charged within two weeks of 'making use of insolent and contemptuous language to the schoolmaster', and given five days solitary at Port Arthur.[29] And one of the smallest, Walter Paisley, just 4 feet 1½ inches (125 cm) tall, almost immediately engaged in 'insubordinate conduct toward the superintendent',[30] costing him seven days solitary, and when he was found 'amusing the boys in the cells last Sunday by reciting an obscene story'[31] he suffered another seven days solitary, and soon after fifteen lashes for misconduct and hitting another boy with a spade.

Nevertheless Booth dutifully reported to Governor Arthur, just a few weeks after the drunken and troublesome initiation, that 'the boys are going on very satisfactorily indeed', and he was 'fully confident' that His Excellency's plan for 'these misguided little creatures…cannot fail to eventually bring into the right path the majority, if not the whole of them'.[32]

Arthur cited Booth's confidence when, a month after Puer opened, he finally revealed to his superiors in London that he had established a juvenile Port Arthur. He thought the surrounding seas of Tasman Peninsula and soldiers guarding the only land access meant the boys could be readily managed from the existing Port Arthur base and still be protected from its moral contamination, saving the British Government the greater cost of creating an entirely separate prison. Arthur promised the boys would be kept 'quite apart and quite distinct from the convicts under sentence' at Port Arthur by Commandant Booth, 'a most admirable person for such a situation…he is kind and humane, active and most determined'.[33]

In what would be a continuing pattern of deviation from the truth of Point Puer, neither Booth nor Arthur admitted Puer was born of the same forces of economic expediency and moral panic which led to boys being exiled from Britain. Or that the first boys arrived intoxicated and without sufficient bedding, a medical officer or free men to teach trades and literacy, and would be housed in roughly built and inadequate accommodation with insufficient resources to adequately classify, separate and educate boys to a point of being 'saved'. Or that 'quite distinct' separation from adult convicts was impossible as Puer could not survive without water and supplies being brought daily by convicts from Port Arthur — the site was dismissed by Booth's successor, William Champ, as 'a wretched, bleak barren spot without water, wood for fuel, or an inch of soil'[34] — and the boys' supervision was largely in the 'contaminating' hands of adult convicts.

With Britain continuing to exile its unwanted, by the end of its first year Point Puer held 161 boys, within four years more than 450, and by the time of Sparkes and Campbell's arrival in 1841, about 700. Despite Lord Stanley's concession that transportation of itself would not change 'bad' boys without adequate means for their reformation, and pleas from Arthur to the Home Office and Colonial Office for more resources — 'we are all in great measure the creatures of education'[35] and 'in no part of the world is the influence and teaching of the divine, the exertions of the schoolmaster, so essential as in Van Diemen's Land'[36] — Whitehall remained fixated on the expediency of exile rather than its necessary expenditure.

Booth, like Arthur, was frustrated that London was constantly 'increasing the number of young prisoners [yet] seemed to want to leave the cost entirely to the local treasury' and ignored most requests for improved accommodation, maintenance, clothing and other essentials, and that 'nothing had been decided concerning the future of these children'.[37] He had unsuccessfully called for qualified teachers to accommodate transported boys on their voyages, for a full-time clergyman, books for boys to read, and for a penny for every shilling of the value of a boy's labour to be invested and handed to them when they ultimately received a ticket of leave.

He was well placed to dispense discipline and punishment, but his resources to offer hope or reward were non-existent. He occasionally issued an additional blanket for warmth, a handful of

THE LOST BOYS OF MR DICKENS   107

raisins to the good boys each Sunday, and to some departing boys 'some appropriate book' such as a Bible or prayer book.[38] But the ambition and inducement of eventual release with some trade and literacy skills and transfer to a hiring depot in Hobart Town — 'almost the only reward in my power to hold out for good conduct'[39] — was itself problematic. Boys only progressed to a trade workshop if their religious and literacy progress, and behaviour, was deemed satisfactory, but the lack of qualified teachers and buildings and circumstances meant progress was minimal and did not allow every boy to do a trade.

Commandant Booth faced an unwinnable battle in the empire's 'war' against juvenile crime. He received more and more 'young boys...more hardened in crime, more daring in exploit, more reckless of punishment, and more troublesome in prison than adults'[40] and was expected to dutifully punish their 'mischief and wickedness...some not more than ten years old [who] blended the trickery of boyhood with the villainy of age'[41] and turn them onto a new path in a remote facility with inadequate resources and experience in juvenile management, Christian mentoring, schooling and trade training.

Booth was a similar age to many of the Puer boys when he was also sent far from home at age fifteen, but his childhood was not one of 'trickery and wickedness' or fighting to survive. His Royal Navy father sent him from a substantial family home in Basingstoke to the care of an uncle in India in pursuit of an appointment at the East India Company, before he embarked on his own military career. He arrived in Hobart Town in February 1833 as a 32-year-old captain with a detachment of the Royal North British 21st Fusiliers and a regimental motto he took to heart, 'no one provokes me with immunity', and was quickly appointed Commandant at Port Arthur.

Governor Arthur cited him as a 'most admirable and determined person' for the task, and by Sir John Franklin as one whose 'superior mind pervades powerfully...especially the station set apart for the

boys at Point Puer...this very difficult and important command'.[42]
But Booth's military determination and mind was not matched by
any experience in dealing with juveniles, some reportedly as young
as seven, eight or nine,[43] nor did he have any experienced officers.
A day before the first boys arrived Booth learned Governor Arthur
had chosen Lieutenant John Montgomery of the 63rd Regiment as
their first superintendent despite knowing Montgomery 'has been
exceedingly addicted to drinking and it has brought him almost to
utter ruin'.[44] Montgomery, who lived at Point Puer with his wife and
children, shared the optimism for a 'school of reform for those young
in years but old in iniquity' and commented how happy it would
have been for many of these 'unfortunate creatures'[45] if England
had adopted similar measures at home, but Booth soon despatched
him to Port Arthur, unhappy that 'a most improper scene'[46] had
taken place. Booth put one of his 21st Fusiliers, Lieutenant William
Macknight, 'a very efficient young fellow' he referred to as 'McSnout',
in charge to restore order.[47]

Booth lacked the resources to adequately house and supervise
the growing number of boys, let alone educate, train and morally
reform them. He often had enough trouble keeping the boys
clothed: visiting French explorer Captain Cyril Laplace found the
boys 'generally dirty and their clothes falling in rags'[48] and Booth
admitted their 'wretched state...three fourths of them are almost in
a state of nudity'[49] and that the lack of clothing and blankets caused
'very many of the minor crimes'.[50]

His only free administrative officers at Puer were a general
superintendent, gaol superintendent, catechist and clerk. Other
than a few visiting Weslyan missionaries, the only free men willing
to work in the penal hardship were a master cooper, shoemaker,
tailor, carpenter, gardener, two overseers (one a former convict), and
a boat-builder (a convict with a ticket-of-leave). About forty other
'least objectionable' convicts he deployed from Port Arthur to help as
overseers and instructors in school and trades such as stone cutting,

sawyering, quarrying, baking, cooking, storekeeping, bookbinding, bricklaying and washing. One was William Jones, sentenced to death for high treason after the sensational armed rebellion by Chartists at Newport, Wales in 1839 before the sentences were commuted to transportation for life. He was in charge of the blacksmith boys before being removed for having 'an evil effect' on them.[51]

It was not an outcome envisaged by chief police magistrate Josiah Spode, a member of the Convict Assignment Board which originally called for boys to be isolated from Hobart Town and from the 'contamination' of adult convicts. He could not 'conceive that a system under which the schoolmaster may be, and actually is, the most expert thief or forger, the overseer the best burglar, the teacher may be a murder or accomplished swindler, can be allowed to continue'.[52]

British prison inspector Benjamin Horne succinctly described it as 'an absurdity'.[53] Education, just an hour a day for Puer's first decade, was in the hands of a sole catechist-superintendent, two convicts nominated as 'schoolmasters' and about forty 'monitors' chosen from among the boys themselves, 'without regard to any other qualification than that of being rather more advanced in the rudiments of knowledge than their companions'. The only resources were a small blackboard and a few Bibles and religious-moral tracts, 'not so much as a map of the world'.[54]

It was, Booth wrote in his diary, 'a trying situation', such that he found himself 'breaking constitutionally rapidly' and that he was 'sick at heart from the number of boys [he was] obliged to punish'.[55]

His 'obligation' reflected his sense of duty to eradicate 'bad' habits of 'wicked' boys as punishment and a deterrence to others, and a military background which embraced strict discipline of men but not juveniles with ingrained degrees of 'wickedness' and no respect for authority.

While Arthur and Booth initially favoured the proverb 'as the twig is bent, the tree's inclined', a child's nature seen as a pliant twig to be bent onto the 'right path', Van Diemen's Land was a long way from debates in London about how to best turn a 'wicked urchin' onto the right path and the throne of Grace, and a long way from adequate experience, resources and facilities. Their pioneering challenges were underscored a few years later when the first official report of the Prison Visitors and Governor at Parkhurst on the Isle of Wight admitted 'there is no branch of prison discipline which is attended with so many difficulties and upon which so little is practically known, as the proper treatment and management of criminal youth.' And just as Arthur and Commandant Booth had experienced, there were 'no specific instructions for carrying on the…details of duty and discipline have been furnished'.[56]

Puer boys might have been 'misguided little creatures' and 'poor little fellows' but isolation and inadequacies meant it was easier for those 'saving' boys to resort to the unremitting delivery of discipline and punishment as the order of the day, and otherwise find their own means of comfort and survival.

Commandant Booth busied himself with inventions, including a remarkable semaphore system and convict-powered railway line, the first in Australia to carry passengers, and maintained a flowery diary recording dinners with fellow officers as 'ration'd at the Commissariat', or finding 'a number of gaol birds' or 'a brace of lads off for a slaunt' (break) or 'piscatorising with the Seine' (fishing), such offences leading to 'a benefit' (thrashing).[57] He embraced any opportunity to visit Hobart Town to absorb 'fair' female company before marrying a blue-eyed beauty half his age, 19-year-old Elizabeth 'Lizzy' Charlotte Eagle, who became such a diversion that colonial officers felt he spent 'half the day on the sofa by the side of his young and pretty wife'[58] at the expense of his duties. The few visitors he greeted 'with the greatest urbanity'[59] in his home on top of a little promontory, which visiting Frenchman Captain D'Urville noted had a 'tastefully furnished drawing room, where a pile of albums, fashionable ornaments and hundreds of these or elegant knickknacks…souvenirs of all shapes and sizes'.[60]

Booth and his few men and their wives seized on any opportunity to make life in their weatherboard cottages more comfortable, be it music, painting, drawing, backgammon, chess, gardening, collecting, philosophy, or needlework. Any birthday, birth or anniversary, and any visit of foreign explorers, the governor or fellow officers from Hobart Town was a cause for feasting and dancing. German-born Thomas Lempriere, his commissary officer, created a small natural history museum for his collections and carved a benchmark into the Puer rocks to begin measuring sea levels and tides, records still used today, and was a prolific portrait painter.

But amid their own amusements and indulgences, foremost for Booth and his men was to survive in their careers by doing their 'duty'.

It had been drilled into them by Governor Arthur, notwithstanding his personal and Christian sentiments, that they were in a gaol colony and everyone had to 'keep in mind that these boys have been very wicked, and that they are transported in order by their punishment that other boys may be deterred…consequently the mode of treatment must be such as is calculated to make them feel this'.[61]

Lempriere echoed the assignment: 'A penal settlement is, and ought to be, an abode of misery to those whose crimes have sequestered them from the society of their fellow creatures. Were it a place of comfort, the very object for which such establishments are formed, the punishment and reform of malefactors, would become nugatory'.[62]

Thousands of boys like Sparkes and Campbell would not enjoy birthday fun, feasts, music, or visitors. For them Point Puer was an 'abode of misery'.

9

A BOYS TOWN

The simple fact was that…he was…being reduced to a state of brutal stupidity and sullenness for life by the ill-usage he had received.
— Charles Dickens, *Oliver Twist*

The 'Boys Town' entered by Henry Sparkes and Charles Campbell in 1841 was nothing like Nottingham, Aberdeen or London — nothing like anywhere else on earth. The first night in the isolation of Her Majesty's Prison for Boys at Point Puer saw some crying out in misery, just as poet William Blake wrote in *A Little Boy Lost*, 'the weeping child could not be heard…they stripped him to his little shirt, and bound him in an iron chain'.[1]

Weeping or hardened, this was an extraordinary place where everyone, from Commandant Booth and his officers to small boys, was compressed between Colonial Office orders and penal colony realities. Man and boy alike had their own need to survive, and make their own choices, each to leave an indelible imprint. Those who had experienced Point Puer and Port Arthur did not think a truer word than that of Dickens, 'that self-preservation is the first law of nature'.[2]

For Commandant Booth and his men, their self-preservation primarily depended on punishment, discipline and not allowing anyone to escape. Just as they dealt with men convicts, boys were simply classified good or bad. If they behaved, they were classified as a 'general' prisoner, housed at the northern end of the point in a whitewashed weatherboard barrack adjacent to the U-shaped workshops, superintendent and catechist cottages. The 'bad' were separately housed about 600 yards (500 m) away in a collection of weatherboard cells and yards, for 'new', then 'second class' or 'third class' crime boys.

Looking about them, Sparkes and Campbell could see the 'good' and 'bad' separated by a tract of land empty except for a patrol of sentries and a small chapel, 75 feet (22.5 m) x 40 feet (12 m), which also acted as the school-house, symbolically elevated off the ground.

And they heard that between their arrival and any eventual form of freedom, they faced three steps. First was simple hard labour: clearing hard land with a spade, hoe and grubbing axe in the hope of producing cabbages, potatoes and turnips; constructing tracks; carrying sawn timber and firewood and washing.

If their labour and behaviour was satisfactory they might then have the reward of some basic trade training which 'must prove very useful when assigned or lent to the settlers'.[3] It might be training in carpentry to make wheelbarrows, coffins, school desks, garden gates, small boats or fittings for a new Gothic church at Port Arthur; shoemaking for the boys and overseers at Puer; nail-making for boots and building; tailoring of prisoner clothing; blacksmithing to make and repair pick axes and sharpen tools for the stonecutters, who did much of the work for the Port Arthur church; or perhaps shingle-splitting, coopering, baking or gardening.

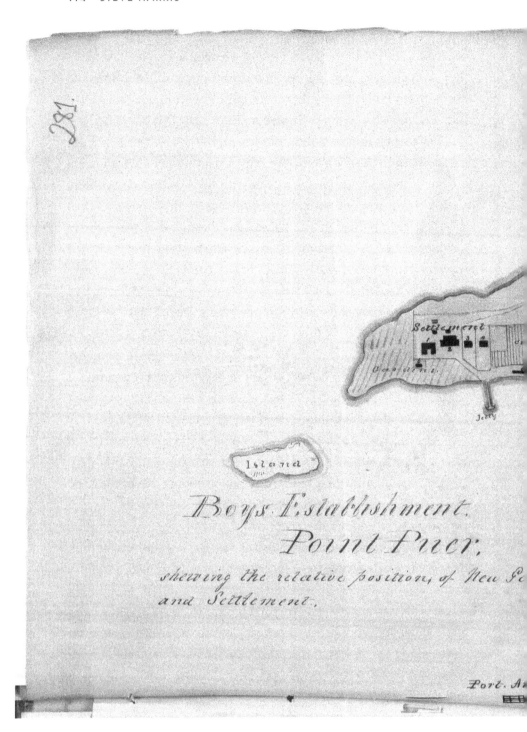

1839 Map of Point Puer showing two separate sections: the 'Trades' area to the left
for well behaved boys with a chance of reform, and the 'Punishment/Gaol' section for
'bad' boys, which is where the murder occurred.

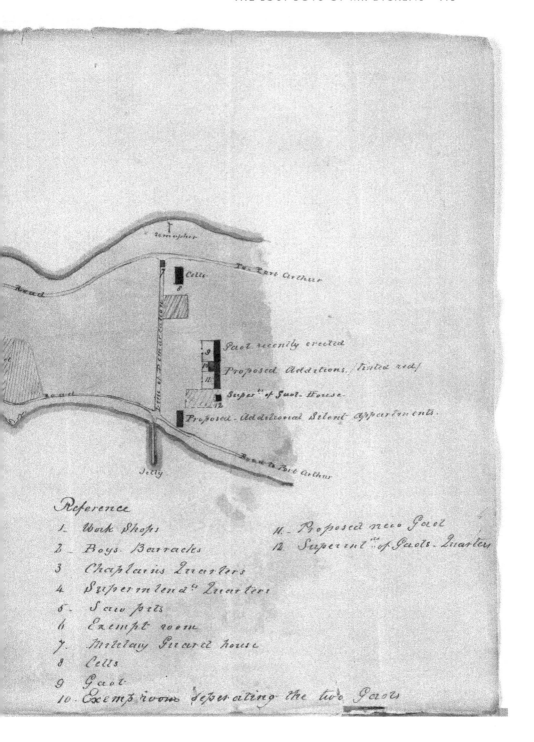

Reference

1. Work Shops
2. Boys. Barracks
3. Chaplains Quarters
4. Superintendᵗ Quarters
5. Saw pits
6. Exempt room
7. Military Guard house
8. Cells
9. Gaol
10. Exempt room Seperating the two Gaols

11. Proposed new Gaol
12. Superintᵗ of Gaols Quarters

Digital Reconstruction of the Point Puer Boys' Prison c1843, (John Stephenson, Digital Heritage Studio 2019).

After acquiring a satisfactory level of trade skill, and some competency in basic reading, writing and arithmetic, they might be eligible to be returned to Hobart Town to some probationary freedom. But, it was firmly stressed, only if their conduct was also in total compliance with the commandant's code of unrelenting discipline.

They were roused around 5am to roll and stow their coarse canvas hammocks or thin mattresses and blanket and rug. They had to wash at tanks or in the cold sea, when the weather and tide permitted, receiving twenty lashes if they refused, be mustered for a young catechist or missionary's prayer at 6am, and then stand and wait for breakfast at 6.30am. After another muster at 7.30am they marched off to their labour or the trade workshops for four hours, breaking at noon for some 'play' — during which they could 'amuse themselves in any innocent and rational manner...quiet and ordinary...within the prescribed bounds'.[4]

After dinner at 1pm they were mustered again to return to work until 5.30pm, with just an hour allocated to 'education'. Supper was at 6.30pm, after which boys had some more playtime in summer, or in colder months had someone read aloud to them before a final muster at 8pm, a scripture reading and prayer before 'bed and silence' at 9pm with 'lights...burning in the barracks all night and a watch kept constantly'.[5]

On Saturday and Sunday they were inspected by a surgeon from Port Arthur to check if they were suffering from any disease and remained fit enough for their labour, and at morning and evening divine services heard an 'approved sermon'.

Each Sunday, boys were also issued with a few ounces of soap for the week and a clean shirt, the only fresh item in their standard issue, a jacket and trousers 'made of tanned sheep skin',[6] a grey cloth waistcoat, striped shirt, a leather or scotch cap, and 'strong' boots. Stockings and socks were not provided.

Their meals, collected for groups of ten or twelve by boys

designated by Booth as 'corporals', were also regimented and monotonous. Breakfast and supper were 9 oz (255 g) of bread and a pint (500 ml) of gruel. The midday dinner was generally a pint (568 ml) of soup, 12 oz (340 g) of meat reduced by boiling and extraction to 6 oz (170 g), with 9 oz (255 g) of bread and 6 oz (170 g) of dumplings. A weekly ration provided one pound (453 g) of vegetables usually boiled down into the soup and a half-pound (226 g) of potatoes served with the meat. Even Booth admitted many were 'unable to consume' the rations, leaving boys in a 'debilitated state'. He engaged in paper warfare for months trying to secure an extra ration of tea and 'two-sevenths' of sugar to help them digest 'their meal of thick gruel every evening',[7] but the colonial surgeon, enjoying the accumulation of an official salary, private practice income, land grants and mansions, was adamant such sweeteners were 'unnecessary'.[8]

Sparkes and Campbell would have quickly learned from other boys that the difference between 'good' and 'bad' lay in Commandant Booth's endless list of offences: disobedience or insubordination, misbehaviour at meals or school or chapel, indecency or gross misconduct, abusing or threatening overseers, 'conniving' at riotous conduct, being 'illegally at large' or absent without leave, refusing to work or follow orders, fishing, singing in the cells, playing cards, pilfering buttons, damaging government tools, stealing vegetables, having bread or meat rations or thread and leather improperly in their possession, possessing tobacco, eating other boys' food, losing any government-issued items such as knife, fork or and cap, stating a wilful falsehood, bad language or profanity, fighting, throwing stones, or any 'ill-use' or 'maltreatment' of another boy.

Booth's view was that the value of discipline existed 'in the certainty of punishment', and so demanded that 'the most trivial crime or irregularity is not permitted to pass without punishment'.[9]

With so many offences, his zealotry, and British criminal law demanding he try every 'major' offence magisterially on oath, Booth had to deal with up to sixty offenders on his daily visits to Point Puer, the sort of offenders described by Birmingham lawyer and judge Matthew Davenport Hill:

> (He) is a little stunted man already – he knows much and a great deal too much of what is called life – he can take care of his immediate interests. He is self-reliant, he has long directed or mis-directed his own actions and has so little trust in those about him, that he submits to no control and asks for no protection. He has consequently much to unlearn – he has to be turned again into a child.[10]

Point Puer boys could not be turned again into children. They had never been children in heart or mind, and their childhood had long been forfeited. They were no longer even seen as children, but as 'stunted men', 'depraved little felons', 'aged dwarfs', 'corrupt little rogues' and 'wicked urchins'.

At noon each day, Booth reviewed all the offences written up on a slate by the overseers and constables, selectively deciding whether to summarily deal with them as the penal governor by recording them in a 'Minor Record', or as a colonial magistrate hearing more serious 'misconduct' offences to be included in the 'Major Record' and 'police character' files.

Minor offences initially led to confinement to the muster ground to 'scavenge' rubbish and weeds during breaks from digging up new ground, denial of any 'play', isolation from school or trade training, being forced to work two hours longer, and loss of dumplings at dinner. If they still evidenced what Booth regarded as 'a mutinous disposition' or 'more determined violation of the regulations',[11] subsequent offences meant a thrashing, time in 'the gaol' with extended labour 'fettered to a chain in separate stalls…breaking stones',[12] solitary confinement, or an extension of their sentences.

Thrashings were recorded as 'punishment on the breech'. Boys were forced to lower their pants, stand on a wooden plank and lay at almost ninety degrees over a specially built wooden bench or 'pony' with arms and legs tethered, then be thrashed in front of all the boys on the bare buttocks or lower back by up to thirty-six 'stripes' or 'lashes'. Used was a birch rod or a leather lash, the latter sometimes knows as a 'No. 1' instrument 'for younger boys, a heavier 'No. 2' for those over fourteen.

Described by Wesleyan chaplain Reverend John Manton as a public flagellation,[13] such summary punishment was widely used in British homes and schools, seemingly endorsed by the biblical proverb of 'spare the rod, spoil the child'. The British Army enthusiastically embraced flogging, although many former convicts who read the popular memoir of a British Army lieutenant agreed with him that floggings reflected more on the character of the commandant than those in his charge.

But prison authorities felt being thrashed on the bare buttocks in front of one's peers was effective humiliation and pain, and it became what Dickens described as 'a very contagious kind of thing'.[14] Some felt too contagious; Vicar-General of New Holland and Van Diemen's Land, William Ullathorne, calling the lash 'the great persuader',[15] and others arguing it merely hardened the disposition of the offender, destroyed any sense of shame and induced 'the recklessness of character which is the natural consequence of hopeless degradation'.[16]

Booth described such severe punishment as a 'benefit' and maintained it was 'never resorted to until every other means have been tried without effect'[17] but corporal punishment rose from twenty percent of punishments in Puer's first year to forty, then fifty-five to seventy percent in subsequent years.[18] A former convict wrote that he 'suffered at Point Puer the average amount of punishment served out to others of my headstrong and easily persuaded companions', his 'average' amounting to 528 lashes over his six years.[19] Boys like Samuel Holmes, the 14-year-old inspiration for Dickens' Artful Dodger, in his first two years received 104 lashes for being insolent to the superintendent, singing in the cell, absenting himself, and 'determined opposition' to an overseer.[20] And William Bickle, just eleven or twelve years old, endured 172 days in solitary and 300 'lashes' to his buttocks.[21]

Penal surgeon Dr Henry Jeanneret fell out with Booth over the extent of his public floggings, and John Frost, the Chartist uprising leader transported for life for treason, said that within days of starting work in Booth's office as a police clerk he 'was completely horror struck by the cruelties committed by the Government authorities, and the sad consequences that resulted from a convict code not equalled in severity in any part of the civilised world'.[22] He claimed the commandant 'often witnesses this punishment with as much indifference as he if were looking at some philosophical experiment'[23] and told British audiences that in Van Diemen's Land humanity was 'the greatest offence that an officer could be guilty of'.[24]

One newspaper claimed new arrivals 'had scarcely been under the control of Booth for a week before boys ten years of age were tied to the triangles and lashed with the cat for the most trivial offences'.[25] Triangles were a feature at Port Arthur where Booth's flagellators, usually brutish convicts, bloodily employed a cat o' nine tails, a rope whip made of nine knotted thongs and soaked in salt water, on bare backs, but Puer records referred only to 'stripes' and 'lashes', although visiting French explorer, Captain Jules Dumont D'Urville, noted boys working while 'several constables of forbidding countenance were walking about with a whip in their hands'.[26]

Sparkes and Campbell could see the whips and the birch rods and the small cells for solitary confinement, a punishment embraced by the British Government after prison inspector William Crawford, in the year Puer opened, visited America for a London committee investigating the 'alarming increase in juvenile delinquency in the metropolis'. Crawford lauded solitary isolation: 'Day after day, with no companions but his thoughts the convict is compelled to reflect and listen to the reproofs of conscience...the folly of their former self-willed and vicious conduct'.[27] Booth well knew Port Arthur prisoners despised the black hole — 'the brain is the seat of all pain, very dreadful',[28] one prisoner described — and he repeatedly sought extra solitary cells at Puer and employed it as punishment in about seventy-five percent of cases, often leaving boys there 'until they manifest a disposition to amendment'.[29]

Booth felt it took about two years to 'break'[30] most boys of their bad habits, but if black hole stints or thrashings did not have the desired effect then those he initially described as 'nice boys' and 'poor little fellows' quickly became 'an abominable little monster' or 'incorrigibly obstinate'[31] who suffered his final punishment: time at the hell of Port Arthur. This was despite his own deputy Lempriere seeing this would 'do away with the benefit intended by the Point Puer establishment [as] the consequences may easily be foreseen',[32] and Quaker missionaries James Backhouse and George Washington Walker warning that 'the evil tendency of human nature'[33] was for bad men to contaminate those around them. But the commandant was at ease in sending boys to Port Arthur for a stint in a solitary cell if none was available at Puer, or for 'amendment' through a 'temporary' stint in irons alongside adult convicts in a chain gang. Some 'temporary' transfers lasted months — in one six-month period eighty-nine boys were sent to Port Arthur but only nine were received back — and some never returned.

New boys like Sparkes and Campbell could quickly sense that the challenge of survival on the streets of London, Aberdeen or Nottingham had been transported with them to Point Puer. They were still in a world where man and the law was not their friend.

Choices had to be made, once more, as to where their best life 'chance' lay: to adhere to the code of Booth and his men or the code of street boys. Neither was one of kindness or fairness, or without pain.

Time would soon tell if they would be two more of the 'wicked children' who 'progressive' people like Lady Jane Franklin felt could have their 'natural and inherited corruptions whipped out of them'.[34]

Or two of those who Booth felt could never be put on the right path,[35] and might evidence, as one newspaper sensed, 'tokens of perverse powers and dispositions — in them you may view the future nightly marauder, and the base assassin'.[36]

10

AN UNNATURAL BALANCE

You think you will die, but you just keep living, day after day after terrible day.
— Charles Dickens, *Great Expectations*

After the Archbishop of Dublin told the House of Lords that 'we have surely made trial long enough of [seeking] to cure a man of vice by putting him in a way of acquiring new vice',[1] Britain had ceased sending convicts to Sydney in 1840, which led to a record surge of 3462 convicts in the year of Sparkes and Campbell arriving,[2] and confusion as to why, as the *Hobart Courier* lamented, penal 'science' could accept that convict vices and colonization so demoralized a community that it had to be discontinued in New South Wales, yet still be visited on smaller Van Diemen's Land.[3]

The truth of Point Puer also remained an open question.

Commandants and governors repeatedly sent official despatches extolling their progress in 'saving' boys, but in personal diaries and conversations acknowledged the task was impossible without more resources and major changes to juvenile crime laws and punishment. Booth's private view was that insufficient resources and an absence of plans for their future meant he would merely be sending boys from Puer at the age of eighteen to become 'nothing but future recruits for Port Arthur'.[4]

Some boys resolved to endeavour to be 'good' and hope for a new and different life once their sentences were completed, but many continued to engage in offences to either feel better about themselves or look better in the eyes of others. Some because they were hungry or bored. Others rebellious or vengeful because the tyranny of constant hardship and thrashings hardened them to the point of indifference. And others driven by the bullying tyranny of fellow boys.

While Henry Sparkes and Charles Campbell initially did not attract any fresh 'bad' ink from the quills of Commandant Booth and deputy Thomas Lempriere, it is unlikely they were being 'good' and quietly taking in the ways of this Boys Town. More likely, they had graduated through Booth's minor and unrecorded punishments, such as confinement to the muster ground, being made to 'scavenge' weeds and rubbish, reduction of rations and playtime.

Graduation to the 'crime' class was seen by many as a badge of honour and sign of 'manhood', and seven months after his arrival in January 1841, Sparkes entered the Major Record for having some workshop material improperly in his possession. Despite Point Puer being established in large part to protect boys from contamination of older youths and men, Sparkes was rowed across the bay to the adult Port Arthur settlement to spend three days in solitary on bread and water. It was a severe punishment for a first recorded 'major' offence: perhaps all the solitary cells at Puer were full, or Booth judged Sparkes to be one of the 'abominable little monsters'.

The most monstrous were those nobs who ran the same bullying system seen on the *Euryalus*. British government visitor Benjamin Horne described a 'fagging system…as in any of our great public schools at home'.[5] Older or more hardened boys forced others to steal for them, hand over food rations, take the blame for their offences, and stay silent about any forbidden activity. Boys in workshops were compelled to bring out items such as needles, thread or leather, and when searched and identified by overseers 'they are punished… without giving a single hint of the influence which has been exerted over them'.[6]

Horne reported that:

the boys have been able to, over the whole institution, establish a sort of tyranny of public opinion among themselves to which every boy in the place is a slave and to which he must submit almost at the peril of his life'.[7] 'No boy must give information against another, however much he may be injured…a boy is detected with a bloody nose or the marks of a severe beating, but it is impossible to find out who did it unless one of the officers has witnessed some part of the occurrence, and even in that case the injured individual solemnly declares that it was only play.[8]

When no one could be induced to inform on culprits who had thrown pots out of a window, every boy seen close to the window was given fifteen lashes. When not a single boy felt inclined to name the ringleaders of 'a furious attack' on an overseer, 'the commandant sentenced the whole of the boys — about 400 — to three months on the muster ground during free time…made to stand erect until their meals were ready'.[9] When visiting writer David Burn joined Booth on a night tour of the boys' wards:

The odour of tobacco smoke was discerned and as the possession of tobacco is an offence against the regulations, notice was given that the entire ward would he placed in charge until the smoker was known. When we came away they had not discovered the offender and in consequence every man (sic) was made to sleep in a silent apartment.[10]

The boys' code of silence was severe. One boy told officers that if he gave evidence against another for attacking an overseer he would have to 'leave Point Puer instantly for he could not consider himself safe a moment after he had done so',[11] even if the offender was removed to Port Arthur.

Lempriere described the code as 'an *esprit de corps*', one in which 'even in this degraded rank of society, the boys would rather undergo any punishment than have it said amongst adults that they had recanted'.[12] Its principal law, Horne reported, was 'the maxim of the whole fraternity was that everyone must tell as many lies as may be necessary for himself and the community'.[13] He could see some 'savage virtue' of 'honour among thieves' if the esprit fidelity was spontaneous but as it was 'the result of the fear of kicks and blows it can only be described as cowardice caused by brutal tyranny'.[14]

Sparkes and Campbell faced the twin tyrannies and cruelties of man and boy, and, like all newly arrived boys, had to quickly decide how they would best survive Point Puer. Whether they would acquiesce to official discipline and punishments, simply endeavouring to get through their sentence as quietly as possible in the hope of some probationary freedom and perhaps a new and better life. Or whether they would resist and rebel, be admired as 'flash' and acquiesce or even become part of the boy's code of bullying and lies rather than risk being loathed as a 'dog' or 'skunk'.

As William Miles described after his interviews with juvenile prisoners in London: 'The daring offender is a member of the prison aristocracy…severity of punishment is by them converted into a scale of merit…they never [have] any feeling of shame or disgrace'.[15]

Sparkes and Campbell could see 'merit' if they were game enough to smoke outside the superintendent's quarters, pick tobacco from the pocket of the catechist — something for which one boy received twenty-one days in solitary on bread and water — misbehave during Sunday services, steal fruit or a fowl from officers' gardens, or break into their quarters to steal. But such 'artful dodges' were not enough for others 'trying to emulate the men in everything' in the pursuit of personal or peer esteem. 'There is not a little scoundrel amongst them but one who thinks himself a hero when placed in the dock before the commandant, tried in the same manner as the men'[16] because, as Horne observed, 'it tends to make the offender a much more important personage in his own eyes'.[17]

These boy-men shocked visiting French explorers Captain Cyrille Laplace and Captain Jules D'Urville. Laplace, who achieved fame for his navigation of the globe on *La Favorite* said 'on these young faces I could find nothing childlike, but features that were hard, emphatic and coarse; in their expression the insolence of crime mixed with the careless indifference of youth'.[18] And some were more than insolent, D'Urville observing 'one of these brats, scarcely 3 feet high [90 cm]' was charged with threatening an overseer with a knife. 'I have never seen a more brutally evil and impudent face. If this child goes on in the same, one day he will become a monster that will have to be stifled.' When Booth sternly promised the gallows if the boy did not change his ways, he was sharply told, 'my father and mother have shown me the way and before I am hanged I shall kill this constable.'[19]

Whether Sparkes was a 'brat' or 'evil', he endured the 'penal science' of solitary confinement and silence at Port Arthur, living his own Oliver Twist experience:

> Oliver remained a close prisoner in the dark and solitary room to which he had been consigned...he only cried bitterly all day, and when the long, dismal night came on, spread his little hands before his eyes to shut out the darkness, and crouching in the corner, tried to sleep: even and anon waking with a start and tremble, and drawing himself closer and closer to the wall, as if to feel even its cold

hard surface were a protection in the gloom and loneliness which surrounded him.[20]

The Port Arthur punishment seemed to harden Sparkes. He was found two weeks after his return with being 'absent without leave', a catch-all term for many offences. Boys repeatedly risked punishment by sneaking off to the steep 60 feet (18 m) cliffs to the west and north of the settlement, 'climbing among the rocks, hiding or disappearing…like land crabs'.[21] Here they savoured highly-prized and strictly forbidden tobacco, used pilfered buttons to gamble on marbles and hand-made dominoes, or used makeshift fishing lines from threads torn from their hammocks and clothing. Up to six boys were absent on any given night, perhaps for some petty pilfering, or to meet up with other boys and men from Port Arthur to trade food, tobacco, tools, clothing, illegal weapons or sex.

Boys 'in trouble' with officers or their peers often tried to stay in the bush with stolen food, hidden by accomplices, and others made more enduring escape attempts. But boys could not overcome the formidable cliffs, bush, seas, or Booth's zealous measures. He had armed soldiers patrolling the surrounding area, another twenty soldiers and a line of fierce dogs at the only exit off Tasman Peninsula, a 110 yard (100 m) of strip of land called Eaglehawk Neck, and a remarkable semaphore network in which thousands of numerical codes enabled quick messages such as 'boy absconded' and 'double the patrols'. Booth proudly showed visitors trophies of failed escape attempts, such as a canoe cut from a hollow gum tree, a charcoal-filled mattress, and 'an extraordinary machine'[22] which two Puer boys had filled with provisions and tools, only for their mutilated bodies to be recovered three weeks later. Other boys were more desperate to escape. Officers had an aversion to reporting that conditions were so onerous for some they would take their own life, such deaths merely recorded as 'fell over the rocks' or 'accidental fall', but others were more forthright. Reverend William Butters, a Wesleyan chaplain at Port Arthur, wrote, 'a boy at Point Puer made an

The line of dogs at Eaglehawk Neck to help prevent prisoners from escaping Port Arthur. *North view of Eagle Hawk Neck which joins Tasman's Peninsula to the main land of Van Dieman's Land*, Charles Hutchins, lithograph, 1845. Image courtesy National Library of Australia, nla.obj-135601456.

unsuccessful attempt to hang himself',[23] and newspapers continued to report 'more than one of these unhappy children sought a happy release from their sufferings by a voluntary death'.[24]

Whether Sparkes was hiding away, playing or engaged in nefarious deeds, his 'absent without leave' brought him before Commissary Officer Lempriere, who sometimes deputised for Booth and had little time for boys he described as the 'depraved stock'[25] of 'ignorant and wicked parents'.[26]

He gave Sparkes another three days in solitary, this time at Point Puer. Unlike the black holes of Port Arthur, rough buildings and scant resources at Puer meant its solitary was not one of complete darkness, silence or isolation from their companions, or being restricted to officially supplied rations. The boys laughed it off as a 'coil', because they 'can coil themselves up like a rope, sleep and enjoy their otium cum dignitate' or 'leisure with dignity'.[27] Solitary confinement was Booth's most common punishment but he admitted that while many came out 'better' for a short time, their companions and 'a fatal pride' meant they soon forgot any good resolutions and 'they become just as dangerous as before'.[28]

'Fatal pride' was feature of life in the penal colony, 'the vice of the lowest and most debased creatures no less of the high and self-assured'[29] and fresh from solitary, an unchastened Sparkes was absent without leave three more times in the following weeks, for which he received fifteen lashes, another seven days in solitary and another eighteen lashes. Lashes were badges of manhood, seen as 'a manly sort of punishment generally inflicted upon grown up convicts',[30] and if any boy evinced any sign of pain fellow boys jeered they were a 'pebble' rather than a 'stone' and boasted that they could 'take as much on their faces'.[31]

After the thrashings, Sparkes engaged in further disobedience: in early November he was given another five days in solitary for unspecified 'disorderly conduct', in early December another three days solitary for 'wilfully destroying his government shirt', during which he was found to have again engaged in 'most disorderly conduct' and given an additional five days in solitary, and then further 'most disorderly conduct in cells' which meant another eight days in solitary, including Christmas Day.[32]

In just five months of his first year at Puer, Sparkes was absent without leave five times and guilty of misconduct five times, sentenced to thirty-four days in solitary and thirty-three stripes or lashes, on a familiar cycle that hardened boys and, in turn, hardened judgments against their continued 'badness'.

Sparkes marked the first anniversary of his arrival with yet another absence without leave, and this time his determined attitude was more severely punished: two months hard labour in chains, breaking rocks with a stone hammer.

The ordeal quietened him for a few months, then in April he was found guilty of misconduct 'in having his bedding destroyed', and misconduct in 'exposing his person improperly', for each of which he spent five days in solitary.[33] Whether Sparkes' 'most disorderly conduct' or 'exposing his person' were related to any homosexual activity is not clear. Sodomy was a word that could not be uttered by Christians, often referred to in official despatches as ****. One of the underlying reasons for Puer was to prevent young boys from 'moral contamination' in the barracks at Hobart Town, so Booth was determined to keep a veil over its existence.

His diary contained references such as having to go 'to Point, tried and punished two or three boys for horrid crimes'[34] and he repeatedly sought additional solitary cells for dealing with what he called 'moral crimes', but details were not fully recorded. He ordered exiled Chartist leader John Frost, who was working as a clerk in Booth's office, to record opaque terms of 'gross misconduct', 'most indecent conduct', 'disorderly conduct in barracks at night', 'putting out lamps in the barracks at night' and 'being in the water closet for some have to be improper purpose' so such 'abominable' offences could be heard under his jurisdiction and not be referred to Hobart

Town. Booth 'smothered the thing', Frost said, because his superiors in Hobart Town and London 'wanted to conceal the state of society among the prisoners'.[35]

Nevertheless the colony's Executive Council formally pressed Booth on 'the suspicion...that a certain very revolting offence was of frequent occurrence at Point Puer'.[36] The commandant averred he was 'quite horror struck' by the claim. 'There is nothing both publicly and privately that I look to more closely', he reported,[37] citing careful watching of boys at the cliff rocks and random checks and lights burning all night in the sleeping quarters. But he carefully said he would not rule out sodomy 'in an unqualified manner as the utmost vigilance of man may be evaded'. It was difficult to know how to 'detect such horrid proceedings' as the sleeping quarters were 'much crowded for room' and there were 'some evils attendant'[38] on convicts he was forced to use as overseers.

Chartist leader Frost later told audiences in Britain that 'scarcely a boy' did not fall victim, and related the case of one 'exceedingly nice lad' who resisted bigger boys before they seized him and took him into the bush. Despite his cries of 'Help, help, murder, murder, mercy, mercy, oh God, oh God' he and others could do nothing. 'If we had attempted anything the big boys would have killed us. The authorities knew these things as well as we did.'[39] Prison inspector Benjamin Horne also reported boys' 'apparent familiar acquaintance with a vice which a Christian should scarcely mention'.[40] In his first week at Puer, 'I heard this crime familiarly alluded to three times'[41] and noted Port Arthur men and Puer boys frequently absconded together and 'unnatural vice is familiar, between boys and overseers'.[42]

Whether Sparkes' exposure and misconduct were part of what Booth wanted to smother, his subsequent offences were now treated more severely, the commandant noting three times he was a 'very bad boy'. In three weeks of November, Sparkes was in trouble multiple times, found guilty of unspecified 'misconduct' offences and given sentences of twenty-five and twenty 'stripes' and seven days in solitary. The first half of 1843 was no different, sentenced in January for insolence (five days solitary), in March for 'absence without leave' (ten days solitary) and again in April (thirty stripes, his heaviest thrashing) and in May for 'misconduct' (ten days solitary).

By this stage he had been at Puer for a little over two years. After the first seven months saw nothing serious recorded, the subsequent twenty months saw Sparkes sentenced to a total of eighty-three days in solitary, 108 'stripes' and two months hard labour in chains.

Unlike Sparkes, Charles Campbell did not take long after his arrival in November 1841 to be in serious trouble and the fact he was one of the smallest boys made no difference, either to him or Puer officers. Within nine weeks he was in trouble three times for 'misconduct in maltreating a fellow boy'.[43] The form of maltreatment was not recorded: perhaps he was intent on showing he was as tough as anyone else, or attacked boys for being an informing 'dog', or possibly it was another opaque term for sexual activity. Whatever the reason, his first recorded offence was serious enough for Thomas Lempriere to immediately impose fifteen stripes. Two days later he was again punished for 'maltreating' a fellow boy, this time Lempriere imposing twenty-five stripes. And just four days after this, for the same offence, Commandant Booth, sensing that physical thrashings were not evincing the right 'amendment', ordered solitary confinement for three days.

Campbell's behaviour then appeared to settle, with no major offences for the next nine months. But then in another burst of offences, Booth found him guilty of 'misconduct' twice in one week, imposing four days solitary on 18 October, and then another seven days on 24 October, plus on the same day an additional seven days for 'insolence'. He was then 'absent without leave' in early November, Booth welcoming his recapture with a 'benefit' of twenty-five stripes. This brought Campbell's total punishment in his first year at Puer to twenty-one days in solitary and sixty-five stripes.

The year 1843 saw Campbell and Sparkes continue to be found

guilty of insolence and misconduct, and, for the first time, in mid-March they were both punished on the same day for the same offence — being absent without leave — and received 10 days in solitary.

Sparkes was again absent without leave in April, along with fellow *Hindostan* boy, William Fletcher, and this time received his heaviest thrashing of thirty stripes. Two months later Campbell's 'insolence' invoked thirty-six stripes, also his heaviest physical punishment.

As the icy fingers of winter gripped Point Puer, the records of the two boys were not markedly different to many of the other 700 boys, each with their own boundaries when it came to intimidation, ambition, pain, loyalty, justice and truth.

Boys had to survive and hope that some form of escape would come one day, ever watchful for those men and boys who said they would look after them if you did something to please them, because they always came back for more, and it was harder to escape their hold than get out of a cell or break off an iron.

Sometimes it meant boys would find themselves doing things they once couldn't imagine doing.

Just two years after arriving in exile, Henry Sparkes and Charles Campbell were about to find themselves in something that seemed unimaginable, even in the mind of Dickens, even in the story of an Empire's lost boys.

11

A HORRIBLE MURDER

No man knows 'til the time comes what depths are within him.
— Charles Dickens, *Our Mutual Friend*

On 23 June 1843, George Rose, assistant superintendent for the Point Puer Boys Prison crime class, was trying to keep warm as he stood waiting for the eighteen 'worst' boys to assemble for their afternoon muster in the gaol yard after the finish of their allocated dinner time. Unexpectedly, one of the smallest boys approached him.

It was red-haired Charles Campbell. 'The overseer of the boys is lying down in the yard,'[1] he said, as troubling as it was casual.

Hugh McGuire was one of the Port Arthur convicts assigned to help supervise Puer boys and had only been in the overseer role for two months. He was perhaps 30 years old and well-built, so there was no obvious reason for why he might be lying in the yard. Rose knew McGuire had been tasked with watching the 'worst' boys, and all convict overseers had to be on their guard against boys who strived to 'emulate the men in everything'.

Some boys had already emulated men when it came to violence, having access to potentially lethal weapons such as stone hammers, chisels and spades, and the opportunity to secrete knives or manufacture their own. News of any violence at Port Arthur spread like wildfire at Puer. 'If one man beats out his comrade's brains with a hammer or another commits suicide, the circumstances with all the disgusting details is soon know to and talked of among the boys.'[2]

Soon after Sparkes' arrival, back in 1841, Puer was alive with talk of how Patrick Minnighan, also known as Minahan, 'a most determined looking young man…a reckless hardihood'[3] had taken a stone hammer to James Travis, 'a mere lad' who had informed on his preparation for an escape attempt from a chain gang at Port Arthur, and how, standing over the dying boy, Minahan had declared, 'there lies one bloody dog, stiff enough!'[4] John Childs, described as 'a probation lad'[5] struck another boy on the head with a stone hammer after being called a 'dog', the Colonial Times reporting it as nothing unusual: 'There was no particular feature in the case. Troy called Childs a dog, and Childs knocked him on the head for it.'[6] One group of boys was said to be so angered by another who consistently told 'skunk' tales 'they pushed him over' the cliffs, although authorities portrayed it as an accident.[7] William Scrimshaw burnt another boy with a red-hot iron. Henry Belfield, the illegitimate son of a surgeon, bashed and knifed a fellow prisoner.

George Rose well knew boys also had no time for most of their convict overseers, who they saw as merely older versions of themselves. Boys quickly identified any 'good' overseers they could work with — those willing to turn a blind eye to offences of black-market trading of food, clothing, tools, tobacco, or sexual activity — and those prepared to go even further and 'connive…to avoid becoming unpopular'.[8] Overseers trying to insist on compliance would 'only provoke ridicule'[9] and be 'insulted or maltreated at every opportunity'.[10]

Just as Commandant Booth had escalating punishments if his first did not produce an 'amendment', so did the boys. The first warning to overseers came in the form of a 'crowning', the tipping of a nightsoil tub over them, or perhaps the killing of a pet cat. Boys would also make 'disgraceful charges'[11] that they sought 'to take liberties with them'.[12]

Some overseers invited revenge, especially those who Inspector Horne said evidenced 'the well-known fact that a slave in power becomes an intolerable tyrant',[13] or who authorities had to remove for 'still more atrocious' offences than those occurring at Port Arthur.[14] The House of Lords heard from the colony's solicitor-general that being an overseer was 'the most wretched and dangerous and the most miserable life that a person could lead in the colony', a life risking 'most murderous assaults'.[15]

Making his way after Campbell into the gaol yard, George Rose would have been fearful of what he would find. No one at Puer could forget the day in 1840, when visiting Frenchman Captain D'Urville attended one of Booth's hearings and was shocked by a small boy who had threatened an overseer with a knife and vowed he would kill the man. Even fresher in Rose's mind was 'a very wild happening'[16] the previous year when, at a given signal, boys extinguished the night lamps and with bricks pulled from fireplaces launched 'a furious attack' on an Austrian-born overseer Frederick 'Adolphus Augustus' Bundoch, 'who was very much disliked'. The victim's 'screams of murder'[17] brought others to his rescue, but not before he was severely wounded and placed in the hospital for three months.

Could this be the day Benjamin Horne had recently warned of, that while boys had not yet fully copied men in 'the highest class of crimes' this was 'no proof that some of them will not eventually do so'?[18] The day when Commandant Booth and everyone in Van

Diemen's Land might confront something not seen, a case of boys committing a murder at Point Puer?

Inside the gaol yard Rose's worst fears were confirmed. Just as Campbell had said, McGuire was indeed lying on the ground and 'bleeding in the head'.[19] He had arrived in the colony less than a year before. After serving nine months for poaching in his native Scottish border town of Peebles, 22 miles (35 km) south of Edinburgh, he had been gaoled again for an assault but then broke out in his prison clothing and was captured and transported for fourteen years for 'theft'. McGuire was marked in his gaol report as a 'bad character' but he gave Booth no trouble when he was despatched to Saltwater Creek, 15 miles (25 km) north of Port Arthur, where about 400 convicts cultivated cabbages, potatoes and turnips.[20]

The commandant rated his Port Arthur behaviour as 'good' or 'very good'[21] with no offences recorded, and with his good build, avowed Protestantism and rare ability to read and write, seemed to be a convict with prospects of staying on the right path himself and worth the risk of assignment as an overseer at Point Puer in March 1843.

In his first eight weeks at Puer McGuire's conduct was regarded as 'orderly' and 'good',[22] and 'very kind and humane' to the boys.[23]

But whether he was truly good and kind, or had been over-zealous in his newfound responsibility, McGuire was now lying on the ground, barely alive with a bloody head wound.

Rose's mind must have raced. Was this another case of revenge against an overseer seen to have over-stepped the mark? Or perhaps even the first case of boys emulating Port Arthur men in committing an apparently senseless crime because they were 'tired of this life and resolved to do something [and] be hanged'[24] or because 'I'd rather be dead than alive as I am now'?[25]

Charles Campbell and seventeen others were staring, silently and sullenly, 'all in a body, looking at [McGuire] at about three or four yards distance'.[26] Rose eyed them all. He looked first at

Campbell, but there was no way of knowing if his alert was out of any real concern for McGuire, if he had been despatched by other boys, or was just trying to appear tough. Rose next looked at Harper Nicholls. Sentenced in York to seven years transportation for stealing a gelding, he was one of 'the most powerful'[27] of the boys, one he knew had 'some quarrel the evening previous' and been before the magistrate just thirty minutes ago on a charge of 'indecent conduct'.[28] He also looked at Daniel Miller, 'a much stouter and taller fellow',[29] and John Smith, 'a strong-looking youth',[30] who had also been before the magistrate that morning. Others he eyed included William Fletcher, a 'rather tall' lad of eighteen who had spent nearly four years on board the notorious *Euryalus*, Michael Shea 'a stout, resolute looking fellow', and Henry Sparkes.[31]

Which of these boys had attacked McGuire? Many of them had been reported by McGuire for various offences, Campbell and Sparkes receiving their heaviest thrashings in McGuire's short time as overseer, and several had just been before the magistrate. Was it a spontaneous revenge attack by one or two boys taken to the magistrate that morning, or another well-planned mob attack? And could boys have been bullied by others to exact some revenge on their behalf, and threatened if they informed?

Word of the assault quickly spread as Rose sent out alerts to Captain Arnold Errington, commanding officer of the 51st light infantry regiment at Port Arthur and the day's visiting magistrate while Commandant Booth was on leave, Point Puer superintendent John Mitchell and Puer gaol superintendent John Hepburn. They all knew Booth, due to return the following day, would be most displeased. 'No one provokes me with immunity' was his regimental motto, and a murderous attack on an overseer was severe provocation, and he would be determined the culprit, or culprits, be immediately identified and punished.

Rushing to the gaol yard the three officers passed McGuire being carried away by convict overseers for medical attention at

Port Arthur. They could see he had 'a wound over his right ear, his arms…hanging down'[32] but he was still conscious, and none thought the wound necessarily fatal.

Captain Errington, who had only been Port Arthur's regimental head for five months, immediately addressed the boys. He demanded to know who had struck McGuire and threatened that if the guilty boy or boys did not come forward, he would take action against them all.

The sullen silence was broken. But not by Charles Campbell, who had alerted Rose to the attack. It was Henry Sparkes: 'It was me that done it.'[33]

Errington might have thought his decisive threat had delivered his culprit, but gaol superintendent Hepburn knew the boys better, familiar with their propensity for elevating status through bravado and 'gameness' or falsehoods. And he knew that threatening to punish all if a culprit was not identified was a well-tried but mostly unsuccessful tactic, boys refusing to reveal the guilty and silently accepting punishment rather than inform on others in an unacceptable 'dog' act, even when they themselves were innocent. And as Inspector Horne had recently detailed, the boys code was to tell as many lies as was necessary for oneself, or for the whole fraternity.

Hepburn looked at Sparkes, who recently had twenty days in solitary and thirty stripes for 'misconduct' and being 'absent without leave'. He was a likely candidate, perhaps angry that McGuire had caused his most severe thrashing, or perhaps that the overseer was about to report him for another offence. But Hepburn knew boys did not admit to any wrongdoing, even of relatively minor offences, so perhaps Sparkes was falsely claiming to be the culprit to gain some status or had been intimidated by bigger and older boys. Hepburn told the boys he would not take Sparkes' statement as the truth, or take anyone else at his word, unless others came forward to verify it.

With blood and unanswered questions in the air, Captain

Errington left to see if McGuire could reveal who had struck him. The overseer was conscious enough to relate that he had been standing between the two gaol yards separating larger and smaller boys. A boy named White was near him, he said, but he couldn't say if he had struck him, and yes, the boys Campbell and Sparkes were standing near him, but he had 'no quarrel' with them and had not made any threat to take them before the magistrate. 'I cannot swear by whom the blow was inflicted,' he told Errington.[34]

By week's end, on the last day of June, McGuire succumbed, 'Died at Port Arthur of fracture' noted on his record.[35] Those running Point Puer were now confronted with the hard truth that boys were capable of much more than mischief, insolence, profanity, misconduct and 'crowning' of overseers. One or more of them was so wicked as to be capable of a murderous attack. The body of Hugh McGuire was the proof.

An inquest was held the same day by Commandant Booth, acting as coroner, and a panel of seven jurors. It found McGuire came to his death by 'a blow or blows' on the right side of his head.[36] The wound was severe: Dr Frederick Brock, in charge of surgical cases at Port Arthur hospital, reported a gash on the right side of the head, about an inch (2.5 cm) long and three-quarters of an inch (2 cm) wide, penetrating the skull bone as far as the dura mater, the outer covering of the brain.

The weapon causing the wound was less clear, the inquest panel deciding it was inflicted by either one of the stone hammers kept in the crime yard, or a stick.

But as to who used a stone hammer or stick, Booth and his panel were in no doubt. After taking 'statements' from officers and some of the bigger boys in the crime class, including William Fletcher, John Smith, Harper Nicholls, Michael Shea and Daniel Miller, they found 'such blows having been struck by Henry Sparkes and Charles Campbell'.[37]

The inquest was unambiguous, and Commandant Booth

determined. Boy convicts were there to be punished and possibly reformed. If any Puer regulation was breached, the guilty had to be punished. That was how 'the system' worked and dumping night soil or throwing bricks and stones was one thing, but the fatal smashing of an overseer's skull was punishable by death, even if that meant a noose would go around a boy's neck.

The commandant now had to report to the colonial governor, Sir John Franklin, revealing the truth that under his command all the strict discipline and punishment had not only failed to turn two boys onto the 'right path', but failed to prevent murder in broad daylight. It was an uncomfortable despatch. Booth had basked in Governor Arthur's approbation of his 'zeal for the public service manifested by the general good order and discipline of the station',[38] and diarised his anxiety when Arthur was recalled: 'oh que je suis miserable...doubts arise!!!'[39] although Franklin had quickly reaffirmed Booth's appointment.

But the murderous news came just as there were questions swirling about the general state of discipline at Port Arthur and calls for the commandant's removal because of the failure to 'put a stop to the blood sheddings at Port Arthur',[40] a dramatic manhunt underway after an infamous outbreak led by Martin Cash, and settler discontent about convict-turned-bushrangers.

A day after the inquest, Booth wrote 'with extreme regret'[41] to tell Sir John of 'a serious circumstance that occurred at the crime class gaol of the juvenile establishment on the day previous to my returning from leave of absence'.[42]

Having cannily established that the attack did not occur directly on his watch, Booth detailed how on the morning of the attack McGuire had charged 'a boy by the name of Nichols for disorderly conduct and threatening language', for which he was severely reprimanded. Booth did not mention any of the other boys who also appeared before the magistrate, merely that after returning Nichols to the gaol yard McGuire 'took his dinner' and then, ten minutes

later, 'was immediately knocked down and fell insensible'. He said
McGuire became 'perfectly sensible' and able to give a deposition
after the depressed part of his skull was raised, before dying six
days later.

Booth was also keen to paint a picture that an overseer he had
recently chosen would not have been so severe on boys to invite a
murderous attack, and that under his command the boys were strictly
managed. 'The deceased was by no means harsh in the performance
of his duties, indeed, perhaps poor man, not sufficiently strict.'[43]

McGuire could not identify his attackers, Booth told the
governor, but an inquest drew 'evidence…that two wretched boys…
very bad characters, admitted themselves to have inflicted the
wounds, which was corroborated afterwards by two other boys who
belonged to the same yard', and after a 'very patient hearing' the
inquest jury concluded McGuire had died of head blows 'struck by
Henry Sparkes and Charles Campbell'.[44]

He had committed them to stand trial in Hobart Town and was
forwarding all the inquest 'evidence' to the Attorney-General because,
as difficult as it must have been to admit, he was 'apprehensive that
there may be a legal flaw in the principal evidences as the magistrate
(Errington), in his anxiety to ascertain the perpetrators of the cruel
act, threatened to punish all who were present unless the offenders
were given up'.[45]

Booth's anxiety was that while his inquest was satisfied with
evidence 'identifying' Sparkes and Campbell as the culprits in a
horrible murder, 'the law will, I fear, consider this evidence given
under the influence of fear', which if ruled inadmissible could mean
the first murder at Point Puer going unpunished.

Booth assured the governor 'there can be no doubt' Campbell
and Sparkes were the murderers, but intimated they might have
been acting under the influence, or perhaps intimidation, of others,
referring to 'the instigators to the deed Nichols and Parkins [sic],
boys of very bad character and who have much evil influence

over their companions'.[46] He strongly recommended the governor authorise their removal from Point Puer to another penal settlement, presumably Port Arthur. The commandant did not provide any evidence about the instigators, or indicate why the inquest did not assign some culpability to them, or whether he would summarily punish them himself. (Nichols had been found guilty of 'gross misconduct' three times in the preceding weeks and had been released after ten days in solitary just before McGuire's murder. The identity of 'Parkins' is unclear.)

Booth's inquest and his report to the governor about Sparkes and Campbell's guilt was unequivocal, despite questions or doubts: the unusual 'confession' of Sparkes, the inconclusive death-bed statement of McGuire, the boys' known code of telling lies to protect themselves, and the commandant's comments about others being the real instigators.

Of eighteen boys at the scene, Sparkes and Campbell were deemed as solely responsible. So as Hugh McGuire was on his final transportation journey to the Isle of the Dead, Campbell and Sparkes were put on a convict-built schooner, the *Eliza,* to take them to Hobart Town to face a Supreme Court trial for murder and the prospect of standing on the scaffold to be hanged by the neck until they were dead.

The semaphore network ensured the message from Tasman Peninsula reached Hobart Town in fifteen minutes, and the *Colonial Times* men began typesetting that 'two lads' were on their way 'charged with the murder of a free [sic] overseer by striking him on the head with a stone hammer'.[47]

The newspaper men must have had the feeling this could be a trial of enormous substance, not just for Sparkes and Campbell, but for others in the system of transporting and punishing convicts, and the notion of 'saving' young boys. John West, co-founder and editor of the *Launceston Examiner* (in the north of the colony) was driving a national argument that transportation was socially and morally wrong. The House of Lords had been told Van Diemen's Land was its 'worst'[48] community of all, as it brought together all the 'bad' of masters and slaves, jailers and prisoners, criminals and executioners. And the *Colonial Times* was questioning whether it was inconsistent with colonists' safety to retain penal facilities 'for the desperate characters that are confined there'.[49] And while some continued to argue that authorities at 'home' should appreciate Commandant Booth's 'discipline and control'[50] others could not believe that a system 'which all parties describe as being destitute of every ingredient of ordinary humanity' could afford Booth any eulogy when 'the public has seen miserable wretch after miserable wretch commit murder in order to go to death on the scaffold…to escape from sufferings, the bitterness of which was unendurable'.[51] And Her Majesty's Government had a report, written by Governor Franklin's former secretary, calling for an end to 'the prevalent doctrine…that criminals once convicted should be but little regarded…if necessary…entirely sacrificed'.[52]

Whether Sparkes and Campbell would be 'entirely sacrificed' would soon be known, but those in newspaper and legal circles might have sensed the trial could see other victims. Commandant Booth and his officers' careers might suffer. The Attorney-General and a defence lawyer, already fierce and bitter rivals in politics and law, might see their reputations swing on whether two boys would have to walk the scaffold. And the colony's first judge, already under fire for being no longer up to the task, would have to conduct a trial which some expected to deliver 'an eye for an eye' and others some mercy for the young. Another 'sacrifice', might be the truth, with the jury having to weigh which evidence, amid the known deceit of boy convicts and the self-interest of Puer officialdom, could be accepted as nothing but the truth.

Even in a colony that already had infamy around the world as a place of excessive criminality, debauchery and capital punishment, and even in a year in which the public had already absorbed reports of convicts using stone hammers to smash in skulls in 'another cold-blooded murder', and other 'atrocious' and 'horrible' murders, and of attacks without cause due 'an old grudge' or because the culprit was 'sick of life',[53] this shaped as an extraordinary chapter in the story of Van Diemen's Land.

Two 'mere boys'[54] had arrived from Port Arthur on Sunday 16 July and were now in gaol awaiting the Supreme Court's sittings starting on Wednesday. 'Their names are Sparkes and Campbell,' the *Examiner* revealed, 'and it is said that the fatal blows were struck by the older boy Campbell, the other looking on, abetting the deed.'[55]

Was that indeed the case? Were Sparkes and Campbell true killers, out of some vengeance, or perhaps victims of a tyranny of other boys, or convenient scapegoating by Puer officers? And could small boys really kill an overseer in broad daylight?

Just more questions in the lottery of life.

12

A TRUTH FROM
THE SHADOWS

Facts alone are wanted in life. Plant nothing else, and root out
everything else.
— Charles Dickens, *Hard Times*

While Van Diemen's Land readied for the trial and judgment on
Henry Sparkes and Charles Campbell, a representative of Her
Majesty's Secretary of State for the Home Department had delivered
a judgment on the secretive Point Puer.

In the months leading up to the bludgeoning of Hugh McGuire,
the pioneering juvenile settlement was undergoing its first review
after nine years. And while colonial authorities in Hobart Town
were shaken by news of boys murdering an overseer, the Home
Department visitor would shake them further with what he had seen.
Benjamin Horne, well-educated and experienced in juvenile matters,

delivered a shocking condemnation: Puer's paths of punishment, discipline and moral reformation were failures, and the treatment of young street boys by the British Government and its agents in Van Diemen's Land meant many were not only condemned to a life of crime but some were capable of murder.

Horne had been tasked with assessing Puer's alignment with juvenile approaches more recently adopted at Parkhurst Prison on the Isle of Wight. He had been educated at Edinburgh Session School 'in the best form',[1] appointed by the Poor Law Commission to develop workhouse schools in Norfolk and Suffolk, studied teacher-training at Glasgow Normal Seminary and was master of the Battersea teacher residential school.

Before his departure, Horne had to familiarise himself with Parkhurst and 'appreciate the nature of the discipline of Parkhurst and the character of the arrangements which it depended upon for its success'.[2]

Parkhurst was, like Puer, another experiment and expedience to address the problems of 'children of the perishing and dangerous classes',[3] as reformer Mary Carpenter described them, and rising concerns about convict 'slavery'. In a rundown former Napoleonic Wars military hospital and children's asylum, unwanted juvenile delinquents would be transformed from undesirable criminals to desirable 'skilled migrants' through the same programme of discipline, trade and moral training that underpinned ambitions of Point Puer four years previously. Parkhurst had improved 'separation and silence' elements and resources, and greater public and government scrutiny than Puer, but the 'migrant' development still encompassed prison dress with a meagre diet, 'silence on all occasions', separation, 'wearing an iron on the leg' and 'uninterrupted surveillance'[4] — and their destiny was still exile. To the first of 1500 boys between twelve and eighteen being set to be sent from Parkhurst to Australia and New Zealand the Home Secretary, Sir James Graham, made it clear to the 'migrants' they were 'doomed to be transported'. They 'must bid a long farewell to the hopes of revisiting his native home, of seeing his parents, or of rejoining his companions. These are the hopes and pleasures which his crimes have forfeited,' he said.[5]

Horne's brief was to escort ninety-two Parkhurst boys to New Zealand, then assess whether the colony of Port Phillip (now Melbourne) would accept any such 'skilled migrants', and then finally move to Point Puer for six months to review its operations and implement recommended changes.

Notwithstanding impressions from Hobart Town of Puer being 'one of the most successful, gratifying and benevolent experiments in modern times', Sir James painted Puer as a boys' ultimate doom where 'the most rigid discipline…with forced labour and instruction…severely maintained to an extent which amounts to hardship and to unremitted punishment…and degradation awaits him and his sufferings will be severe'.[6]

The better behaved Parkurst boys would go to any colony prepared to accept them, such as Western Australia, which agreed to take about thirty boys as free and assisted migrant-apprentices with a conditional pardon as long as the word 'convict' was never mentioned, but any 'intractable or incorrigible' boys would be 'instantly dismissed…and transported to Point Puer by the first ship that sails'.[7]

After unloading his cargo of Parkhurst boys at Auckland, to the surprise and dismay of officials worried New Zealand would become one of 'England's moral dunghills',[8] Horne's arrival in Hobart Town created anxiety among officials and supporters who had consistently lauded the Puer experiment.

Horne appreciated that authorities in London wanted to maintain the 'terror' of punishment, but also be seen to be responding to social reformers, philanthropists, some magistrates, newspapers, police and prison administrators despairing at the cycle of deprivation, delinquency and imprisonment, and the absence of true solutions. As feminist-reformer Caroline Cornwallis would write in a prize-winning essay, 'we shall have to look deep and inquire long, perhaps...[to] discover where the first fault lies.'[9]

Wherever the faults in Britain's laws and social institutions, Benjamin Horne found the 'solution' of Point Puer so replete with faults that he recommended spending cease and Puer be closed.

Horne's visit would have unsettled Governor Sir John Franklin, who was much more interested in polar exploration and cultural pursuits than penal science and convictism. When he and his influential wife Jane made an obligatory visit to Port Arthur and Point Puer, Sir John merely suggested some boys should perhaps learn the 'higher branches of gardening' while Lady Jane had no time for 'wicked children who have never had their natural and inherited corruptions whipped out of them'[10] and did not 'hesitate to deprecate the restrictions on the flogging of boys at Point Puer'.[11]

Franklin's private secretary and friend Captain Alexander Maconochie, a former Naval officer and first professor of geography at the University of London, had already embarrassed him by writing a report for the English Society for the Improvement of Prison Discipline that castigated the convict system of 'slave labour'[12] and 'slave holders'.[13] Maconochie argued strongly 'there is a science of each'[14] in punishment and reform, and the former should not be so cruel and vindictive to be at the expense of a convict's self-respect, or desire and capacity to learn habits of honesty and industry.

Forced to dismiss Maconochie, Franklin was sensitive to what Horne might find at Point Puer and demanded on Horne's arrival in February 1843 that his report go directly to him. But struggling with convictism and its economic pressures, and reeling from Arthurite Colonial Secretary John Montagu telling London that its governor was an 'imbecile', Franklin could have no idea what he would soon face.

Just a few months after Horne sailed from Hobart Town to Point Puer, Her Majesty's ruler had two challenging documents on his desk, and they would form a perverse context as his rule came to an end. His reputation had begun in the Battle of Trafalgar on the *Bellerophon*, which became the first prison hulk for juveniles, and now he had a scathing report from Horne on Point Puer juvenile prison and a letter from Commandant Booth revealing that on the settlement designed to 'save' Britain's street boys a supervisor had been bashed to death. A quill and a stone hammer had each unmasked the truth of Point Puer, the divergence between promise and outcome, official despatches and reality.

Franklin had no choice but to leave the truth of the murder to be resolved in the Supreme Court, where his Attorney-General, Thomas Welsh, would face their shared nemesis, Edward Macdowell, defence counsel for the boys. Franklin had dismissed Macdowell as Attorney-General in 1841 in favour of Welsh, leading the angry barrister to pen an editorial in the *Van Diemen's Land Chronicle* declaring Franklin's performance resembled the 'imbecility of the latter days of the Roman empire'.[15]

Franklin also had Horne's report on his desk for months, but with news of the murder on its way to London, he had no choice but to now despatch it. Britain wanted its delinquent boys out of sight and out of mind, but Horne's report and news of boys on trial for murder would lift the veil over Puer.

Horne made it clear that Point Puer settlement lacked the rudimentary conditions and resources necessary to meet a charter of punishment and reform, and so could not 'fulfil the intentions of the Law on one hand, nor the expectation of the Christian and the Philanthropist on the other'.[16]

Horne could not even give a 'pass' mark to punishment, the foremost priority of the Colonial Office and its far-flung administrators. Commandant Booth and his subordinates were 'at great pains' to detect any offences among the 716 boys present, often dealing with up to fifty or sixty boys on a single day, and 'very strict in punishing them'. But they were often 'faults which can scarcely be considered criminal', the court-like appearances inflated the boys' sense of self-importance, and while 'a removal to the jail is very little feared by a bad boy' the whole approach merely tended to 'degrade and harden'.

The severity of discipline and absence of proper facilities, resources and instruction, or a clear pathway toward an honest working life and freedom, meant boys who were part of 'a habitual class of paupers' in Britain were not finding the 'right path' in exile. Instead of becoming good and useful members of society after their punishment expired, they were becoming part of a 'habitual prisoner class' which would see them at risk of being 'a nuisance and expense to the colony'[17] for years and condemned to become adult convicts at Port Arthur.

Whatever the averred hopes for Puer, Horne said the site was poorly chosen in the first place, 'too much…sacrificed to mistaken notions of economy'.[18]

Basic conditions shocked him. The barracks were all so crowded hammocks had long been discontinued. 'The appearance at night sleeping upon the bare floor can be compared to nothing but that of a horde of gypsies in a large barn, the only difference being that the said gypsies have generally a little straw under their blankets which the Point Puer boys have not.'[19] In regards to their clothing and hygiene, Horne said 'cleanliness is said by some to be next to Godliness but this maxim does not appear to be acted upon by many of the boys' in the absence of 'military drill and daily inspection' to promote habits of cleanliness, neatness and obedience. The more 'worthless boys' were generally 'the most ragged and dirty'.[20]

Reformative resources and efforts were also grossly inadequate. Puer failed to employ every means to rouse the 'almost dormant feeling of self-respect',[21] such as a chaplain visiting boys 'in the silence and seclusion of his cell…(to) use every proper means to instruct and reclaim him'.[22] Religious knowledge was 'extremely meagre',[23] boys being 'almost totally ignorant…incapable of comprehending the…Chaplain', and their singing at divine services was 'screaming… almost intolerable'.[24]

And as for education, most well-conducted prisons and houses of correction in Britain employed one or more teachers, but Puer had no free and well-trained school masters, merely the 'superintendence' of a Catechist, assisted by two convict 'schoolmasters' and forty 'monitors' chosen from convicts and boys whose only qualification was being a little more advanced in 'the rudiments of knowledge'.[25] Other than the Holy Scriptures, any books were those 'laid aside in good schools in Britain for several years',[26] and a map of the world was non-existent. Most of the boys could not read 'without such an amount of blunders and spelling as totally obscures the sense', and there was no attempt to teach them to understand even 'the meaning of comparatively easy words and phrases'. Boys who had been more than four years at Puer could still not read easy words of one syllable, writing was 'very poor' and any progress in arithmetic 'closely bordered on the miraculous'.[27]

Using mostly convict men as overseers and school masters was an 'absurdity' that had to end. Many connived with the boys 'to avoid becoming unpopular',[28] leaving boys free to wander, 'steal anything they can lay their hands upon from the Officer's quarters and the gardens...in broad daylight',[29] abscond into the bush with secreted provisions, or engage in 'unnatural vice...familiar, between boys and overseers'.[30]

The jail buildings and solitary cells 'resembling sentry boxes' were so poorly built that boys could readily mix and converse freely, 'sleep on the floor almost as closely as they can lie', remove boards so 'provisions may be conveyed to them' or 'break out of them and abscond'.

'He has as much food as before, his labour...is not more severe...and is performed in the open air...he associates with companions of the same character as himself, and does not consider separation from his class in the school any great loss.'[31] This meant punishment had little deterring influence, but was efficient in doing harm. 'A boy who has perhaps a little moral principle remaining is sent to the jail for two or three months, associates daily with other boys still worse than himself, and returns to the general class thoroughly corrupted.'[32]

As for the frequent use of the lash, Horne felt it merely tended to degrade and harden, and after repetition became 'useless' as some boys took pride in their endurance 'and consider flogging a manly sort of punishment'.[33]

Horne called for a cessation of spending on Point Puer and its closure in favour of a new 'penitentiary' on Maria Island, on the east coast. It should be dedicated to 800 boys housed in separate cells along the lines of Parkhurst and 'enclosed by a substantial wall of sufficient height to render escape difficult if not impossible'.[34] Punishments ought to be reduced, boys exempted from criminal convict laws and regulations and provided an improved pathway to become apprentices and free men. Puer's secrecy should also end, with a panel of qualified visitors to provide regular reports.

But as Hobart Town absorbed the news of boys killing an overseer and wondered what would emerge at the trial of Sparkes and Campbell, Benjamin Horne had a clear understanding of the forces in play at Puer and what would emerge.

Writing just before the murderous attack, he highlighted the boys' code of silence and intimidation, 'a sort of tyranny…to which every boy in the place is a slave and to which he must submit almost at the peril of his life'.[35]

Boys had not yet emulated Port Arthur men in the 'highest' crime of murder, but Horne presciently concluded this was 'no proof that some will not eventually do so'.[36]

And if:

> a case of a very serious nature [were] to occur, no boy would give evidence against another, or if he pretended to give any it could not be relied on, for it seems to be a maxim of the whole fraternity that everyone must tell as many lies as may be necessary for himself and for the community.[37]

If one admits that he has committed some act of disorder of which four or five are suspected and for which one or all must be punished, you are by no means certain that the self-accuser is the culprit.[38]

He may be either an individual foolhardy enough to undertake the punishment for the others or he may have been selected to bear the blame, and no one would dare to offend his companions and hazard their resentment for fear of undergoing the most severe punishment which the law permits a magistrate to inflict.[39]

He cited the case where one of the boys refused to give evidence to convict another for attacking an overseer because he would then have to 'leave Point Puer instantly, for he could not consider himself safe a moment after he had done so, even although the other boy had been removed to Port Arthur'.[40]

His was a conviction that boys were truly capable of one day committing a murder, but also capable of ensuring that the truth of such an event might remain elusive. His report shone a light on the darkness of Puer, exposing the self-serving reports formerly presented to the Mother Country, that its children would be overjoyed with such food, lodging, clothing and instruction available at Puer, and how the grand experiment was producing evidence of infamy being lost in industry and sin giving place to grace.

Despite his belief that some Puer boys might eventually be capable of murder, Horne, who temporarily remained as the settlement's first and only qualified teacher, could not have envisaged that boys in his classroom would soon be on trial for stone-hammering an overseer to death. And that he might draw some grim satisfaction that his report coincided with Hobart's newspapers reprinting London commentary decrying that English and Welsh courts were still processing 15,000 juveniles a year, some for still trifling charges 'such as stealing an orange, a few apples or two biscuits', and putting children as young as nine in prisons which were contaminating enough for adults but 'still more ruinous to the morals of the young'.[41] And that the ultimate, most ruinous outcome was his own unmasking of the code of 'brutal tyranny' and hardship which might lead to the 'highest' crime.

13

A TRIAL BEGINS

Take nothing on its looks, take everything on evidence. There's no better rule.
— Charles Dickens, *Great Expectations*

On a wintery Sunday 16 July 1843, the 70 foot (21 m) wooden schooner *Eliza* — built by convicts at Port Arthur, named after their nemesis' wife and featuring a carved woman's bust figurehead — unloaded Henry Sparkes and Charles Campbell, who were then escorted by soldiers to Hobart Town Gaol to await their destiny.

Everyone was keen to see what these 'boy killers' looked like. There was nothing remarkable about their appearance or demeanour, just two more roughly clothed boys, sullen and small 'in stature and appearance...mere boys', as newspapers described.[1] Just two more real-life Oliver Twists, who had long lived with the law not being their friend.

The Court House, Hobart Town, print, 1834. Image courtesy Libraries Tasmania, SD_ILS:655280.

Regina v Sparkes and Campbell was listed for Thursday 20 July, in Australia's first Supreme Court, the stone heart of colonial administration and judgment in Van Diemen's Land. In a clutch of convict-built buildings, everything about a convict's behaviour was monitored and judged under the laws of man and God: the Supreme Court, Government House, St David's Cathedral and town gaol with its scaffold deliberately in full view.

When John Pedder became the colony's first Supreme Court Chief Justice he took the mediaeval oath of judicial office and the oath of allegiance to the crown, incorporating a personal obligation to God. Lord Chief Justice Hale's sentiment was that the administration of justice was entrusted for God, King and Country. As Pedder's New South Wales peer, William Burton, put it, 'to do justice is a divine command…we must obey God'.[2]

The court was not completely finished when it was hastily opened in 1824 to best New South Wales by a week. Behind a white picket fence the two-storey Georgian building with a classical portico entrance looked substantial enough, its brown stonework and arched windows fitted with small panes of glass, and in one corner an odd circular turret which housed a small water closet for the judge. But it was widely seen as a gloomy and inadequate building. It was 'Lilliputian', the *Colonial Times* complained,[3] with insufficient space for lawyers, jury, press and public. The lawyers' blue table was designed only for 'taper gentlemen'[4] and if the jury happened to be 'twelve good men and fat'[5] or even one corpulent juryman was present, the whole court would be 'thrown into confusion to know what to do'.[6] There were also frequent complaints about poor acoustics and the street noise of carriages and workmen, bad ventilation, and inadequate heating against the chill of a Hobart winter.

But it was a stage for the grand theatre of life, where the accused, prosecutor, defence counsel, witnesses, judge and jury were all, as Dickens had written, ordinary men pursuing their own means of survival and sense of truth and justice. It was a popular 'place of public amusement' where at no expense one could enjoy 'as sport the awful exhibition of human infirmity by men who are constituted arbiters of life and property...the decisions of the judges become as common a subject to bet upon as the result of a horse race, the bets being regulated on the colour of (Chief Justice) Mr Pedder's nose'.[7] Some looked forward to the human drama of men and women, young and old, facing judgment for crimes of murder, infanticide, bushranging, highway robbery, rape, sodomy with man or beast, sheep and cattle stealing. More than 200 souls had already been sentenced to be hanged, the noose swinging more often in Van Diemen's Land than any other colony, and the prospect of a hanging 'at the usual hour' appealed as 'amusement' to people who warmed to the public spectacle of the condemned 'dancing' on the end of a rope, or keen to hear any dramatic last-minute confession.

But before a hanging there had to be a judgment, and before that a trial, although most of those packing into the court felt this would be another day of everyday Supreme Court drama: a swift and harsh judgment, with no appeal process, and no waiting for a hanging sentence to be carried out. It seemed inevitable that the crime of blood, the biblical dictum of *lex talionis* — an eye for an eye — would soon see Chief Justice Pedder don his familiar black cap to pronounce the death sentence, and the hangman, himself a convict, prepare his 'rope and soap for two'.

Reporters from the *Colonial Times* and other newspapers did not see any 'amusement' inside the Supreme Court, and often neither compassion nor justice. Time and again they were reminded of the Boz sketches of the Old Bailey, where Dickens observed that:

> nothing is so likely to strike the person who enters [a court] for the first time as the calm indifference with which the proceedings are conducted; every trial seems a matter of business. There is a great deal of form but no compassion; considerable interest but no sympathy...you can scarcely

believe that the result of the trial is a matter of life or death
to one wretched being present.[8]

And this was a matter of life and death for Henry Sparkes and
Charles Campbell. When the boys were brought up from their cell
into the courtroom their appearance, and the charges, soon arrested
the thinking that this was an unambiguous murder destined to end
with a familiar outcome.

Observers were first struck by their size and youth. They
were described as 'mere boys',[9] 'boys',[10] 'very small in stature…and
appearance…and young'.[11]

And struck by the indictments read by the clerk of the court.
The first count charged Sparkes with 'having, on 23 June, with force
of arms, and with a certain stick in his right hand, and with malice
aforethought, feloniously struck and beat Hugh McGuire on the
right side of the head, inflicting a mortal wound, of which the said
Hugh McGuire did languish and live until the 29th day of June, on
which said day, from the effects of such mortal wound, he died'.[12]
The second count charged Charles Campbell with 'being present
and feloniously aiding, comforting, assisting and maintaining, with
malice aforethought, the said Henry Sparkes, in the committal of
the felony'.[13]

Then the names were inverted, charging Campbell as the
principal and Sparkes as the abettor.

Then more counts charged both together with having 'severally
struck, beat and thrown down Hugh McGuire, with malice
aforethought, against the peace of our Lady the Queen, her crown
and dignity', using 'certain sticks' or 'certain stone hammers'.[14]

The atmosphere in the court changed, with many a furrowed
brow, raised eyebrow and murmuring: one dead man, two boys
charged, but multiple and conflicting counts. Masking any disquiet
he might have felt, Chief Justice Pedder looked at the two boys,
barely visible above the bar of the dock.

The prosecuting Attorney-General, Thomas Welsh, immediately

sought an adjournment as two 'material'[15] witnesses had been sent for but had not yet arrived from Port Arthur, and he suggested 'the propriety'[16] of the Court assigning counsel to the accused boys.

Judge Pedder weighed the request for defence counsel. A new English law in 1837 provided for the accused to have defence counsel if they could afford it, and it was 'normal' for Port Arthur prisoners on murder charges to have counsel, but Pedder 'did not want it to go abroad that in all capital cases a counsel was to be appointed'. He had even told some accused of murder that he could not justify 'putting the public to the expense of assigning counsel to him', as it would 'do him no good, nor the public either'.[17] But perhaps wanting to ensure two boys had the fairest possible hearing, and sensing the ambiguity of the charges and likely evidence, Pedder assigned Mr Edward Macdowell, who was already in the court on numerous cases, to defend the boys.

He then adjourned the case to the following day, Friday 21 July, and the boys were led back to the Murray Street gaol. But the case was again adjourned until Monday as the Attorney-General still wanted more time for the arrival and examination of two 'fresh' witnesses from Port Arthur.

Sparkes, Campbell, the press and public were forced to wait. As were the jurors, already irked by being forced to leave their homes and businesses, some as far as 20 miles (13 km) away and forced to remain in Hobart Town at their own expense and without jury compensation. And on Monday 24 July, their hopes of returning home were again dashed, the case adjourned for another day.

In their cell, Sparkes and Campbell must have wondered about the two new witnesses causing the delays, and, as ever, their chances. Would Puer boys expected to give evidence choose, as William Miles described to the House of Lords, to 'not betray his comrade' or 'plunder his bosom friend'?[18] What were their chances of being found guilty? If so, what were the chances of the jury making a plea for mercy? And would the judge endorse such a plea to the

Governor? And would Her Majesty's ruler accede before he left the colony?

Out in the street and in the pubs of Hobart Town, their fate was the major topic, along with an on-going manhunt for a gang of escapees, and the hope that new rewards of a conditional pardon and 100 acres or 100 sovereigns would end the 'terror...of deadly marauders'.[19] In the corridors of power, there was also anxiety about a collapsed economy and a record number of 5329 more unfunded convicts. And anxiety about Point Puer's morality: a new Commissariat Office advertisement declared Point Puer was in need of '180 Sacred Histories, by the Society for Promoting Christian Knowledge, 500 Church Catechisms, and 400 Prayer Books'.[20]

By the time the town's numerous clock bells rang out their competing declarations that it was 10am on Tuesday 25 July, the courthouse was full, and full of expectation.

With Antarctic air blown up from the most distant part of Van Diemen's Land territory, Macquarie Island 930 miles (1500 km) away, and streets hazardous due to a frost layer over mud and puddles, Judge John Pedder left his manor house in the pretty village of Newtown where his wife Maria waited for any responses to their advertisement for a lady's maid ('required to understand plain needlework, as well as millinery and dressmaking'), housemaid and a coachman ('no married man need apply').[21]

Inside his chamber room, Pedder's mind was not on domestic matters. Some were calling for his head. The *Colonial Times* acknowledged the only Chief Justice the colony had known was 'a high bred gentleman' able to contain his temper and undertake his duties with dignity and conscientiousness but said a judge ought to possess other qualities, 'especially a clear and perfect knowledge of the law, and a peremptory determination to decide upon the law'.[22]

The charge of doubtful legal expertise and indecisiveness was hurtful but not unfamiliar. Early in Pedder's career convict-writer Henry Savery castigated his style by referring to his wife as 'Mrs

Sir John Lewes Pedder, pre – 1850, painting, 1850s. Image courtesy
Libraries Tasmania, PH30/1/280.

Doubtmuch'.[23] Governor Arthur lauded his 'unbending integrity'[24] but he and Sir John Franklin both found him 'tedious' in decision-making with 'a habit of looking for difficulties'[25] and responding to such difficulties by 'rambling through a long search of half analogies and semi-precedents'.[26] A distinguished surveyor-general James Calder called him Sir Petulant Pedder,[27] previous Attorneys-General Joseph Gellibrand and Alfred Stephen complained he raised 'every technical objection that would prevail in England'[28] and the most recent, Edward Macdowell, had the year before been critical of judicial 'ignorance' and commented in Latin that 'the Greeks suffer for the misconduct of kings'.[29]

With unusual boldness the *Colonial Times* called on Pedder to resign while he could retain 'some respect and esteem'.[30] His task had been so 'onerous...solemn and awful' for so long it had 'impaired' his mind and body.[31] Pedder himself could hardly disagree. His Charterhouse-Trinity Hall-Tory-upbringing to become 'a perfect English gentleman',[32] and a brief and unrewarding career in commercial law in the Temple Inns, was no preparation to being chief judge in a penal colony. He faced questions and crimes he had never dealt with, and had to administer a judicial code 'written in letters of blood...justice pure and simple',[33] which often clashed with his personal sense of justice and Christian belief. Colleagues described his struggle between painful duty and pained heart when he had to impose the death sentence, particularly when he had to condemn the young to the noose, as he had done just a year previously, 'tears rolling profusely down his cheeks'[34] when sentencing a former Puer boy for 'an unnatural crime of a most repulsive description'.[35] Pedder himself acknowledged 'terrible attacks in the head' when he faced 'any unusual occurrence'.[36] Now he faced several 'unusual occurrences': calls for his resignation, legal controversies after a recent case delivered a guilty verdict on a capital firearms crime but no punishment,[37] and political questions about his role in the 'falsehood, treachery, meanness and perfidy'[38] of a dossier condemning Sir John Franklin.

Some in colonial circles wondered if this day's Point Puer murder case would affirm that his mind and body were exhausted or perhaps that he could not face condemning another teenager, either due his Christian beliefs or perhaps that while English law of 'doli incapax' did not apply to boys of Sparkes and Campbell's age, they had never understood the consequences of being seduced by the Devil and straying from the right path.

The crowded Supreme Court stood and hushed for his entrance wearing the gown and wig of an English barrister and what Henry Savery described as 'the solemn melancholy visage' of a 'valetudinarian (hypochondriac)…who took snuff regularly'.[39]

Patting his pocket to reassure himself and remind everyone why he had the nickname of 'Snuffbox',[40] Pedder took his seat, and the jury, lawyers, press and public squeezed back into their places to wait for two javelin men to deliver what everyone had come to see: two boys said to be killers.

In their rough Puer garb, there was nothing remarkable about their appearance, save for Campbell's red hair, but their small stature and hardened faces made it hard to discern their age. They had probably not grown much since they arrived at Puer two years before when Sparkes measured 4 feet 7 ½ inches (141 cm) and Campbell just 3 feet 11 inches (119 cm). The Courier said they were not easy to see, 'Campbell more particularly so, his head being only above the dock'.[41] The Launceston Examiner said they looked 'very small and young', but having been 'at Port Arthur [sic] more than two years, probably are much older than they look'.[42] If their various court and convict records were accurate — and many boys did not know when they were born, or deliberately falsified their age — they were probably fourteen to sixteen years old.

They stood silently, neither exhibiting 'any sense of the degradation of their position, or any apparent fear or anxiety as to the awful result which might await them…they rather seemed to regard themselves in the light of heroes'.[43]

After an anxious wait Pedder finally commenced Regina v
Sparkes and Campbell. The boys' fate would swing on Thomas Welsh
prosecuting against their defence barrister Edward Macdowell. The
two Irishmen were enmeshed in the fierce machinations of colonial
life, the cloak of courtroom civility not masking their enmity:
Macdowell, the colony's most able barrister and father of the bar,
had been replaced by Welsh as Attorney-General following his
open hostility to the Solicitor-General. He frequently questioned
his successor's 'manliness' and legal qualities, while Welsh
addressed Macdowell as 'my learned friend or I'd rather say the
learned gentleman'.[44]

There was much anticipation as to the courtroom theatre of
Welsh's 'gentlemanly style and manner' and Macdowell's 'forensic
eloquence'[45] and especially his 'particular forte, without a shadow of
doubt, [his] sarcastic irony'.[46] This 'keen and cutting weapon', which
had previously wounded the Governor, was something he wielded
with 'no common skill and no trifling sagacity and effect'. It 'cuts
into the very bones and marrow of his victim'.[47] And it was still fresh
in people's minds that Macdowell had recently bested Attorney-
General Welsh on another convict hammer murder case because
of an incorrect date in his paperwork, the courtroom drama so
affecting Welsh that 'he fainted and was carried out of the court'.[48]

The Attorney-General rose to present the Crown case probably
anxious to avoid another embarrassing loss to Edward Macdowell,
but cognisant that the primary role of colonial prosecutors was
to present evidence to the jury and question witnesses, not act as
advocates who might 'strain a case against a prisoner' and pursue
vengeance or their own view of justice. It was 'simply to bring it to
the jury'.[49] On this day, the Attorney-General had to first bring to the
jury an explanation as to why it faced so many counts to consider.

'With respect to the offence itself, this particularity was not at all
necessary,' he said, as there was no doubt McGuire had been fatally
bashed at Point Puer. 'But it had been rendered necessary by the

extraordinary discrepancy...found to exist in the evidence, which the jury would have to weigh well and deliberately.'[50]

An inquest had found Sparkes and Campbell to be the murderers, but while there were 'several points of corroboration' in the inquest depositions of four Puer boys who said they witnessed the murder, there were 'massive discrepancies'[51] and the jury would have to ascertain 'any reasonable doubt of the truth of the witnesses'.[52]

Welsh told the jury he had done his best to 'reconcile the contradictory evidence, but candour obliged him to confess that he had not been able to do so'. The 'massive discrepancies' meant he had 'difficulty in arriving at any satisfactory conclusion as to the manner in which the deceased met his death'.[53]

Everyone must have wondered what was going on in the jurymen's heads. An inquest had unequivocally condemned Sparkes and Campbell as killers, but now four weeks later, and with more time and all his experience, the Attorney-General was basically telling them he found the truth too elusive for him to find, so it was up to them to effectively decide what was 'manifest discrepancy' and what might be 'manifest lie'.

And the Attorney General now had to admit another difficulty, something which had been 'officially communicated to him'. This was the 'interference' of Magistrate Errington, who had 'expressed himself to the effect that he could not have supposed that boys so young could have behaved so cowardly; he also said that he would flog them all if they did not tell who did it'. While Captain Errington did not suppose that McGuire's wounds were then mortal it was 'extremely indiscreet in him to make this threat,' Welsh said.[54]

And while he 'would observe that the prisoners had confessed to the deed' before Captain Errington's arrival, the Attorney-General had thought it proper to delay the initial proceedings to send for two additional witnesses.

'God forbid,' the Attorney-General said, making the most of his difficulty, 'that while conducting a prosecution on the part of the Crown I should ever withhold any portion of the evidence that might tell in favour of the prisoner, or keep back anything that might by possibility cast a doubt upon the testimony of the witnesses on behalf of the prosecution.'[55]

Closing his opening remarks, the court heard the Attorney-General make another startling admission. It was, he said, 'an extraordinary circumstance…that there appeared no motive for the deed, on the part of the prisoners at the bar…in fact, the deceased Overseer was ever kind even to a fault.'[56]

By the time Welsh resumed his seat, the trial was already very different to what had been expected. It had begun as a seemingly unambiguous murder, the guilt of Sparkes and Campbell already concluded at an inquest and their condemnation a matter of course. But now the courtroom was absorbing the fact that the prosecution was not sure if Sparkes or Campbell was the primary killer or which weapons were used, that the inquest evidence had so many discrepancies that the truth of what happened to overseer McGuire was unclear, and that while the boys were said to have 'confessed' there was no evident motive.

Eyes raced around the room. The jury would have been forgiven for feeling irritated by the unexpected complexity and the faded hope of a quick exit, the judge for taking an extra-long draught of snuff. Looking at those deciding their fate Sparkes and Campbell could only try to sense if 'chance' was running with or against them.

And as the Attorney-General prepared to bring in his Crown witnesses, no one knew what evidence would be manifestly truth, discrepancies or lies.

14

A CHAIN OF DECEIT

*Lawyers hold that there are too kinds of particularly bad witnesses —
a reluctant witness and a too-willing witness.*
— Charles Dickens, *Pickwick Papers*

George Rose was the first to swear to 'tell the truth and nothing but
the truth'.

The assistant superintendent recalled how after Campbell told
him 'the overseer of the boys is lying down in the yard'[1] he had gone
to the larger of two separate gaol yards where he saw eighteen of
the bigger boys, 'all in a body, looking at him [Hugh McGuire] at
about three or four yards distance'.[2] He ordered them to fall in while
he sent for medical assistance for the overseer, who was 'bleeding
profusely',[3] and for John Hepburn, the gaol superintendent.

Seeing a pile of about twelve stone-hammers about 10 yards

(9 m) from where McGuire was lying, just outside the door from the large ward to the yard, he examined them 'minutely'[4] but 'there were none absent, nor was there any particular mark on any, nor any blood…no marks, no blood upon them'[5] and he did not perceive that any of the hammers had been recently washed.

Rose said he also inspected the boys' clothing and their hands, starting with Harper Nicholls who he knew had had been 'in disgrace and trouble' with McGuire. After 'some quarrel the evening previous'[6] the overseer had taken him before the magistrate just half an hour before the attack on a charge of 'indecent misconduct', but he 'observed nothing with respect to his clothes,'[7] nor see anything untoward on his hands.[8]

Rose said he also searched for any other weapons and two boys, William Fletcher and John Smith, had shown him two sticks,[9] one 'which appeared to be a broom handle' and the other more a bludgeon, about 18 inches (45 cm) long 'with a large knob at the end'. These were now produced in court.[10] To Judge Pedder's query Rose said one came from a water cask beside the door where McGuire had been found, and the other from a shelf inside the ward. Neither should have been there at all, he said, but when he examined them he could not perceive anything untoward.

Asked about Sparkes and Campbell, they also 'had no stains'[11] on their clothes or signs of recent hand washing. And he could not recall either having any dispute with McGuire or over any charges he had laid against them. 'Till I saw him lying…he was very indulgent and kind to the boys…very kind and humane, not severe to the boys but much otherwise.'[12]

Edward Macdowell, standing at the blue barristers' table, asked Rose to explain the layout of the scene, and mark on a plan where he was standing and where McGuire was lying. Rose said the rules were that the large and small boys in the crime class could not move from their own ward and yard to the other, nor communicate with the other. Anyone seeking to do so would have to pass through the door where McGuire was standing. 'It is possible a boy might have gone from one to the other, but I do not think they did'[13] because it was 'forbidden'[14] and it was 'McGuire's duty to prevent boys passing from one yard to another.'[15] Rose explained that in addition to the large boys he was supervising, about ten smaller boys were in the second ward and yard. Macdowell let his questions sow their own seeds of doubt: Campbell, especially, was obviously not one of the 'larger' boys.

Rose said Fletcher and Smith handed him the stick and bludgeon five-to-ten minutes after visiting magistrate Captain Errington confronted the group of boys. 'I heard Captain Errington address the boys,' Rose said. 'He said he would try them all the next day if it was not found out who struck McGuire.'[16]

Macdowell may not have been fully aware of the extent of Commandant Booth's private concerns to the Governor about Errington, but as the prosecutor had referred to his 'extremely indiscreet threat' he well appreciated the legal opportunity this presented, and he pressed Rose on exactly what Errington had said.

'I heard the word "tried" used by Captain Errington...not the word 'flogged'. He might have said so without my hearing. On my oath I cannot recollect Captain Errington say "I hope the boy who has struck McGuire will come forward and say so, otherwise I will flog you all"...I did not hear the word "flog" at all...to the best of my recollection he said "unless it is found out I will try you all tomorrow".'[17]

Macdowell seemed well content with the picture of a military captain threatening a 'flogging' to engineer a quick identification of the culprits.

Newspaper reporters watched Sparkes and Campbell as witnesses appeared, mindful of Dickens' reportorial advice to closely watch the faces of prisoners and the 'painful reality' of certain moments, such as when 'a particular witness appears...how he changes his position and wipes his clammy forehead and feverish hands.'[18]

Whatever William Hill Fletcher had to say would be new to Sparkes and Campbell, as he was not one of the four boys whose depositions at the McGuire inquest led to them being charged. A 'lad of about 18…rather tall',[19] he first testified that after his midday dinner he had gone to stand in front of a fire in the small ward, which seemed to contradict Rose's testimony about large and small boys being unable to move from one area to another.

But what he said next rivetted everyone. As soon as he had gone to stand at the fire, he said, the ward door shut on him. When he opened it again, he saw McGuire standing and then 'I saw him knocked down with a stick. I saw it distinctly, he was knocked down with a short stick with a knob at the end'.[20]

> The blow was struck by Sparkes. The stick was twirled round by Sparkes…wrung round the head twice…waved it twice over his own head before he struck the blow…it fell on the right side of McGuire's head.[21]

Then Campbell, who had been standing behind Sparkes with 'a stick in his hand',[22] the brown one now produced in court, 'gave McGuire a blow across the body…a blow across the belly…as he lay on the ground'.[23]

Fletcher said he ran 'immediately'[24] to take the sticks from the two boys, who had landed one blow each. 'I forced the sticks out of their hands',[25] and 'chucked'[26] them into the large ward. 'When I took the sticks away Sparkes said to Campbell 'he's not had enough' and Campbell replied 'I think he must have a little more'.[27] Both prisoners then went to the place where the stone hammers were lying in the corner of the yard and each took one…got two hammers.[28] 'They went with the hammers to where McGuire was lying. I begged them not to injure him anymore.'[29]

But he could not see what they actually did with the hammers. Despite his professed concern and efforts to prevent further injury to McGuire, he had hidden himself in the water closet, he said, and remained there for ten minutes, accompanied for some of the time by another boy, John Smith. When he came out he saw McGuire lying on the doorway steps supported by two other overseers.

After hearing Captain Errington say that 'if the boy was not brought forward who had struck McGuire he would the next day try every one and flog them,'[30] he saw Sparkes and Campbell approach Errington and superintendent Mitchell.

Macdowell jumped to his feet: 'I object to the question as to what the prisoners said.'[31]

Attorney-General: 'The question I am about to ask, is a question which ought to go to the jury.'

Macdowell:

'Tis a proper question, or it is not; it would be idle to find that it was an improper one after the answer was given; it will then be too late; I submit it is not evidence, since the boys may have spoken in consequence of a threat or intimidation from Captain Errington, a fact which the Attorney-General himself extracted.[32]

In what the *Hobart Town Advertiser* saw as 'rather sharp legal skirmishing'[33] the Attorney-General wanted the jury to hear any testimony as to what Sparkes and Campbell were seen to have done or said, especially it was of a confessional nature. Macdowell wanted nothing of the kind. He argued that the first threat 'that he would "try them and flog them"[34] and then on his second visit seeking two witnesses to "have them all flogged if the real offender was not discovered"[35] meant that irrespective of the nature of anything Sparkes or Campbell might have said it was inadmissible as it was done "under the influence of fear"'.[36]

The Attorney-General argued that no one would come forward to voluntarily admit their guilt of a crime which they must know would render them liable to a trial for their lives, merely to avoid 'so comparatively slight a punishment as a flogging'.[37]

But Judge Pedder indicated he was not convinced. If it was a private person who made such a threat, he said, he did not think there would be any objection, 'but a magistrate is quite different; he has tried, probably, these boys, or some of them before, and punished them'. The Attorney-General again pressed that the question was 'good' because the consequences 'flowing from the confession would be worse than the punishment, and the boys must have known it'.[38]

Pedder paused for more snuff, and huskily made his ruling:

> No principle is more clearly established that you shall not receive evidence to criminate a man, of expressions brought out by the immediate consequences of threats, held out by any magistrate or constable. Even a threat to 'lock a man up' has been held to exclude a confession…It is not clear that the minds of the prisoners were free from the fear of punishment and, as the case now stands, I do not admit the question.[39]

Just as Commandant Booth had feared, and the Attorney-General suspected, the language attributed to Captain Errington meant whatever Sparkes and Campbell said to him and superintendent Mitchell was not admissible.

Disappointed, the Attorney-General said he would confine himself to evidence as to what occurred before Captain Errington made his threats and resumed his questioning of Fletcher. But his key boy witness declared that not only was his description of Sparkes and Campbell's actions 'after Captain Errington made these remarks', it was also 'Captain Errington's threat that induced me to make that communication'. Judge Pedder moved to stop him going any further, but as Macdowell wasn't unhappy to point out, 'the jury have it now'.[40] Fletcher, perhaps seeking to retrieve his own esteem, declared, 'I am not afraid of Captain Errington's threat, nor was not then.'[41]

More than one person in the courtroom had the same questions running through their mind. Fletcher had graphically incriminated Sparkes and Campbell, but why would he be motivated to break the boys' code and risk the wrath of his peers by being a 'dog'? Could his story of trying to prevent the continued beating of McGuire be an attempt to deflect attention from himself like an old ruse from childhood days when a boy would steal something and then run away down the street yelling out 'stop thief, stop thief', pointing to another as the culprit? And despite his apparent concern to stop the beating, why would he rush to hide in the water closet while the fatal blows were struck?

Judge Pedder also seemed to have some doubts, asking Fletcher about the stick and bludgeon he said had been used by Sparkes and Campbell before he seized them and 'chucked them'. The boy said Sparkes had held the large stick with both hands, waving it twice around his head before striking McGuire. He later found it under a table, he said, when Rose had left the yard. 'No one else was present when I found the stick,'[42] he said. He had not found the 'bludgeon'.[43]

More than one person was a tad confused. Assistant superintendent Rose had testified that he had seen stone hammers in the yard but had made no mention of seeing two sticks until, he said, Fletcher and another boy, John Smith, handed them to him, and that they had been retrieved from a water closet and a shelf. Now Fletcher was saying he had retrieved one from under a table.

Macdowell rose to his feet, probably concerned that despite the legal argument around Captain Errington's threat that the jury might still see Fletcher's evidence as unambiguously condemning the boys as murderers. Reporters in the court wondered if they would now see Macdowell question witnesses in the style that was often the talk of the town: 'Didn't he sheet it home to the witness? Didn't he give it to him? Did you see how he fixed his eye while he was castigating him to the full bent of his humour?'[44]

Macdowell sheeted home his questions. Why, he asked Fletcher, when he claimed he saw Sparkes and Campbell with the sticks near

McGuire, did he not approach or warn the overseer? 'I did not know what they were going to do.'[45]

And when he saw the blows struck, as he claimed, why did he not do anything then? 'When I saw the blow struck I did not give any information, perhaps the other prisoners would have prevented me.' Only when McGuire fell senseless 'did I interfere to prevent him getting more', and 'forced' the sticks out of the boys' hands, after which, he said 'they went and got two hammers.'[46]

As to why he did not force the hammers from them: 'I was afraid of them.'[47]

And why did he not raise the alarm? 'Because it is a rule among the boys at Point Puer that when a boy tells he is called a tell-tale, a dog.' This prompted some laughter in the courtroom.[48] And what were the consequences? 'One boy would tell another if he told anything…when a boy got the name of a dog he was beaten.'[49]

Why did he go to the water closet? 'For my own safety…I was so overcome with the sight…I could not go to speak to anyone. I was crying. I could not speak. I went there solely to seek my own safety.'[50]

Fletcher said it was only after all the boys had been removed from the gaol yard, and after Captain Errington said 'two boys have come and criminated themselves but I shall not believe them until two witnesses come forward and say they saw the action, and if you don't I'll flog every one of you', did he talk to John Smith, who was then having dinner with Harper Nicholls. While he couldn't say whether they had the same view as he did, Smith 'saw the same as I did' and after they had 'talked it over together' they went forward and spoke to Mr Rose.[51]

The next boy witness was John Smith, described by the *Hobart Town Advertiser* as 'a strong looking youth…a miscreant and a ruffian'[52] who admitted he had been before the magistrate on the morning of the attack for 'throwing his cap in the fire.'[53] He said McGuire was standing in the doorway with a piece of bread in his hand when Sparkes came from behind and struck the overseer.

Sparkes had a 'bludgeon' stick, Campbell a longer broom handle, and 'they both gave him a piece'.[54]

Asked to show how the bludgeon was used by Sparkes, Smith made a circuit over his head and struck out. He said McGuire had blood flowing from his head, and moved a little but did not speak, and 'they struck him two more blows on the head, then threw the sticks away'[55] and said 'let us go and get the stone-hammers'.[56]

At this evidence the silence of the two boys in the dock was broken. 'Sparkes [was] observed to shed tears…cried a little.'[57] Some wondered if they were tears due to a second boy's incriminating evidence, or perhaps a sign of remorse or despair over what Dickens called the 'painful reality' of what his life had become. Others thought it was possibly a realisation that his 'it was me that done it' words that were designed to elicit the esteem of other boys were now a false and perhaps fatal boast.

Smith told the court he went into the water closet to 'get out of the way' when Sparkes and Campbell were moving towards the stone hammers. 'I went there because I was shocked at the sight… could not stand it.'[58]

Like Fletcher, Smith pointed the finger at Sparkes and Campbell, but he also contradicted several aspects of Fletcher's version of events. 'I did not see anybody take sticks from them. I didn't see Fletcher any part of that time.' And while he went to the water closet, 'I can't recollect Fletcher coming in…I'm quite sure that Fletcher was not in the water closet when I went in.'[59] And while Fletcher said he had 'chucked' both sticks away and no one else was present when he found the broom handle stick, Smith said the two of them went together at Rose's request to find any sticks, he finding the 'bludgeon' behind a water-cask and Fletcher the long stick under a shelf holding bed hammocks — 'the shelf was high…he was obliged to climb up to find it…he had to get it from under three beds'.[60]

And while Fletcher said Sparkes and Campbell had each hit McGuire once, Smith maintained he saw McGuire struck twice by both Sparkes and Campbell, 'each of them in the head'.[61]

Pressed by Macdowell, he did not see the boys use stone-hammers because 'I couldn't bear to see it [I] went away…I did not see them with stone-hammers'.[62]

And why did he hide in the water closet rather than raise the alarm? 'Boys who tell what they see are called 'dogs'.…kicked and knocked about like dogs.'[63]

Macdowell was also curious about another matter. Despite Fletcher's evidence that they had 'talked it over together' Smith swore he had no conversations with Fletcher before talking to Rose about what he had seen. 'I didn't know that Fletcher had seen any part of it…[or] knew anything about it until he went to Mr Rose.' But confusingly he also said: 'I had told Mr Rose first that if Captain Errington wants two witnesses, Fletcher and I saw it done'.[64]

Endeavouring to insinuate the possibility that Smith, like some other boys, might have had their own motive against McGuire, Macdowell asked why he was inside having his dinner so late. Smith admitted 'I was down getting tried before the magistrate, that was the reason. Nicholls, Miller and myself were down getting tried. McGuire had taken us down that day.'[65] The three had returned from the magistrate's hearing together, but when the blow was struck he was the only one still inside with his dinner, as Nicholls and Miller had taken theirs outside. 'I can't tell you why Nicholls and Miller left the table and went into the yard with their dinners.'[66]

The next witness, Daniel Miller, 'a much stouter and taller fellow than either of the prisoners',[67] was adamant the weapons which killed McGuire were the stone hammers. He swore they had 'no sticks whatsoever…I saw him knocked down with a stone hammer[68] but, confusingly, also said, 'I saw the sticks in Sparkes' hands and Campbell's when he was knocked down.'[69]

He said the boys had taken two hammers from the pile in the yard while McGuire was inside having his dinner, and hidden them behind the ward door.[70] Five minutes later McGuire emerged and 'I saw him knocked down with a stone hammer…both the prisoners struck him with hammers…Campbell and Sparkes struck them, blows were struck with two hammers…about three blows were struck after McGuire fell'.[71]

Miller said he did not move from where he was sitting, but 'sat quietly, looking on…I did not move from my seat',[72] while Sparkes and Campbell, he said, walked up and down for three minutes before they returned the hammers to the pile, after which Campbell went to Mr Rose and told him 'overseer McGuire was lying most dead in the yard'.[73]

To the Attorney-General, he said he did not see Harper Nicholls at the time the blow was struck, but saw him 'walking up and down afterwards'.[74]

To Macdowell, Miller said he saw Sparkes and Campbell move the stone hammers about five minutes before McGuire was struck. 'I saw them shut the door close back on the hammers',[75] and seen the two hit McGuire two or three times before putting the hammers back.

Many in the courtroom must have now struggled with evidence about the weapons: sticks in a doorway attack and then stone hammers, or just stone hammers? Stone hammers hidden in advance before a door, or retrieved from a pile in the yard?

A fourth Puer boy, William McShea, 'a stout, resolute looking young fellow',[76] said he heard the noise of McGuire falling from the doorway and when he turned to look he saw Sparkes and Campbell emerge 'each a stone hammer in their hands' and beat the overseer 'with stone hammers' while he was on the ground.[77]

'I heard Harper Nicholls say "don't hit him on the head anymore with the hammers"…they gave a few more blows…and then threw the hammers among the rest.'[78]

As for his own attitude, McShea told Macdowell: 'I didn't want to interfere. I didn't care about it, provided I didn't get into any trouble myself. I heard Campbell tell Mr Rose that McGuire was lying half dead in the yard before I thought of mentioning it to anyone. I didn't care about it, that is my only reason.'[79]

As for the hammer produced in court it was definitely the one used in the attack: 'I know it by a bit out of the corner.'[80] He said he had mentioned this and what he had seen after superintendent Mitchell told him 'it would be a blanch on my heart if I concealed who it was'.[81]

Four Puer boys had finished their evidence for the prosecution, the number of questions growing with each: Was the murder committed by sticks or stone hammers or both? What exactly were boys other than Sparkes and Campbell doing at the time of the attack? Why would larger boys be 'frightened' of smaller boys? Why would street-hardened boys with no love of overseers be 'crying' and 'shocked'? Why were some of them so keen to portray themselves as trying to prevent McGuire's continued beating, or maintain they were in a water closet at the time? What to make of boys who said they feared being beaten as 'dogs' but were so willing to incriminate Sparkes and Campbell? And why was Harper Nicholls so often mentioned but not called to give evidence?

With lingering questions about the boys' evidence, the Attorney-General now began calling other Point Puer officers: John Mitchell, a Cornishman who had arrived in the colony as a road surveyor before becoming Point Puer superintendent, John Hepburn the gaol superintendent, Captain Arnold Errington, commanding officer of the 51st Light Infantry Regiment, and Frederick Brock the Port Arthur surgeon.

Hepburn was one of the two 'material' witnesses whose late arrival had caused the delays in the trial's commencement. The former Naval officer had been brought to Van Diemen's Land as Sir John Franklin's superintendent at Government House, a personal favour after Hepburn had helped save his life on an Arctic voyage, before moving to Point Puer to oversee the worst boys in the gaol section.

He told the court: 'I saw overseer M'Guire [sic] lying senseless on the ground; I desired the boys

to fall in; while they were in the act of doing so, boy Sparkes said...'[82]

'Objection!' roared Macdowell, reiterating his earlier argument that evidence under threat of a flogging was inadmissible. But Judge Pedder, despite having disallowed questioning of William Fletcher, was content for a government witness to proceed.

'Neither Mr Mitchell nor Captain Errington were present,' Hepburn said of Sparkes' conversation. 'It was before they arrived. No threat or encouragement was held out. Sparkes had stepped out and said: "It was me that done it."[83] Hepburn told the court his response was: "I know of no more boy likely to commit such a crime, but I shall not take your own word...I would not believe it until some other boy came forward".[84]

Macdowell seemed sceptical about Hepburn's 'confession' evidence. Given the prosecution's anxiety about evidence being contaminated by Captain Errington's threats, it seemed convenient that its last-minute witness was adamant that Sparkes had 'confessed' before Captain Errington had addressed the boys, without threat or encouragement. To Judge Pedder, Hepburn admitted 'I did not attend the inquest',[85] and was first examined in the case 'yesterday'.[86]

All eyes now turned to Captain Errington, army officer, magistrate at Port Arthur and visiting magistrate at Point Puer. One who had seemingly threatened all the boys if any culprits were not identified.

When arriving at the scene of the attack, he told the Attorney-General, McGuire was being carried away to the Port Arthur dispensary, 'apparently dead, from a blow I observed on his right ear; to me he appeared dead'.[87]

'Having arrived at the gaol, I saw Mr Hepburn; I endeavoured to ascertain who had done it. Upon entering the yard I felt...'[88]

Macdowell again roared his objection that the witness's feelings were not relevant. Judge Pedder agreed such evidence could not be heard.

To Macdowell, Captain Errington said 'I endeavoured, unsuccessfully, to ascertain who had done it'[89] before returning to Port Arthur to question McGuire, despite earlier saying he was 'apparently dead' before making a second visit to Point Puer. Yes, he knew the boys Fletcher, Smith, Shea and Nicholls, but recollected speaking with Fletcher and Smith only on his return.

Surgeon Brock, in charge of surgical cases at Port Arthur and Point Puer, described McGuire's wound when he arrived at the Port Arthur hospital: a depressed fracture on the right side of the skull, just over the ear, which penetrated the dura mater. The scalp wound was about one and a half inches long and lacerated at the edges. The portion of bone depressed was nearly two inches wide.

'My first impression was it was with stone hammers, from the appearance of the wound.'[90] When the Attorney-General showed him a hammer and the bludgeon stick, he said either could have been the weapon, but 'I still think it most likely by a hammer'.[91]

After McGuire died in the early afternoon of 30 June, Brock had examined the body at the inquest and, apart from the head wound, found two puncture wounds in McGuire's thigh — 'a very blunt stick would be likely to produce such wounds'.[92] But in answer to Judge Pedder, 'there was but one single great wound, and by one blow I should say'.[93]

At this point the Attorney-General sought permission for a reading of the deathbed statement of Hugh McGuire. He said it had been taken by Captain Errington on the day of the attack and read to McGuire. The Captain had testified, 'It is signed by Hugh McGuire, I saw him sign it.'[94]

Everyone in the court wanted to hear McGuire's statement. He had been standing in a doorway when he was struck from behind, he said. Sparkes was near the door and Campbell standing behind him, but he could not say whether any of them had struck him. 'I do not know who knocked me down.'[95] He did not see any weapons and had 'no quarrel with either Campbell or Sparkes. Nor did I threaten to bring either before the magistrate, I had no quarrel with anyone today'.[96]

'I cannot swear by whom the blow was inflicted…I do not know who knocked me down…this statement is true.'[97]

While the court room was still absorbing the murdered man's words, the Attorney-General made a surprise call for another witness: Harper Nicholls, the boy whose named had been frequently mentioned as having been before the magistrate on the morning of the attack on a charge of 'indecent conduct'. The prosecutor explained that he did not have any questions for Nicholls, but under a legal convention he called him as a material witness in 'further evidence' which had come to light since the inquest-committal, and which the defence and jury ought to have before them.

The Attorney-General might have wished he was not expected to oblige the convention as Nicholls, described as 'the most powerful in appearance of any of the boys'[98] proceeded to further contradict some of the already contradictory evidence.

As to the attack on McGuire: 'I did not see him receive any blows.[99] I did not see him receive any blows while lying down.'[100]

Of Campbell and Sparkes: 'I saw neither of them there.'[101]

And of evidence that he had pleaded with them: 'I did not say to either of the prisoners "don't beat him on the head".'[102]

With a rising murmuring in the courtroom Nicholls left, the fifth Puer boy to give evidence, the fifth variation on what transpired. On that note, Attorney-General Welsh, fulfilling his duty to outline the 'evidence' as best he could, closed the case for the Crown.

No one could tell what the jury was making of it all. Were all the boys, perhaps including Sparkes and Campbell, engaged in a 'tyranny' of deception and lies to ensure that the evidence was so contradictory and confusing that no one would hang? If Sparkes and Campbell had truly 'confessed to the deed' was it merely seeking a badge of honour when they were unaware McGuire's injuries would prove fatal? And if they were the true perpetrators, were they acting alone or at the behest of, or under intimidation by, others? Were other boys more complicit? And was the evidence of some Point Puer officers a bid to ensure boys could not kill an overseer without someone paying the ultimate price?

Judge Pedder might have wondered if the Crown evidence had convinced the jury the boys were evil devils deserving to hang, just as other juries had readily condemned young boy and girl teenagers for 'unnatural offences', sexual assault and infanticide. Or whether they wanted to hear from Edward Macdowell, who now rose to his feet, pulling his robes about him in readiness for his final address, one that might determine whether Sparkes and Campbell were two boys about to be 'saved' or condemned to hang.

15

A PUER JUDGMENT

Let no man talk of murderers escaping justice and hint that providence must sleep.
— Charles Dickens, *Oliver Twist*

Many in the packed courtroom could only look into the faces of the key players in this life and death lottery, trying to see where the truth might lie. The eyes of Sparkes and Campbell were on their counsel as he readied for his pivotal performance on the Supreme Court stage. Prosecutor Welsh perhaps worried what his rival had in store. Chief Justice Pedder, again drawing on his snuffbox, maintained his melancholy visage, weighing a clear-cut murder without clear answers and the fate of two boys swinging in the balance. The twelve jury men, squeezed on the small jury benches, knew they would soon confront a full day of conflicting evidence and the life and death question of whether to condemn or acquit.

Newspaper reporters were among those wondering what to make of Sparkes and Campbell, who they would not hear from, and their five Point Puer companions. One reporter wrote down the thought which crossed the minds of many, that the boys making statements condemning Sparkes and Campbell, or claiming indifference, were 'among the oldest and most powerful of them — certainly much more so than the prisoners'.[1]

And what to make of Point Puer itself, where boys purportedly being put on 'the right path' had variously said of the killing: 'I didn't care about it', 'I didn't want to get into any trouble myself', 'the rule is not to tell', 'I didn't want to interfere', 'I went to the water closet', 'I had no heart to tell of it', and 'I sat quietly looking on'?

Reporters wondered how a murder could have been 'wantonly perpetrated without exciting in the breast of the youthful one compassionate emotion for its hapless victim, not a detestation of the crime sufficiently strong to bring its author to justice'. Surely even their fear of other boys could not be accepted as an excuse for 'their criminal indifference'.[2]

Some were convinced Sparkes and Campbell were boy killers and deserved to have an appointment with the hangman, or that even with the discrepancies in evidence McGuire's slaying demanded retribution. Others were thinking that while the two might not be entirely innocent they were no more guilty than several other boys.

But now all eyes in the courtroom, 'crowded almost to suffocation',[3] turned to Edward Macdowell, and the pencils of newspaper reporters hovered expectantly over their notebooks.

Macdowell began his defence by focusing on the doubts inherent even in the very charges against Sparkes and Campbell. In one count, he 'observed',[4] Sparkes was charged as a principal and Campbell as accessory; in another count, Campbell was charged as principal and Sparkes as accessory. In one count, the murder was alleged to have been committed with hammers; in another, with sticks; and in a third, with hammers as well as sticks.

With due respect to 'my learned friend', he 'did not pretend to be critical upon the many counts which the Attorney-General had introduced into the information', but in law 'undoubtedly one count would have been sufficient'.[5]

Having absorbed that legal skewer, the Attorney-General had to listen for another hour as his rival, with so much professed respect, sarcastically complimented him for the manner in which he had introduced and run the case and then attacked almost every aspect of the Crown evidence.

Macdowell was much obliged 'to my learned friend…for the fairness and candour…in which he allowed his own doubts as to the manner in which the offence had been committed to appear on the face of his information'.[6] Driving home the message that the case had opened with doubt, he reminded the jury the Attorney-General:

by his own finite understanding, as he was pleased to term it… was unable to satisfy himself as to the manner in which the offence had been completed…And if the Attorney-General, with his long experience, after full examination of the depositions was unable to arrive at that conclusion, was it not too much to call upon the jury, upon such conflicting testimony, to arrive at that conclusion and to consign these two boys to an ignominious death.[7]

It was true the law allowed that offence stated in a particular way might be proved to have been committed in another, but the law never said, 'nor did common sense allow', that when an offence was said to have been committed in two different and conflicting ways by witnesses who swore they were present at its commission, that both accounts could be believed, or that one result could be deduced 'from varying and contradictory testimony'.[8]

'It is true that a slight variance in evidence is often a test of truth, and the best proof that the story was not concocted between the witnesses,' he said. 'But here, if one witness is to be believed, the other must have spoken false.'[9]

Macdowell now worked his way through the 'sworn truth' of the Puer boys.

William Fletcher swore McGuire was hit with sticks and then by stone hammers because the overseer 'had not enough', while Daniel Miller swore he saw no sticks used, only hammers. Fletcher, John Smith and William McShea said they saw Sparkes and Campbell strike blows, while Harper Nicholls said he did not see any blows and did not see Sparkes and Campbell.

Could anyone believe bigger boys, like John Smith, 'a stout fellow who saw the bloody deed…and yet instead of interfering tells you he ran into the water closet to get out of the way' and Fletcher, who swore that 'he became overcome with his feelings and went to cry…in the water closet'?[10]

And if the jury believed Fletcher that he had taken the two sticks from Campbell and Sparkes and thrown them away before retreating to the water closet, 'how could they believe…John Smith, who swore that he positively saw the prisoners themselves throw away the sticks, and did not see Fletcher near them during the whole time they were beating McGuire?'[11]

Beyond this contradiction, Macdowell asked with 'considerable animation',[12] was there 'nothing self-contradictory in Fletcher's testimony? How was it that he was able to snatch the sticks from the hands of both prisoners without any resistance on their part, and yet afterwards his resolution so failed him that when they went for the hammers he had no interference to offer, and could only go to the water closet and relieve his feelings with tears?'[13]

Fletcher said he had talked with Smith before communicating what he claimed to have seen to Captain Errington, yet Smith swore he had no such communication. It was also a 'curious felicity' which led Fletcher to the very place where the stick was later found, climbing 5 feet (1.5 m) to find under three beds 'the very thing of which he was in search, and which he must have had some good reasons for knowing where to find'.[14]

And what of the 'discriminating eye' of William McShea, who on the basis of only once seeing a particular stone hammer was able to identify it in court as one used by Campbell because of a mark 'which the jury could hardly have discerned when pointed out?'[15]

Not only in the manner of the offence, Macdowell said, but almost every circumstance connected with it did witnesses for the Crown contradict one another. Pausing to allow the jury to absorb his outline of the 'manifold and extraordinary discrepancies' alluded to by the Attorney-General, Macdowell now sought to convince the jury how it should see them.

'The true solution of all these discrepancies, of all these contradictions, and all of the suspicious circumstances, can be found by looking at the time and circumstances when and under which the witnesses had first come forward to give their testimony,' he told the court.[16]

When was that? Not 'til after Captain Errington, with a zeal whose vigour, however honourable in him, however excusable was its source, namely the horror created by the first impression of the act, still in a vigour beyond the law had assembled these boys... drawn them into a line and told them that unless someone would come forward to tell who beat McGuire he would try them and flog them all.[17]

This represented 'a strong temptation' for boys to affix the whole blame on one or other of them. As Campbell had been the first boy to reveal that McGuire was bleeding on the ground, this rendered him, in the words of Fletcher, a 'dog' and thus 'a fit victim for accusation'.[18]

Fletcher, he reminded the jury, had not taken any action because he would be called a 'dog'. Miller, who was 'reposing in dignity by the water tank at the time...he had not time to tell of it' and Michael Shea, who he could only describe as 'a miscreant and a brute' swore he said nothing because 'it was nothing to him, it was of no concern of his. This was the account given of their own conduct by the witnesses who...gave their evidence under a threat of flogging'.[19]

Sounding as sincere as possible, Macdowell said he very much 'regretted' Captain Errington had made such a threat because of the difficulties it raised with justice, and meant the jury had to exclude from their consideration all after-admissions allegedly made by Sparkes and Campbell, and to 'look with the greatest suspicion upon all the evidence which had been by such means procured'.[20]

And so, he said, nothing remained for the jury but the 'very respectable' testimony of John Hepburn, the Puer superintendent, the Crown's last-minute witness who maintained that even before Captain Errington had addressed the boys Sparkes had come forward to state 'it was me that done it'.

His evidence was 'entitled to consideration', Macdowell said, 'but it ought to be recollected that at that time no one suspected that McGuire had been dangerously beaten, and that all Sparkes had to fear from such a confession, true or not, would be a slight punishment, which would probably relieve the rest of the boys from further blame or injury in the matter'.[21]

As to Hepburn's words that he knew no boy more likely to commit the act, pausing here to make the biting aside that given all the evidence the jury could 'not believe that there existed in fact any high state of morality in any portion of the community at Point Puer',[22] the superintendent still would not believe Sparkes without any boy coming forward.

'That the unfortunate man fell victim to the brutality of some boys was sufficiently evident,'[23] Macdowell said. And it was regretted, 'deeply, for the sake of this community, that the boys at the establishment of Point Puer were not under better management… there was only one overseer present at the time and that upon that man the cruelty and vengeance of the boys were exercised'.[24]

But more fundamentally he 'regretted for the administration of justice that the real murderers would not be discovered'. The jury would be 'compelled to arrive at the same conclusion with the Attorney-General, namely that it was impossible by whom, and in what manner, McGuire had come to his death'.[25]

Although the jury would be 'unable to find who were the actual murderers',[26] Macdowell firmly told them they had evidence that, of all the boys present at the time of McGuire's murder, 'the probability was that the prisoners at the bar were the least concerned'.[27]

It had been sworn that while McGuire had no quarrel with either Sparkes or Campbell there was evidence that other boys present 'had the strongest motives for entertaining ill-will to the overseer'.[28] Harper Nicholls and John Smith, and two other boys who were not produced, had been that day convicted before the magistrate and sentenced to solitary confinement and other punishments, 'through the instrumentality and, in one instance, the accusation of McGuire'. These boys 'had a motive and an inducement to take vengeance on the overseer...left unprotected among them,' he said.[29] And, as assistant superintendent Rose had testified, he had not seen the bludgeon stick with a knob on it until that day. 'Who brought it to the prison? Who so likely as the boys who had been getting tried that morning?'[30]

Glancing at Sparkes and Campbell, Macdowell sheeted home his clear and concise conclusion: 'There existed no evidence, no suspicion, no probability of a motive.'[31] The conduct of the two boys was consistent with this statement, Campbell giving the first notice of the attack while all the other boys 'concealed the offence.'[32]

So, Macdowell said, the jury must deliver a verdict of acquittal 'on the merits of the case, and not one of mercy',[33] perhaps deliberately raising 'mercy' in case anyone on the jury was not convinced by the merits of his argument. A guilty verdict would 'punish the only boys among those who were present at the commission of the crime who were really guiltless of it', rendering an awful result, an ignominious death. 'Even the tender years of the prisoners would not be expected to protect them if their verdict was one of condemnation.'[34]

Macdowell resumed his seat and Judge Pedder patted his snuffbox before proceeding to give a detailed summary of the evidence and the matters which he thought the jury ought to properly consider. More than one person in the courtroom would have wondered if they would have to endure another of the judge's 'tedious' recitation of statutes, previous decisions and half-precedents, and his aching propensity to ensure every possible concern or doubts on behalf of any prisoner was at least put on the table for the jury to consider, adding to a jury's 'confusion and confoundedness' rather than clarity.

The newspaper reporters were not making many notes, perhaps feeling they had many pages of good reading in hand without straining to hear and record Judge Pedder's 'husky tone of voice, frequently altogether inaudible, making constant breaks, or hesitations, and taking large quantities of snuff as he proceeded'.[35]

He began by reminding the jury not to attach undue weight to the mere circumstances of a prisoner being put on trial. In England a trial occurred only after a grand jury of twenty-three first decided on the necessity, whereas in Van Diemen's Land the Attorney-General was effectively a one-person grand jury deciding who should face trial.

As to the evidence about a 'confession', Pedder had told many a jury any confessions ought to be treated 'with real jealousy…they ought to be clear and direct and not to be made out by inference and not obtained by the influence of hope and fear'.[36] This was specially the case with conflicting evidence. And on that point, the judge's jaundiced view of life in the colony was that it was 'the most dangerous doctrine possible that a juryman should be bound to believe any man merely because of evidence on oath'.[37] It was possible even the most upright person 'might be brought to the gallows upon the evidence of any scoundrel'.[38] It was only two weeks previously that Judge Pedder objected to evidence from a witness who himself appeared to have participated in a crime, as to do so would encourage men to simply give evidence against accomplices 'with the crime he himself has shared' to avoid punishment.[39]

Pedder's oft-laboured but oft-delivered message was to impress upon the jurymen that had to be guided by the probabilities of the case, and the credibility of all the facts presented. They ought not acquit prisoners 'because there was an improbable possibility that they might be innocent', but they could acquit a prisoner if they were satisfied there were sufficient doubts, beyond what was reasonable doubt, about their guilt. But if there were no such doubts, and the jury was satisfied of guilt, then they ought to return a verdict of guilty.

On 'reasonable doubt', Pedder embraced the theological roots of criminal justice, and how English Chief Justice Matthew Hale had drawn on the threads of law, philosophy and Christianity: 'It is always safer to err in acquitting, than punishing, on the part of mercy than the part of justice…the best rule in doubtful cases is rather to incline to acquittal than conviction…it is better five guilty persons should escape unpunished than one innocent person should die.'[40]

Many times Pedder had explained to a jury that if the evidence was not sufficient to convince them beyond reasonable doubt of prisoners' guilt, then under the 'benignity and reason' of the law they had to acquit. But if they were so convinced of guilt beyond reasonable doubt, then the law required them to declare them guilty and the benignity of the law would be satisfied in fairness and impartiality.

In this case, the jury had to be satisfied that Hugh McGuire's death had resulted from blows to the head, and then satisfied, after weighing the conflicting evidence, and weighing the motives and veracity of witnesses, that it was beyond reasonable doubt that either Sparkes or Campbell, or both of them, had landed those fatal blows. But if they were convinced that while McGuire had been killed by boys in his charge but not convinced beyond reasonable doubt that Sparkes and Campbell, either as principal or in concert, had felled the overseer, then it had to resolve in favour of acquittal.

In conclusion, Judge Pedder left the evidence 'to the jury to judge entirely of its credibility'[41] and after more than ten hours in the jury box, the jurymen stood at 9.20pm to leave the courtroom to weigh their judgment.

Their faces did not convey what was on their minds or what they might soon be saying in the jury room. Some were perhaps convinced the boys had been witnessed in a murderous act and had confessed, and if an inquest and Commandant Booth were convinced of their guilt, that was good enough. But others were perhaps more concerned with all the discrepancies in the evidence, and if even the Attorney-General couldn't decide whether Sparkes was the murderer, with Campbell as his assistant, or whether it was the other way around, or whether they were equally guilty, or whether they used sticks or stone hammers or both, how could the jury? Some might have felt 'we know this sort of boys will do and say whatever it takes, so how can we believe any of them?' And others might have recalled the defence lawyer's little aside that the truth of any evidence from anyone at Point Puer, including those in charge, was open to question.

Those waiting for the jury's verdict probably anticipated a division over whether there was reasonable doubt, or that McGuire's murder could not go unpunished and someone had to pay the price.

But the wondering and waiting was of short duration. In less than ten minutes the signal came back to the courtroom: the twelve jurymen had made a decision.

As the jury shuffled back into place, Sparkes and Campbell, perhaps dreading that a swift judgement meant they would soon walk the scaffold, personified Dickens' description of those in the dock: 'The prisoner watches the countenances of the jury, as a dying man, clinging to life to the very last, vainly looks in the face of his physician for a slight ray of hope…you can almost hear the man's heart beat.'[42]

Just as the author had experienced, 'a dead silence prevails as the foreman delivers in the verdict', and indeed the packed courtroom silenced and held its breath as the foreman was asked if the jury had reached a verdict on the charges against Henry Sparkes and Charles Campbell.

He replied simply: 'Not guilty.'[43]

Every man and two boys breathed out as one. Judge Pedder's gavel pronounced the long day over and retired to shed his robes and anxiety, perhaps recalling the words of his NSW compatriot, Justice William Burton, that 'we often see truth indeed represented naked, but justice is always decently clad to the feet.'[44] Attorney-General Welsh and defence counsel Macdowell also departed, another duel lost and won, as did the twelve jurymen. Each was looking for some libation relief against a long and trying day, and their role in a rare case of a Van Diemen's Land murder going unpunished.

Henry Sparkes and Charles Campbell were led away to Hobart Gaol to rejoin their five peers and await their return to Point Puer. One or more of them knew the secret truth of who killed Hugh McGuire, and whether the conflicting evidence was merely boys pursuing their own self-interests, or a devilishly clever 'dodge' to ensure none could ever be convicted of the murder, a deadly elevation of their street crime days when boys agreed 'I winna tell if you dinna tell'.

The only indisputable truth was that Hugh McGuire was now buried on the Isles des Morts at Port Arthur, murdered by one or more of the Mother Country's unwanted boys being 'saved' at Point Puer. Reporters rushed back to their newspaper offices where printers would busily set the type that would tell readers of an extraordinary chapter in the 'fluctuations of life' in Van Diemen's Land. One that had begun with RUHTRA TROP TA REDRUM type and had since revealed its true form and meaning. It was a story of murder. A very Puer murder.

POSTSCRIPT

Whether Henry Sparkes and Charles Campbell had bashed Hugh McGuire to death, were complicit in a broader murder plot, had 'confessed' merely to impress others, or were perhaps completely innocent, could not be established.

When justice in Van Diemen's Land often saw an accused sentenced to severe punishment merely on 'suspicion', what colony officials and Commandant Booth thought of being bested by a collection of 'little felons' committing murder was not recorded. And any knowledge of Benjamin Horne, the British inspector-school master who warned that boys could become murderers, went with him to his grave soon after the murder trial. Just after his report finally reached London, a Puer boy was tasked with using a stone hammer to chip out a headstone on the Isle of the Dead, close by the grave of Hugh McGuire: 'Sacred to the Memory of Benjamin [sic]

Horne, Head Master School Point Puer [sic] died 27 De [sic] 1843, aged 33 years, sincerely [sic] regretted by all who knew him'. The cause of death was not recorded.

But the Press was in no doubt of the injustice. 'The guilt rests solely with the boys,' the *Courier* said.[1] It could not believe that despite nearly twenty boys at the scene there was not sufficient evidence to detect or convict the murderers. Such an outcome might be expected with men 'experienced in the commission of crime and practised in the arts of its concealment', but in this case a murder was wantonly perpetrated 'without exciting in the breast of the youthful one compassionate emotion for its hapless victim — nor a detestation of the crime sufficiently strong to bring its author to justice'.[2]

Even to a colony well used to violence and evil it was extraordinary that boys could not only commit murder but evince such 'criminal indifference', saying they 'did not care about it' or 'had no time to tell of it'.[3] Several months later, the *Cornwall Chronicle* was still perturbed: 'Our readers cannot have forgotten the murder by the convict boys…and the acquittal of the parties…from the prevarication and loose and disjointed testimony of the witnesses who were, in fact, accomplices.'[4]

The truth behind a 'perfect' murder would remain known only to Sparkes, Campbell and their companions, all returned to Point Puer to complete their remaining days as boy convicts.

Guilty, complicit or innocent of the murder, the two boys continued to draw the attention of Commandant Booth and his regime, with constant offences of 'misconduct', insolence, disobedience, indecent language, improper possession of food, absenteeism and absconding. They were often punished on the same day for the same offences, and a year after the trial they were both found guilty of absconding and despatched to Port Arthur for eighteen months and two years respectively. They spent six months in the coal mines where Booth sent his worst prisoners, and he marked their papers as boys 'of extremely bad character'.

In the two years after the murder trial, Sparkes received sentences totalling sixty 'stripes' and sixty-four 'lashes', spent thirty-three days in solitary confinement, and more than six months in hard labour at Port Arthur, often in chains. In the three years after the trial, Campbell was punished thirty-one times, receiving 151 days in solitary confinement and 228 lashes, and periods of six and twelve months in hard labour at Port Arthur. He assaulted fellow prisoners and threatened overseers, and his sentence was extended by eighteen months. He was moved to the Cascades convict station on Tasman Peninsula with a note that he 'be kept under strict reformate treatment'.[5]

In early 1849, he was sent to Fingal probation station for three months to 'test his conduct'. He kept sufficiently quiet to receive a certificate of freedom in September 1849, but it did not mean he had finally found the 'right path'. In September 1850, he was charged with a fellow *Lord Goderich* boy of breaking into a hut at Oatlands to steal opossum skin rugs and blankets. From Campbell Town gaol he 'got over the wall'[6] and robbed another farm before being recaptured in Launceston. Once more before Chief Justice Pedder, he was sentenced to ten years transportation for both thefts. While waiting to be sent across oceans to an island hell once more, this time 2000 miles (3200 km) to Norfolk Island, he threatened overseers at the Hobart Prison barracks.

Having been exiled to Hobart Town and then further isolated to Point Puer, in May 1851 Campbell began another period of exile on an island that, like Tasmania, at times was known as an island of 'paradise'. The New South Wales Governor Sir Thomas Brisbane saw the Pacific isle, 1000 miles (1600 km) north-east of Sydney, as the best place for the worst felons, as prisoners would 'forever be excluded from all hope of return' and experience the 'new plus ultra...of convict degradation', a place of the most extreme punishment short of death.[7]

Only 15 square miles (40 km²) in area, Norfolk overshadowed even the 'emancipation or death' regime in Van Diemen's Land. Prisoners were kept in chains for most of the time, quarrying stone and felling timber. Punishment for even petty offences, such as smoking or chewing their tobacco ration outside permitted times and places, could lead to thirty lashes and months in solitary darkness in so-called 'dumb cells'. A convict involved in an 1834 uprising declared to Supreme Court Judge Sir William Burton, 'let a man's heart be what it will be when he comes here, his man's heart is taken from him and there is given to him the heart of a beast.'[8]

What was in Campbell's heart was known only to him, but he was now twenty-one, no longer the diminutive boy on his arrival at Point Puer, 17 inches (45 cm) taller at 5 feet 4 inches (1.6 m). He was listed as a Roman Catholic with a 'ruddy' complexion, able to read and write, with skill as a 'stone cutter'.

Numerous other Point Puer boys were transported to Norfolk. Many were involved in a bloody uprising and had been hanged for it. And in March 1852, Campbell recognised another among new arrivals: Henry Sparkes. He had received his free certificate around Christmas 1845, but struggled to survive. In 1847 after being allowed to stay a night in a hut at Avoca, 50 miles (80 km) south-east of Launceston, he helped himself to the owner's waistcoat and handkerchief and soon found himself before the familiar face of the Chief Justice. Pedder 'recalled the prisoner', but perhaps sensed the now twenty-year-old had endured a tough life or was just too troublesome to be kept in prison and recorded a sentence of two years in prison with hard labour but ordered he not be kept in gaol but 'on the roads'.[9]

Sparkes' record grew as he bounced between road gangs at Ross and Campbell Town in the midlands of the colony, with the usual offences of 'misconduct' and idleness leading to numerous ten-day sentences to solitary confinement, but also 'assaulting a fellow prisoner' for which he was sentenced to twelve months hard labour at Port Arthur, this further extended for improperly having tobacco, snuff and another man's boots in his possession, and breaking one of the convict-powered railway wagons.

The pattern continued in 1848, with punishments for absconding, insolence, misconduct, disobedience and improper language. Allowed some freedom in January 1849, Sparkes appears to have eked out a living in the countryside, perhaps with occasional labouring work, cadging food or theft. But in 1851, Sparkes, now described as being a 'tailor/labourer', was charged with stealing clothes from a mill at Jerusalem and was sentenced, for the second time in his life, to seven years transportation.

He arrived at Norfolk Island, in early March 1852, reunited in exile with Campbell. Their days of living a life of 'chance' had seen death sentences recorded against them as 'artful dodgers' in Aberdeen and Nottingham, a noose prepared for them as teenagers in Hobart Town, and much of their lives had been spent in punishment. Now as adults they were in a 'hell in paradise', but their shared time in a new hell did not last long.

Just two months later and a few days short of his first year at Norfolk, Charles Campbell was dead, aged twenty-two. Whether Campbell's death was due to violence, suicide or illness is unknown, but his short life was over, his final record a simple 'died at Norfolk Island 8 May 1852'.[10]

In the days before his death, the *Colonial Times* quoted a military officer relating that Norfolk's cruelty was:

> beyond belief...it is a common thing to see the miserable wretches driven to work until the blood oozes out of their shoes and streams on the ground...a mutinous spirit appears everywhere, the lives of officials are threatened...it is believed, in the end, a general outbreak will take place.[11]

And in the same month of Campbell's death, the *Freeman's Journal* in Sydney quoted 'a respectable individual' who said the treatment was 'so barbarous as to induce them to prefer death to life'[12] and two weeks later the first Catholic Bishop of Hobart, Robert Willson, demanded the British Government close Norfolk after seeing so many prisoners looking like 'living skeletons...an appalling spectacle'.[13]

The death of his co-accused seemed to have little impact on Sparkes. He continued to be punished for misconduct, smoking, disobedience, improper language and falling asleep, but also for fighting and abusing bullocks. In 1000 days on the island, he racked up more than 2400 days of punishment sentences, mostly hard labour in chains, before he was back at Port Arthur for Christmas 1854 where he received remissions on his remaining sentence for unexplained 'meritorious conduct'.

Released in May 1855, Sparkes was assigned to Ellenthorpe Hall, about 10 miles (16 km) west of Ross, where George Clark ran a farm of 20,000 sheep while his wife Hannah took in young ladies from leading families to attend her fashionable 'finishing' school. But in late December Sparkes' name featured in a 'wanted' notice:

> From the service of Mr G. C. Clark, Esq., Ellenthorpe Hall, Henry Sparks, per *Hindostan*, tried at Richmond 20 October 1851, seven years, labourer, 4 feet 8 inches, complexion fresh, hair dark brown, eyebrows brown, eyes blue, native place Nottingham, blue mark inside right arm, top of left hand injured, much pockpitted.[14]

Details of his remaining life are unclear, although the expiry of his sentences was reported in November 1858. He is believed to be the Henry Sparkes, recorded as being a labourer aged thirty, who married seventeen-year-old Harriet Nicholls in Oatlands, just 18 miles (30 km) from Ross, on Boxing Day 1860; who as a 'blind octogenarian'[15] was denied 'compassionate allowance'[16] from Oatlands Council due insufficient funds; died of 'senility' at Whitefoord, just south of Oatlands, in 1901 aged 88, and whose 'widow Harriett Sparkes', who was killed by an express train in a nearby tunnel in 1908.[17]

In a colony prejudiced against them, boys kept their Point Puer past to themselves, but it left an indelible imprint on their lives, such that their past was never shed. UNESCO has recognised the world heritage value of such convict records of Australia, citing the forced emigration of 165,000 individuals as marking 'the beginning of the modern age of globalisation by government agency'.[18] And within that heritage lies the unique story of 3000 boy convicts, and the significance of Point Puer in the history of the British Empire and the world's approach to children and criminal justice.

If government-sanctioned slavery is seen as perhaps the greatest stain on the British Empire, then the forced exile of thousands of boy convicts to the extremities of the globe to endure severe punishment amid the faint promise of a better life is perhaps its greatest crime. In an unprecedented measure of state intervention, a generation of boys were made orphans of their mother country in its war on juvenile crime, stolen away to a new colony of punishment, and held in circumstances that made many even more the enemies of the law and society and manacled their life prospects.

It's often said that history is written by victors, but the history of victims can sometimes be more truthful and revealing. And if one embraces the value of a 'bottom-up' or 'history from below' approach to understanding culture and values, and accepts Nobel Prize winner William Faulkner's view that jails are 'the true records of a…community's history',[19] then seeing history through the eyes of convicts like Charles Campbell and Henry Sparkes offers a powerful prism.

In the remotest part of the British Empire, without formal British Government approval, instructions or appropriate resourcing, Point Puer was the first prison built exclusively for boys, and a seminal foundation in the world's contemporary attitudes and debates around juvenile crime management.

In the long journey of criminally treating juvenile children as adults to society more broadly accepting age distinctions and reformatory-orientation, Point Puer Boys' Prison was an historic marker. Just as commissary officer Thomas Lempriere's carved tidal marks in the rocks off the Isle of the Dead at Point Puer remain scientific benchmarks for monitoring sea levels today. A primitive but revolutionary attempt to bring elements of juvenile strategies now employed throughout the world as authorities continue to wrestle with how to best repress juvenile criminality, rescue the at-risk, and rehabilitate. Before Parkhurst Prison on the Isle of Wight, the 'ragged schools' of education in Britain, the Mettray agricultural establishments in France, reformatory farm schools and institutions in England and the network of houses of refuge in America, Puer had taken primitive but pioneering steps to bring together a 'revolutionary mixture of geographical separation; economically driven penal labour; technical, religious and scholarly instruction; bounded play, monitorial and incentive systems'.[20]

Revolutionary in ambition, but for the 3000 boys in the Point Puer experiment, a failure in delivery. While the stated intent was to 'save' and transform boys, Puer was a largely unplanned facility on a poorly-chosen site with insufficient resources and facilities to provide adequate accommodation, supervision, moral reformation and trade training — although Benjamin Horne regarded the trade training that did exist as superior to that taught at Parkhurst — and was too exposed to older Port Arthur convicts. Perhaps the harshest verdict was that of Chartist leader John Frost: 'If I had 12 sons and it was left with me whether they should be transported or hanged, I should at once say to hang them soon rather than allow them to go to Point Puer.'[21]

And the Point Puer punishment was more profound than the years of sentence. Men transported for seven years could spend a year on a probation station and be granted a form of freedom, but boys on the same sentence could not leave Puer until they were at least sixteen and deemed literate, skilled and 'good'. But resources to make them literate and skilled were inadequate and being seen as 'good' was a challenge when even minor offences led to a perpetual and hardening cycle of more and more punishments and reinforcement as 'a bad boy'. Many 'graduated' as boys poorly equipped in mind and body for life as free men, their diminished childhood having morphed into diminished adulthood.

Recent studies suggest they also had a higher mortality than those at Port Arthur, or elsewhere in the colony or England, as a result of their impoverished childhoods of disease and poor nutrition, imprisonment, and risks of injury in their labour punishments. Perhaps fifteen percent, like Charles Campbell, died while under sentence and perhaps forty percent did not live to forty.[22] Juvenile transportees, if they survived to age twenty, had an average lifespan of fifty-five years, seven less than the average Tasmanian male.

Boys like Campbell and Sparkes were, as Quaker missionary Frederick Mackie described in 1850, 'the fruits of an evil system'.[23] Some managed to melt into Tasmanian society or migrate to another colony, developing their skills in shoemaking, masonry, carpentry or boat building. Jeremiah Melbourn, transported for stealing three pairs of trousers in Cambridge, utilised his stone mason skills to help build Princess Bridge in Melbourne. James Henry Ashton, sentenced at Essex Assizes for fourteen years for stealing a broach, formed the grandly titled Ashton's Royal Olympic Circus and for thirty-five years as Golden Ashton toured eastern Australia as the foundation of the famous Ashton company today. Another who buried his Puer background and forged a new and respectable life was Henry Smith, who became secretary of the Hobart Marine Board and was embraced by the Tasmanian Club. And one of the oldest boats in the Maritime Museum of Hobart is a wooden dinghy built by Walter Paisley, the youngest and smallest of Puer's first intake after being sentenced at thirteen for house-breaking in Buckinghamshire. He became known as 'a celebrated woodman' but retained his Puer persona as 'quick-witted...and it was said, not too honest'.[24]

Many boys remained 'not too honest' because they were returned to Hobart Town basically homeless, penniless, barely literate and often only capable of basic labouring, competing for work against free men in a society prejudiced against them. As one former Puer boy recalled:

> I was discharged to Hobart Town with a suit of fustian prison clothing, without money and without recommendation — not even sixpence to pay my first night's lodging. I was now in Van Diemen's Land, free, certainly, young, homeless, friendless and penniless.[25]

It was the same circumstances which put them onto the streets as children and the criminal path which led to Van Diemen's Land. And again, without anything like Britain's refuges for the destitute they were once more 'reduced to resort to crime to prevent starvation'.[26] Even if they were fortunate to be deemed suitable for assignment, many were rejected by their masters for misconduct, insubordination or indecent language, and 'ordered to undergo severe discipline at Point Puer'[27] or sentenced to Port Arthur.

William Scrimshaw, transported for stealing a coat in Kidderminster, Worcestershire, made his way to Sydney. But after running ahead of a crowd in Surry Hills shouting 'stop thief' he was identified as the real culprit and returned to Van Diemen's Land for another fourteen years. In 1844, he and five others absconded in a whale boat before being apprehended about 300 nautical miles (550 km) away on the northern coast of the colony, again with a death sentence recorded but instead spared by transportation for life to Norfolk Island.

Scrimshaw was one of many Puer boys who did not return from Norfolk. He, William Pearson from Nottingham, James Cairnes (who arrived with Campbell on the *Lord Goderich*), Denis Prendergast and Edward McGinniss were part of an infamous rebellion on Norfolk Island in which three constables and an overseer were bludgeoned to death. They were among twelve executed and dumped in a mass grave. Rebellion leader William Westwood, a Port Arthur convict, spoke for many when he said shortly before his hanging that he had drunk from the 'bitter cup of misery' and been so harshly treated for so long that he and others were called by heaven to execute vengeance, and prayed that at the end of his 'living death…no tyrant will then disturb my repose, I hope'.[28]

Some Puer boys endeavoured to escape but perished in the bush or were lost at sea or perhaps taken by sharks. Charles Brewer, who had been transported for seven years for pickpocketing a handkerchief worth sixpence, was among twenty prisoners who seized a boat conveying them to Norfolk Island but perished in a storm. Others escaped the system by becoming bushrangers in Tasmania or Victoria. Francis 'Captain Melville' McCallum, who lived a year with Aboriginals in Van Diemen's Land before moving to Victoria, cultivated a legend as a 19th century Robin Hood, cultured and courteous to those he robbed. His life of chance ended when he was found mysteriously strangled in his cell, but not before he used a court hearing to make the Australian public aware of the abuses suffered by prisoners on hulks at Williamstown, near Melbourne. Others who became famous outlaws were William Driscoll, known as Dido, and James Gavagan, or James Morgan, who at eleven stole umbrellas from a London doorway but after Puer was involved in the sensational robbery of £25,000 of gold from a ship at Geelong.

Violent death, suicide or execution was the fate of many. Peter Kenny (who arrived on the Lord Goderich with Campbell), James McAllister, John Childs, Hugh Mclean and Henry Belfield were among those executed for using a stone hammer or axe in the murder or attempted murder of tyrannical overseers, fellow prisoners, female companions, or firing at pursuing constables. James Platt joined the last free member of the notorious Martin Cash gang before being caught in a shootout and was executed.

The final words of young convicts like Francis McCallum and

William Westwood, detailing the tyrannical destruction of their bodies and souls, helped fuel efforts by church leaders and reformers, such as newspaper editor and preacher John West, to press for Australia's colonies to unite in rejection of convict transportation.

But the wheels of reform were slow, no less so for juveniles. Benjamin Horne recommended the closure of Point Puer at the time of the murder trial in 1843, and establishing a new facility for 800 boys on Maria Island on the east coast. His report was not sent to new Puer commandant William Champ, for fifteen months. Champ, who would become Tasmania's first Premier, responded by castigating Puer as 'a melancholy, bleak cancer spot'[29] deserving not 'one shilling more' and advocated Safety Cove as a better site offering greater protection from older convicts, despite it being just 2 miles (3 km) away from Port Arthur. And it took two years before a new colonial governor, Sir John Eardley-Wilmot, even acknowledged the Horne report in his official correspondence with London. In October 1845 he revealed he had sanctioned Horne's recommendation of a new settlement at Safety Cove, to be run along Parkhurst lines, but with a key caveat:

> Little permanent good can be effected among the lads on emerging from the establishment so long as they are allowed to associate with the old and adult convicts, especially in barracks...when not able to obtain services or wages.[30]

Eardley-Wilmot said with the growing demand for labour on mainland colonies that boys of good conduct and capable of providing for themselves ought to be 'withdrawn from the contagion of bad example'.[31] But even at the end of 1846, nearly three years since Horne advocated Puer's closure, it remained. *The Courier* was one of many to question why 'the system...continued in almost unmitigated operation'.[32]

Just as economic expediency had led to Puer being established with inadequate resources and facilities, its closure and replacement was also deemed as a cost too high. The number of boys being transported had, however, declined as Britain finally recognised juvenile delinquency as a distinct social phenomenon, curbing its heavy incarceration of juveniles under sixteen and acknowledging juvenile reformatories in Britain were a better option than transportation. In March 1849, the Government of Van Diemen's Land finally proclaimed Point Puer 'broken up...the Home Government having ceased to send out children to this colony who are now retained in the prisons at home'.[33] The remaining 160 boys were transferred to the Cascades probation station on Tasman Peninsula while they waited to be assigned as apprentices to free settlers. Governor Eardley-Wilmot urged Secretary of State William Gladstone to grant a conditional pardon to all boys who had completed a third or a half of their sentences to avoid the 'evil' of them associating with older convicts, and recommended 'well conducted' boys with some trade and literacy skills be sent to another colony in Australia or New Zealand. But the most decisive response from London was to recall Eardley-Wilmot, despite being the only governor with criminal justice experience, for perceived administrative failures.

Point Puer was closed and not replaced, and all convict transportation to Van Diemen's Land finally ended in 1853. With Van Diemen's Land becoming Tasmania, the colony endeavoured to put any 'stain' of convictism behind it, including the stain of Point Puer. While commandant and future Premier Champ described Point Puer as a 'cancer', it was promoted as 'an oasis in the desert of penal government'[34] by influential 19th century historian John West, who said that 'many boys became apprentices and many were lost sight of as prisoners and are known only as respectable men', and 1950s research claimed 'many boys, probably 2000, the majority of those who passed through Point Puer, made good'.[35]

Such generous assessments have since been repeated by other historians, and in Robert Hughes' *Fatal Shore*. But, nearing the 200th anniversary of the founding of Point Puer, its unique place in history, and a more nuanced truth, is undeniable. And while the days of Charles Dickens, convict transportation and Point Puer boys' prison may seem to be of another age, many of the challenges and issues of that time remain at the forefront of life in the 21st century.

Just as Britain wrestled with the Oliver Twists, Henry Sparkes and Charles Campbells of the world, so the world continues to struggle with teenage street gangs, juvenile crime, marginalised immigrant youth and at-risk children, and wrestle with what to do with those deemed 'dangerous', 'deprived' or 'defective'. London and Hobart Town's decrying of the absence of 'any moral or social obligations' among juvenile delinquents echoes around the world today.

And just as William Faulkner wrote, 'the past is never dead. It's not even past',[36] so fundamental questions from Point Puer days remain. What is the 'right' age of criminal responsibility? Is the concept of *doli incapax* still relevant? Why do children as young as ten and eleven murder? Are some children 'evil'? What is the balance of child-family welfare management and the responsibilities of the criminal justice system? How and when should the state intervene for at-risk children? Is there any place for corporal punishment? Is solitary confinement effective and just? Do we have the right balance of prevention, punishment and reformation?

Such questions are hotly debated when the behaviour of youth offends, shocks or panics society. It was thus in Dickensian Britain, and is ever thus. Such as in 1968 when Mary Bell, aged ten–eleven, strangled two male toddler boys to death near Newcastle upon Tyne. In 1993 when two young boys of ten lured two-year-old James Bulger from a shopping centre in Merseyside to be bashed to death. And in 2018 when two 13 year old Irish boys brutally murdered Ana Kriegel. In 1998 when the British Labour Government abandoned *doli incapax* in a 'tough on crime, no more excuses' political strategy. And in 2014 when then Home Secretary, Theresa May, introduced a new 'Anti-Social Behaviour, Crime and Policing Act', after a government White Paper replete with language echoing Dickensian Britain said it wanted to challenge and combat 'dangerous and yobbish behaviour of those who make victims' lives a misery', especially young people 'hanging about' and causing others to feel intimidated and fearful.

When the young commit offences that do not fit a conventional picture of childhood innocence, the community mood still often turns to an Old Testament view of 'evil', that 'adult crime means adult time' and authorities must 'do something' to combat a perceived threat to ordinary citizens and their way of life. In such a climate of panic, demonization and political-media pressure to not be 'soft' on crime, the debate is invariably louder on outcomes and punishment rather than causes and prevention. Questions of how society and its laws best accommodate the transition from childhood to adulthood remain as alive as they were 200 years ago: how to deem when or if the young truly understand right from wrong and the consequences of doing wrong, how and when 'protection' for childhood 'innocence' is removed so they are held accountable; and whether parliaments or courts are best placed to make such judgments.

Just as Campbell and Sparkes and their fellow Puer boys 'exhibited in their conduct neither before or at the trial any sense of the degradation of their position, or any apparent fear or anxiety as to the awful result which might await them',[37] a century and a half later at the Bulger trial Robert Thompson and Jon Venables looked 'bewildered and bored'. Twenty-five years after that famous trial the age under which children in the UK and Australia are presumed criminally incapable is still ten, among the lowest age levels in the world. This is despite other laws prohibiting and 'protecting' children from buying cigarettes, alcohol or fireworks until they are eighteen, or legally engaging in sex or buying a small animal until sixteen or seventeen.

At the time of writing, the House of Lords seemed inclined to pass a 2013 private members bill to raise the age of criminal responsibility in the UK to twelve, Lord Navnit Dholakia arguing the 'anomalous exception' when so many other laws accepted that young children do not have the capacity for making mature, adult-like decisions. The British Government has not supported the bill, but neither has it opposed it. In Australia, where about 600 children under the age of fourteen are incarcerated and children between the ages of ten and seventeen make up thirteen percent of the prison population, the Federal Government is also assessing the potential of lifting the age of criminal responsibility to sixteen.

For those between the ages of ten and thirteen the presumption of *doli incapax* may still be rebutted in Australia by proof that the child did understand the wrongfulness of their actions, but the UK Labour Government abandoned this defence in 1998, Home Secretary Jack Straw arguing a medieval law assuming youngsters ten to thirteen 'incapable of evil' unless the prosecution could prove the reverse was an archaic legal presumption which 'makes it very difficult for youth courts to convict young offenders and start the process of changing their offending behaviour'.

While few in the United Kingdom or Australia would today question the 'rightness' of children not being hanged, whipped, exiled or separated from families, the role and forms of incarceration and punishment remain vexed. Some bemoan the decline in summary corporal punishment, such as the end in the 1940s of court-ordered thrashings, the gradual outlawing of corporal punishment in schools since the mid-1980s, and changing attitudes to parental smacking. Meanwhile, the United Nations, Amnesty International and major medical organisations in Britain and the United States continue to call for solitary confinement to be outlawed for juveniles, experienced by nearly forty percent of boys in British jails, and human rights activists in Australia continue to criticise the use of solitary treatment, often referred to as segregation, seclusion, separation or isolation as breaches of international law on torture.

Much has changed since Charles Campbell and Henry Sparkes were deemed an evil enemy and exiled to Point Puer, but some of the truths spoken by some in the 19th century still resonate: 'All people who have led hazardous and forbidden lives are, in a certain sense, imaginative and if their imaginations are not filled with good things they will choke themselves with bad ones' (Charles Dickens). 'It is generally accepted that among the uneducated the human mind is more prone to evil than virtue' (William Miles).'We are all in great measure the creatures of education…We transgress the laws according to the strength of the temptations which may be raised up within us' (George Arthur). 'If a country does nothing for a man what shall allure him to obedience to its laws?' (Thomas Wontner).

Young people have always challenged or upset adult laws and norms, crime by the young a leitmotif for general social malaise, engendering moral panic or public fear over the contamination or transformation of a community or country. The boy thieves of Dickensian Britain, born in impoverished or hazardous circumstances, were denied parental, moral and educational guidance, and became friends of dishonesty and rebellion with no sense of moral degradation or social duty in their quest for identity and survival. Their story echoes today in the streets of cities around the world, challenging governments and communities.

Amid the beauty of Tasman Peninsula and the archaeological digs of Point Puer, one can hear the voices of those who were stifled from the start, those denied a voice when they lived and not featured in 'official' history. But out of pain and lost dreams they are voices deserving to be heard.

Charles Campbell and Henry Sparkes and 3000 other young boys tell us, as Dickens did in much of his work, that a single event or decision in anyone's life can be the first link of a lifetime chain of gold or thorns. That misfortune or bad behaviour ought not be excessively punished. That the courts of public and political opinion often fail to see the reality below the surface of the lives of others, leading to harshness, disinterest, prejudice, injustice and inhumanity. That moral panic and political and economic expediency, the temptation to 'do something', can have unintended and counter-productive consequences. That 'evils' cannot be resolved through presumptions, dogmas and experiments. That just as some questioned the moral right of 19th century Britain to inflict on others a burden too grievous for itself to manage, so today it remains a question of the morality of shifting unwanted people or problems elsewhere. That suppression, and lack of transparency and accountability can allow those in power to promote a self-serving 'truth'. That many in power in government, law or church are often cloaked more in the mantle of their office than their mettle and integrity.

And finally, the lost boys of Point Puer might point to the words of Psalm 72, inscribed over the Old Bailey Central Criminal Court, 'defend the children of the poor and punish the wrongdoer', and urge all to listen to the children and ask: who is the wrong doer?'

.

We must not think of old times as sad times, or regard them as anything but the fathers and mothers of the present.

— Charles Dickens, *letter*, 1860

REFERENCES

Ackroyd, Peter, 2012, *Dicken: A Memoir of Middle Age*, London: Vintage Books.

Alexander, Alison, 2013, *The Ambitions of Jane Franklin, Victorian Lady Adventurer*, Sydney: Allen and Unwin.

Anonymous, 1913, *Notes of an Officer of the Convict Department: Point Puer*, Hobart: J.W.Beattie.

Arthur, George, 1833, *Observations on Secondary Punishment*, Hobart Town: James Ross.

Bacon, Francis, 1824, *Bacon's Essay of Plantations, 1625: The Works of Francis Bacon*, London: W.Baynes and Son.

Backhouse, James & Walker, George, 1834, *Report of Visit to the Settlements of Tasman Peninsula*, Hobart: Royal Society Tasmania.

Barnard, Simon, 2016, *Marked Men and Women of Australia*, Melbourne: Text Publishing.

Barst, Julie M. 2012, *The Molesworth Report and the Dissolution of Convict Transportation to Australia, August 1838*, London: Britain, Representation and Nineteenth Century History, www. branchcollective.org

Beattie, J.W. (ed.), 1913, *Port Arthur: Van Diemen's Land*, Hobart: Port Arthur Museum.

Bennett, John Michael, 2003, *Sir John Pedder: First Chief Justice of Tasmania, 1824-1854*, Sydney: Federation Press; 2009, *Sir Alfred Stephen: Third Chief Justice of New South Wales*, Sydney: Federation Press.

Bentham, Jeremy, 1842, *The Works of Jeremy Bentham*, Edinburgh: William Tait.

Bigge, John Thomas, 1822, *Report of the Commissioner of Inquiry on the State of the Colony of New South Wales*, London: House of Commons; 1823, *Report of the Commissioner of Inquiry on the Judicial Establishments of New South Wales*, London: House of Commons.

Blackstone, William, 1765-9, *Commentaries on the Luws of England, Vol. 4*, Oxford: Clarendon Press.

Bolger, Peter, 1973, *Hobart Town*, Canberra: Australian National University Press.

Booth, Charles O'Hara, 1838, *Report on the Juvenile Establishment at Point Puer*, London: British Parliamentary Papers.

Boyce, James, 2018, *Van Diemen's Land*, Melbourne: Black Inc.

Boyer, P.W., 1974, *Leaders and Helpers, Jane Franklin's Plan for VDL, Vol. 21-2*, Hobart: Tasmanian Historical Research Association.

British Parliament, House of Commons, House of Lords Select Committee reports and commissions of inquiry, 1822, *State of the Colony of New South Wales*; 1823, *Judicial Establishment of NSW and VDL*; 1831, *Secondary Punishments*; 1835, *Gaols and Houses of Correction*; 1837, *Metropolitan Police*; 1838, *Prison Discipline in VDL*; 1838, *Transportation*; 1842, *Crime and Punishment*; 1844, *State of Large Towns*; 1863, *Discipline in Gaols and Houses of Correction*.

Brand, Ian, 1972, *Port Arthur 1830-1877: A History of Transportation*, Hobart: Jason Publications.

Brenton, Jaheel, Sir, 1842, *Memoir of Captain Edward Pelham Brenton, R.N.* London: J. Nisbet and Co.

Brenton, Edward Pelham, 1834, *Observations on The Training and Education of Children in Great Britain*, London: C. Rice.

Brooke, A. Brandon, D. & National Archives, 2005, *Bound for Botany Bay: British Convict Voyages to Australia*, Kew (UK): National Archives.

Brown, James Baldwin, 1823, *Memoirs of the Public and Private Life of John Howard, the Philanthropist*, London: T. & G. Underwood.

Buddee Paul, 1984, *Fate of the Artful Dodger*, Perth: St George Books.

Burn, David, 1905, *An Excursion to Port Arthur in 1842*, Hobart: J.W.Beattie.

Burton, F., 1986, *The Moral Lever: Education and Teachers of Convicts and Free Children at Port Arthur and Point Puer Juvenile Prison, Tasman Peninsula 1830-1877*, Hobart: National Parks and Wildlife Service of Tasmania.

Burton, W.W., 1840, *The State of Religion and Education in NSW*, London: J. Cross.

Button, Henry, 1909, *Flotsam and Jetsam: Floating Fragments of life in England and Tasmania*, Launceston: A.W. Birchall and Sons.

Bynum, W.F., Hardy, Anne, and Jacyna, Stephen, 2006, *The Western Medical Tradition: 1800-2000*, Cambridge: Cambridge University Press.

Calvert, E. Roy and Calvert, Theodora, 2016, *The Lawbreaker: A Critical Study of the Modern Treatment of Crime*, Oxon (UK): Routledge Revivals.

Campbell, Charles, 1993, *The Intolerable Hulks: British Shipboard Confinement 1776-1857*, London: Heritage Books.

Carpenter, Mary, 1851, *Reformatory Schools for the Development of the Perishing and Dangerous and Classes and for Juvenile Offenders*, London: C. Gilpin; 1853, *Juvenile delinquents, their condition and treatment*, London: W. & F.G Cash.

Castles, Alex, 1975, *The Judiciary and Political Questions: The First Australian Experience 1824-25*, Adelaide: Adelaide Law Review.

Castles, Alex, Stefan Petrow & Kate Ramsey (eds.), 2003, *Lawless Harvests or God Save the Judges, VDL 1803-1855*, Melbourne: Australian Scholarly Publishing.

Chapman, P. (ed.), 1997-2003, *Historical Records of Australia III, VII & VIII*, Canberra: Commonwealth Parliament.

Clark, Carnell Inglis, 1995, *The Supreme Court of Tasmania's First Century*, Hobart: University of Tasmania Law Press.

Clarke, Marcus, 1976, *For the Term of His Natural Life: Short Stories, Critical Essays and Journalism*, Brisbane: University Queensland Press.

Collins, Philip, 1994, *Dickens and Crime*, Basingstoke (UK): Macmillan.

Crawford, William, 1834, *Report of William Crawford, Esq., On the Penitentiaries of the United States*, London: House of Commons.

Dalrymple Alexander, 1786, *A Serious Admonition to the Publick on the Intended Thief Colony at Botany Bay*, London: Sewell.

Dalton, Trent & Lobbecke, Eric, 2018, *Voyage of the Damned*, Sydney: The Australian.

Davie, Neil, 2017, *Punishment, Reform or Expediency? Juvenile Crime and The Prison Hulks, 1822-1843*. Paris: L'Harmattan.

Davis, Richard, 1974, *Exile, Companion to Tasmanian History*, Hobart: University of Tasmania; 2006, *The Tasmanian Gallows, A Study of Capital Punishment*, Hobart: Cat and Fiddle Press.

Derricourt, William (Day), 1900, *Old Convict Days*, New York: The New Amsterdam Book Company.

Dickens, Charles, 1836, *Sketches by Boz, Illustrative of Every-day Life and Every-day People,* London: John Macrone; 1838, *Oliver Twist,* London: Richard Bentley; *1838, The Posthumous Papers of the Pickwick Club,* London: Chapman and Hall; 1839, *Nicholas Nickleby,* London: Chapman and Hall; 1841, *Barnaby Rudge,* London: Chapman and Hall; 1842, *American Notes for General Circulation,* London: Chapman and Hall; 1844, *Martin Chuzzlewit,* London: Chapman and Hall; 1849, *David Copperfield,* London: Bradbury and Evans; 1861, *Great Expectations,* London: Chapman and Hall.

Dormer, Ray & Whalen, Julie, 2003, *An Almost Incredible Academy, The Boys Prison on Point Puer,* paper, Perth: Australian Corrections Education Association conference.

Duckworth, Jeannie, 2002, *Fagin's Children: Criminal Children in Victorian England*, London: Hambledon and London.

Evans, Lloyd & Nicholls, Paul Llewellyn, 1984, *Convicts and Colonial Society 1788-1868*, Melbourne: Macmillan.

Ewing, T. J., 1843, *Statistics of Van Diemen's Land from 1838 to 1841*, Hobart: Government Printer.

Eyre, Joyce, 1939, *The Franklin-Montagu Dispute*, Honours Thesis, Hobart: University of Tasmania Modern History.

Fenton, James, 1884, *A History of Tasmania from its Discovery 1642 to the Present Time*, Hobart: J. Walch and Sons.

Field, Henry, 1884, *The Date-book of Remarkable and Memorable Events connected with Nottingham and its Neighbourhood, Part 2, 1750-1884*, Nottingham: East Midlands Collection No.3.

Forbes, Alexander, 1835, *Thoughts concerning Man's Condition and Duties in this Life, and his Hopes in the World to come*, Edinburgh: William Whyte & Co.

Forster, John, 1872, *Life of Dickens*, London: Chapman and Hall.

Forsyth, William D., 1935 *Governor Arthur's Convict System*, London: Longmans Green.

Fox, Jacqueline, 2012, *John Lewes Pedder: Some New Perspectives on a Colonial Judge*, Hobart: Tasmanian Historical Research Association; 2012, *Constructing a Colonial Chief Justice*, PhD Thesis, Hobart: University of Tasmania; 2018, *Bound by every tie of duty: John Lewes Pedder, Chief Justice of Van Diemen's Land*, Melbourne: Australian Scholarly Publishing.

Foxhall, Katherine, 2011, *From Convicts to Colonists; the Health of Prisoners and the Voyage to Australia 1823-1853*, London: Journal of Imperial and Commonwealth History, Institute of Historical Research.

Frost, John, 1856, *The Horrors of Convict Life: Two Lectures*, London: Holyoake.

Fry, Elizabeth, 1819, *Prisons in Scotland and the North of England*, London: A. Constable & Co.

Fry, Howard T., 1970, *Alexander Dalrymple and the Expansion of British Trade*, Oxford: Routledge.

Gandevia, Bryan, 1977, *A Comparison of the Height of Boys Transported to Australia from England, Scotland and Ireland, c 1840 with Later British and Australian Development*, Sydney: Australian Paediatric Journal 13, Royal Australian College of Physicians.

Gatrell, V. A. C., 1996, *The Hanging Tree: Execution and the English People: 1770-1868*, Oxford: Oxford University Press.

Giblin, Ronald Worthy, 1926, *Notes on the Journal of Captain Charles O'Hara Booth: Sometime Commandant of Port Arthur*, Hobart: Royal Society of Tasmania.

Gilchrist, Catie, 2006, *Male Convict Sexuality in the Penal Colonies of Australia 1820-1850*, PhD Thesis, Sydney: University of Sydney.

Gillespie, James Edward, 1923, *Transportation of English Convicts After 1783*, Chicago: American Institute of Criminal Law & Criminology.

Gorton, Kerin, 2002, *Carters Barracks and Point Puer: the Confinement Experience of Convict Boys in Colonial Australia 1820-1850*, PhD Thesis, Newcastle: University of Newcastle.

Gray, Freda, 2002, *What Leisure, What Pleasure, Vol. 19*, Hobart: Tasmanian Historical Research Association.

Green, Louis, 1967, "Edward Macdowell, 1798-1860", *Australian Dictionary of Biography Vol. 2*, Melbourne: Melbourne University Press.

Gurney, Joseph John, 1819, *Notes on a visit made to some of the prisons in Scotland and the north of England, in company with Elizabeth Fry*, Edinburgh: Archibald Constable and Co.

Harris, Steve, 2015, *Solomon's Noose*, Melbourne: Melbourne Books.

Heard, Dora (ed.), 1981, *The Journal of Charles O'Hara Booth, Commandant of the Port Arthur Penal Settlement*, Hobart: Tasmanian Historical Research Association.

Henderson, Andrew, 1845, *Scraps and Facts of Convict Ships*. Devonport (UK): J. Heydon.

Hill, Micaiah & Cornwallis, Caroline Francis, 1853, *Two Prize Essays on Juvenile Delinquency* London: Smith, Elder and Co.

Hitchcock, Tim and Shoemaker, Robert, 2015, *London Lives: Poverty, Crime and the Making of a Modern City, 1690-1800*, Cambridge: Cambridge University Press.

Hogg, G., 1937, *D'Entrecasteaux: An Account of his Life, his Expedition and his Officers*, Hobart: Royal Society Tasmania.

Holford, George, 1822, *A Short Vindication of the General Penitentiary at Millbank*, London: Rivington; 1826, *Statements and Observations Concerning the Hulks*, London: Rivington; 1827, Letter to the Secretary of State, London: Philanthropic Society.

Hooper, Frederick Cleverdon, 1954, *The Point Puer experiment: A study of the penal and educational treatment of juvenile transportees in VDL 1830-1850*, Master Thesis, Melbourne: University of Melbourne; 1967, *Prison Boys of Port Arthur: A Study of the Point Puer Boy's Establishment, Van Diemen's Land, 1834-1850*, Melbourne: University of Melbourne.

Horn, Pamela, 2010, *Young Offenders, Juvenile Delinquency 1700-2000*, Stroud (UK): Amberley.

Horne, Benjamin, 1843, *Report on Point Puer Boys' Prison, to Governor of Van Diemen's Land*, Hobart: Tasmanian Archives Office.

Howard, Sharon, 2015, *Bloody Code: Reflecting on a decade of the Old Bailey Online and the Digital Futures of Our Criminal Past*, Plymouth: Plymouth University.

Howell, P.A., 1967, "Sir John Lewes Pedder, 1793-1859", *Australian Dictionary of Biography Vol. 11*, Melbourne: Melbourne University Press.

Hughes, Robert, 1987, *The Fatal Shore: A History of the Transportation of Convicts to Australia 1887-1868*, London: Collins Harvill.

Humphery, Kim, 1990, *A New Era of Existence: Convict Transportation and the Authority of the Colonial Surgeon in Colonial Australia*, Sydney: Australian Society for the Study of Labour History; 1992, *Objects of Compassion: Young Male Convicts in Van Diemen's Land, 1834-50*, London: Institute of Historical Studies.

Hyam, Ronald, 1990, *Empire and Sexuality: the British Experience*, Manchester: Manchester University Press; 2010, *Understanding the British Empire*, Cambridge: Cambridge University Press.

Ives, George, 1914, *History of Penal Methods: Criminals, Witches, Lunatics*, London: S. Paul and Co.

Jackman, Greg, 2001, *Get Thee to Church: Hard work, Godliness and Tourism at Australia's first rural reformatory*, No. 19, Parramatta: Australasian Historical Archaeology.

Jackson, Skye, 1998, *From Orphan School to Point Puer*, Hons. Thesis, Hobart: University of Tasmania.

Jefferies, Julie, 2005, *The UK Population: Past, Present and Future*, London: Office for National Statistics.

Johnson, William Branch, 1970, *The English Prison Hulk*, London: Phillimore.

Johnston, Helen, 2015, *Crime in England 1815-1880: Experiencing the Criminal Justice System*, London: Routledge.

Jordan, Thomas E., 1985, *Transported to Van Diemen's Land, The Boys of the Frances Charlotte (1832) and Lord Goderich (1841), Vol. 56-4*, Washington: Society for Research in Child Development.

Kercher, Bruce, 2003, *Perish or Prosper: The Law and Convict Transportation in the British Empire, 1700-1850*, Law and History Review 21, Cambridge: Cambridge University Press.

Kerr, Joan, 1984, *Mary Morton Allport and the Status of the Colonial Lady Painter*, Hobart: Tasmanian Historical Research Association.

King, Peter 1998, *The Rise of Juvenile Delinquency in England, 1780-1840, Past and Present*, Oxford: Oxford University Press.

Kirby, Peter, 2003, *Child Labour in Britain, 1750–1870*, Basingstoke: Palgrave Macmillan.

Kyle, Avril, 1992, *Depraved Little Felons, Vol. 25-99*, Melbourne: Australian Historical Studies.

Leakey, Emily, 1882, *Clear, Shining Light, A Memoir of Caroline Woolmer*, London: J. F. Shaw.

Lempriere, Thomas, 1954, *The Penal Settlements of Van Diemen's Land*, Hobart: Royal Society of Tasmania.

Lennox, Geoff, 2006, *Thomas Lempriere: Companion to Tasmanian History*, Hobart: University of Tasmania.

Levin, Yale, 1940, *The Treatment of Juvenile Delinquency in England during the 19th century*, Chicago: Journal of Criminal Law and Criminology.

Levy, Michael Charles Ivan, 1953, *Governor George Arthur: A Colonial Benevolent Despot*, Melbourne: Georgian House.

Lilburn, Edward, 1840, *A Complete Exposure of the Convict System: Its horrors, hardships and severities, including an account of the dreadful sufferings of the unhappy captives*, Lincoln (UK): Thomas Colmer.

Low, Alex, 2005, *Sir Alfred Stephen and the Reform of the Court System in VDL, Australian Journal of Legal History*, Sydney: Macquarie University.

Maconochie, Alexander, 1838, *Report Prison Discipline in Van Diemen's Land, British Parliament*, London: W. Clowes.

Mackanass, George, 1936, *Sir Joseph Banks: His relations with Australia*, Sydney: Angus and Robertson.

Magarey, Susan, 1978, *The Invention of Juvenile Delinquency in early 19th Century England*, Sydney: Australian Society for the Study of Labour History.

Mathias, Malcolm, (ed.), 1998, *Point Puer Lads, Tried and Transported*, Melbourne: Victoria State Computer and Education Centre.

Maxwell-Stewart, Hamish, 2010," Convict Transportation from Britain and Ireland 1615-1870", *History Compass Vol. 8-11*, Wiley Online Library.

Maxwell-Stewart, Hamish, Hood, Susan, 2002, *Pack of Thieves: 52 Port Arthur lives*, Port Arthur: Port Arthur Historic Site Management Authority.

Maxwell-Stewart, Hamish & Kippen, Rebecca, 2015, "*What is a man that is a bolter to do? I would steal the Governor's axe rather than starve*": Old lags and recidivism in the Tasmanian penal colony, London: J. Routledge.

May, Margaret, 1973, "Innocence and Experience: The Evolution of the Concept of Juvenile Delinquency in the Mid-Nineteenth Century", *Victorian Studies Vol. 17-1*, Bloomington: Indiana University Press.

Mayhew, Henry & Binny, John, 1862, *Criminal Prisons of London and Scenes of Prison Life*, London: Griffin Bohn and Company.

Mayhew, Henry, 1851, *London Labour and the London Poor*, London: Charles Griffin & Co.

MacFie, Peter & Hargraves, Nigel, 1999, *The Empire's First Stolen Generation: The first intake at Point Puer 1834-39, Vol. 6-2*, Hobart: Tasmanian Historical Studies.

McConville, Sean, 1981, *A History of English Prison Administration, 1750-1877*, Abingdon (UK): Routledge.

McGoogan, Ken, 2007, *Lady Franklin's Revenge*, London: Bantam Books.

McKay, Anne, 1958, *The Assignment System of Convict Labour Van Diemen's Land 1824-1842*, Master Thesis, Hobart: University of Tasmania.

McMahon, Anne, 2017, *The Runnymede 1, 1839-40: Transporting Juvenile Prisoners*, Hobart: Tasmanian Ancestry.

Melville, Henry, 1835, *History of Van Diemen's Land*, London: Smith and Elder.

Miles, William Augustus, 1837, *A letter to Lord John Russell concerning Juvenile Delinquency*, Shrewsbury: John Eddowes; 1839, *Poverty, Mendacity and Crime*, London: Shaw and Sons.

Miller, Morris, 1973, *Pressmen and Governors*, Sydney: Sydney University Press.

Morrell, W.P., 1930, *British Colonial Policy in the Age of Peel and Russell*, Oxford: Clarendon Press.

Newlin, George, 1996, *Everything in Dickens*, London: Greenwood Press.

Newman, Terry, 2005, *Becoming Tasmania: Convicts After 1853'*, Hobart: Parliament of Tasmania; 2005, *Becoming Tasmania: Renaming Van Diemen's Land*, Hobart: Parliament of Tasmania.

Nicholls, M. (ed.), 1973, *Traveller Under Concern, the Journal of Frederick Mackie*, Hobart: University of Tasmania.

Nunn, Cameron, 2015, *Juveniles as Human Capital*, Sydney: Australian Society for the Study of Labour History; 2015, *Pure Minds, Pure Bodies, Pure Lips: Religious Ideology and the Juvenile Convict Institutions at Carters' Barracks and Point Puer*, Sydney: Journal of Religious History; Nunn, Cameron, 2017, *Becoming Men: Masculinities and the Juvenile Convict Institutions of Carters' Barracks and Point Puer in Nineteenth-Century Australia'*, Vol. 29-1, London: Institute of Historical Research, Gender & History.

Orr, Stephen, 2014, *Lost Boys of Point Puer, No. 22*, Sydney: Inside History,.

Petrow, Stefan, 1998, *Drawing Lots: Murder at the Port Arthur Settlement in 1835, Vol. 45-3*, Hobart: Tasmanian Historical Research Association.

Plater, David & Royan, Sangeetha, 2012, "The Development and Application in Nineteenth Century Australia of the Prosecutor's Role as a Minister of Justice: Rhetoric or Reality?", *Law Review Vol. 31-1*, Hobart: University of Tasmania.

Prettyman, E.R., 1966, *Some Notes on the Penal Settlement at Port Arthur*, Hobart: Tasmanian Museum and Art Gallery.

Pridmore, Walter, 2005, *Point Puer, and the Prisons of Port Arthur*, Hobart: Walter Pridmore; 2009, *Port Arthur, Convicts and Commandants*, Hobart: Walter Pridmore.

Priestly, Philip, 1985, *Victorian Prison Lives: English Prison Biography 1830-1914*, New York: Methuen.

Radzinowicz, Leon & Hood, Roger, 1957, *A History of English Criminal Law, Vol. 11*, New York: Macmillan; 1990, *The Emergence of Penal Policy in Victorian and Edwardian England*, Oxford: Clarendon Press.

Ramsland, John, 2008, "The Myth and Reality of Point Puer", *History of Education and Children's Literature, Vol. 3-1*, Macerata (Italy): Universita di Macerata.

Reid, Kirsty,2007, *Gender, Crime and Empire*, Manchester: University of Manchester.

Reynolds, George W.M., 1844, *The Mysteries of London, Vol. 3*, London: G.Vickers.

Reynolds, Henry, 1969, "That hated stain: Aftermath of transportation", *Australian Historical Studies Vol. 14*, Melbourne: University of Melbourne; 2006, *Identity, Companion to Tasmanian History*, Hobart: Centre for Tasmania Historical Studies.

Richardson, Ruth, 2012, *Dickens and the Workhouse, Oliver Twist and the London Poor*, Oxford: Oxford University Press.

Richmond, Barbara, 1956, *Some Aspects of the History of Transportation and Immigration in Van Diemen's Land 1824-1855*, Master Thesis, Hobart: University of Tasmania.

Ritter, Dr Leonara, 1999, *Inventing Juvenile Delinquency and Determining its Cure*, Canberra: Charles Sturt University History of Crime, Policing and Punishment.

Robson, Leslie Llyod, 1976, *The Convict Settlers of Australia: An Enquiry into the Origin & Character of the Convicts Transported to New South Wales & Van Diemen's Land 1787-1852*, Melbourne: Melbourne University Press; 1983, *A History of Tasmania*, Melbourne: Oxford University Press.

Romilly, Samuel Sir, 1820, *The Speeches of Sir Samuel Romilly in the House of Commons, Vol. 1*, London: Ridgway and Sons.

Roscoe, Katherine, *Van Diemen's Land 1804-1853*, www.convictvoyages.org

Rosen, Bruce, 1998, *Victorian Childhoods and the Point Puer*

Boys, pointpuer.freeservers.com; 2017, *Murder most foul: The death of an overseer at Point Puer, Vol. 64-3*, Hobart: Tasmanian Historical Research Association.

Ross, Lynette, 1995, *Death and Burial at Port Arthur*, Honours Thesis, Hobart: University of Tasmania; 2005, "The Final Escape: An Analysis of Suicide at the Penal Settlement of Port Arthur", *Journal of Australian Colonial History No. 7*, Armidale: University of New England.

Ross, James, 1837, *Excursions to Port Arthur*, Hobart: Elliston's Hobart Town Almanack.

Ross, Michael & Graeme-Evans, Alex, 1992, *A Short History Guide to Port Arthur 1830-77*, Hobart: Greenridge.

Rowbotham, Judith, 2017, "When to spare the rod? Legal Reactions and Popular Attitudes towards the (in)appropriate Chastisement of Children", *Law, Crime and History, Vol. 7-1*, Plymouth: Solon.

Samson, Jane (ed), 2001, *The British Empire*, Oxford: Oxford University Press.

Scarlett, James, 1842, *Charges Delivered to the Grand Jury of Leicester 1839*, London: John Murray.

Shaw, Alan George Lewers, 1966, *Sir George Arthur, 1784-1854*, Melbourne: Melbourne University Press; 1966, *Convicts and the Colonies: A Study of Penal Transportation from Great Britain and Ireland to Australia and other parts of the British Empire*, London: Faber.

Shipp, John, 1831, *The Military Bijou*, London: Whittaker Treacher and Co.

Shore, Heather, 1999, *Artful Dodgers: Youth and Crime in Early Nineteenth-Century London*, Woodbridge (UK): Boydell Press; 1999, *Cross coves, Buzzers and General sorts of Prigs: Juvenile Crime and the Criminal 'underworld' in the early Nineteenth Century, Vol. 39-1*, Oxford: British Journal of Criminology; 2002, *Transportation, Penal Ideology and the Experience of juvenile Offenders in England and Australia in the Early Nineteenth Century, Vol. 6-2*, Geneva: International Association for the History of Crime and Criminal Justice, Crime, History and Societies; 2003, *Inventing the Juvenile Delinquent in Nineteenth Century Europe*, Oxon: Willan; 2011, "Inventing and Reinventing Juvenile Delinquency", *Memoria Y Civilizacion, Vol. 14*, Pamplona (Spain): University of Navarra; 2011, *Reforming the Juvenile in Nineteenth and Early Twentieth Century England*, Wotton-under-Edge (UK): Prison Service Journal.

Shore, Heather & Johnston, Helen, 2015, "Introduction: Thinking about the future of our criminal past", *Law, Crime and History, Vol. 5-1*, Leeds: Leeds Beckett University.

Slee, June, 2003, *Point Puer*, Port Arthur: Port Arthur Historic Site Management Authority.

Slee, June & Tuffin, Richard, 2003, *Point Puer*, Strahan (Tas.): Escapes Conference.

Smith, Coultman, 1941, *Shadow over Tasmania*, Hobart: J.Walch and Sons.

Stephenson, J. 2019, *Digital Reconstruction of the Point Puer Boys' Prison*, Digital Heritage Studio, Tasmania. www.digitalheritagestudio.com.au

Syme, Joseph, 1848, *Nine years in Van Diemen's Land*, Dundee: W. Middleton.

Symons, Jelinger Cookson, 1849, *Tactics for the Times, as regards the condition and treatment of the dangerous classes*, London: John Ollivier; 1855, *The Reformation of Young Offenders*, London: Routledge.

Thompson, Neville, 1999, *Earl Bathurst and British Empire*, Pen and Sword, Barnsley (UK): Barnsley.

Tomalin, Claire, 2012, *Charles Dickens: A Life*, London: Penguin.

Tuffin, Richard, 2007, *Point Puer: Overview History*, Port Arthur: Port Arthur Historic Site Management Authority.

Turner, Jo & Taylor, Paul, 2017, *A Companion to the History of Crime and Criminal Justice*, Bistol: Policy Press.

Ullathorne, William Bernard, 1838, *The Horrors of Transportation Briefly Unfolded to the People*, Birmingham: R.P.Stone.

Vaux, James Hardy, 1827, *Memoirs of James Hardy Vaux*, London: Hunt and Clarke.

Wakefield, Edward Gibbon, 1832, *Householders in Danger from the Populace*, London: Effingham Wilson.

Watkins, Emma Dr., 2018, *Life-Courses of Young Convicts Transported to Van Diemen's Land*, PhD Thesis, Liverpool: University of Liverpool.

West, John, 2011, *History of Tasmania*, Cambridge: Cambridge University Press.

Whatley, Richard, 1832, *Thoughts on Secondary Punishment*, London: B. Fellowes; 1840, *Substance of a Speech on Transportation, House of Lords*, London: B. Fellowes.

White, Matthew, 2014, *Juvenile Crime in 19th Century*, London: British Library.

Whitman, James Q., 2008, *The Origins of Reasonable Doubt, Theological Roots of the Criminal Trial*, New Haven: Yale University Press.

Wiener, Martin J., 1994, *Reconstructing the Criminal. Culture, Law and Policy in England, 1830-1914*, Cambridge: Cambridge University Press.

Wilson, A.N., 2003, *The Victorians*, London: Arrow Books.

Wolter, R. M., *Sound and Fury in Colonial Australia: The Search for the Convict Voice, 1800-1840*, PhD Thesis, Sydney: University of Sydney.

Wontner, Thomas, 1833, *Old Bailey Experience: Criminal jurisprudence and the Actual Working of our Penal Code Laws*, London: James Fraser.

Wrigley and Schofield, 1981, *The Population History of England, 1541–1871*, Boston: Harvard University Press.

ABBREVIATIONS

ADB, Australian Dictionary of Biography

AOT, Archives Office of Tasmania

BPP, British Parliamentary Papers

CT, Colonial Times

HRA, Historical Records of Australia

HT Almanack, Hobart Town Almanack

HT Courier, Hobart Town Courier

HT Gazette, Hobart Town Gazette

ML, Mitchell Library, Sydney

NA, National Archives (UK)

NRS, National Records of Scotland

RS, Royal Society Collection, University of Tasmania

RSC, Royal Society Collection, University of Tasmania

TAHO, Tasmanian Archives and Heritage Office

THRA, Tasmanian Historical Research Association

UTAS, University of Tasmania

VDL, Van Diemen's Land

NOTES

CHAPTER 1

1 *Courier*, (17 February 1843).

2 Dickens, speech February 1842, www.dickens-online.info/speeches-literary-and-social p. 5

3 Dickens, *Oliver Twist*, (London: Hyde Park Editions, 2015), p. 348

4 *Hobart Town Courier*, (hereafter HT Courier), (16 August 1839).

5 *Colonial Times*, (hereafter CT), (18 July 1843).

6 *Tasmanian*, (7 November 1834).

CHAPTER 2

1 Wontner, Thomas, *Old Bailey experience: criminal jurisprudence and the actual working of our penal code of laws*, (London: James Fraser, 1833), p. 255.

2 Horn, Pamela, *The Rise of Juvenile Delinquency, 1700-2000*, (Stroud: Amberley, 2010), p. 13.

3 Shore, Heather, *Artful Dodgers, Youth and Crime in Early Nineteenth Century London*, (Woodbridge: Boydell Press, 1999), p. 35.

4 Romilly, Samuel Sir, *The Speeches of Sir Samuel Romilly in the House of Commons, Vol. 1*, (London: Ridgway and Sons, 1820), p. 108.

5 Harris, Steve, *Solomon's Noose*, (Melbourne: Melbourne Books, 2015), p. 17.

6 Wakefield, Edward Gibbon, *Householders in Danger from the Populace*, (London: Effingham Wilson, 1832), p. 7.

7 Ritter, Leonora, *Inventing Juvenile Delinquency and Determining its Cure*, paper presented History of Crime, Policing and Punishment, (Canberra: Charles Sturt University, 1999).

8 Richardson Ruth, *Dickens and the Workhouse, Oliver Twist and the London Poor*, (Oxford: Oxford University Press, 2012), p. 219.

9 Wontner, p. 260.

10 Mayhew, Henry and Binny, John, *Criminal Prisons of London and Scenes of Prison Life*, (London: Griffin Bohn and Company, 1862), pp. 406-9.

11 Dickens, *Nicholas Nickleby*.

12 Wontner, pp. 295-6.

13 Ibid., p. 305.

14 Ibid,. pp. 265, 295-6.

15 Beaumont, J.T.B., Middlesex and Westminster magistrate, cited Shore, Heather, *Cross Coves, Buzzers and General Sorts of Prigs, Vol. 39-1,* (London: British Journal Criminology, London 1999), pp. 10-24.

16 Ibid.

17 Miles, W.A., cited *Tasmanian,* (25 November 1836).

18 *Metropolitan,* (June 1836), reprinted *HT Courier* (2 December 1836).

19 Miles, W. A., *Poverty, Mendacity and Crime, Or the Facts, Examinations etc Upon which the Report was Founded,* (London: Shaw and Sons, 1839), p. 45.

20 Miles, p. 121.

21 Ibid., p. 92.

22 Ibid., p. 12.

23 Dickens letter 15 November 1848, cited Tomalin, Claire, *Charles Dickens, A Life,* (London: Penguin, 2012), p. 206.

24 Miles, p. 45.

25 Dickens, *Oliver Twist,* (London: Hyde Park Editions, 2015), p. 419.

26 Shore, *Artful Dodgers,* p. 8.

27 Blackstone, William, *Commentaries on the Laws of England, Vol. 4,* (Oxford: Clarendon Press, 1765-9), pp. 22-4.

28 Horn, p. 10.

29 Magarey, Susan, *The Invention of Juvenile Delinquency in early 19th Century England,* (Sydney: Australian Society for the Study of Labour History, 1978), pp. 11-27.

30 Wontner p. 256

31 Ousby, John, the Rev, *Evidence, Select Committee on Metropolis Police, Vol. 12,* (London: BPP, 1837), p. 167.

32 Gurney, Joseph John, *Elizabeth Fry, Notes on a Visit to Some of the Prisons in Scotland and the North of England,* (Edinburgh: Archibald Constable and Co, 1819), p. 101.

33 *Times,* (3 July 1834).

34 Shore, *Artful Dodger,* p. 9.

35 Mayhew and Binny, p. 472.

36 BPP, *Select Committee on Secondary Punishments,* (1831), p. 33.

37 *Metropolitan,* (June 1836), reprinted *HT Courier,* (2 December 1836).

38 Symons, J.C, *Tactics for the Times, as regards the condition and treatment of the dangerous classes,* (London: John Ollivier, 1849), p. 15.

39 *Tasmanian,* (25 November 1836).

40 Ibid.

CHAPTER 3

1 *First Report of the Commission into the State of Large Towns,* (London: W. Clowes and Sons, 1844), pp. 136, 250, 298-33.

2 Bynum, W.F., Hardy, Anne, Jacyna, Stephen, *The Western Medical Tradition: 1800-2000,* (Cambridge: Cambridge University Press, 2006), p. 16.

3 *Records of The Borough of Nottingham, Vol. 9,* (1849), p. 71.

4 Field, Henry, *The Date-book of Remarkable and Memorable Events connected with Nottingham and its Neighbourhood, Part 2,* 1750-1884, (Nottingham: East Midlands Collection No 3. D14 FIE, Nottingham, 1884).

5 Scarlett, James, *Charges Delivered to the Grand Jury of Leicester 1839,* (London: John Murray, 1842), pp. 10-11.

6 *Nottingham Review and General Advertiser,* (4 January 1839).

7 Ibid.

8 Miles, W.A., *A letter to Lord John Russell concerning Juvenile Delinquency,* (Shrewsbury: John Eddowes, 1837), p. 6.

9 *Nottingham Review and General Advertiser,* (4 January 1839).

10   Nottinghamshire Inspire Archives, C/QSM/1/43.

11   *Miles, Poverty, Mendacity,* p. 47.

12   *Nottingham Review and General Advertiser* (4 January 1839).

13   Wontner, p. 306.

14   Const, Francis, *Selection of Reports and Papers of the House of Commons: Prisons, Vol. 51,* (London: BPP), p. 283.

15   Dickens, *Oliver Twist, p. 350.*

16   *The Sun,* (29 August 1837).

17   Ibid.

18   Nottinghamshire Inspire Archives, C/QSR/150.

19   *Nottingham Review and General Advertiser,* (4 January 1839).

20   Ibid.

21   Nottinghamshire Inspire Archives, C/QSM/1/43.

22   *The Christian Reformer,* or *Unitarian Magazine and Review,* (London: Sherwood, Gilbert and Piper, 1849).

23   C 26/1840/95 National Records of Scotland (hereafter NRS).

24   *Aberdeen Journal* (30 September 1840).

25   Trial papers, JC26 1840/1895, AD14/40/103 NRS.

26   Ibid.

27   CON 18/1/28, Tasmanian Archives and Heritage Office (hereafter TAHO).

28   AD14/40/103/NRS.

29   Ibid.

30   JC 26/1840/95 NRS.

31   Ibid.

32   Ibid.

33   Ibid.

34   Ibid.

35   *Aberdeen Journal,* (30 September 1840).

36   Trial papers, JC26 1840/1895, NRS.

37   Gurney, p. 33.

38   Judge Coleridge, *Yorkshire Gazette,* (4 April 1840).

39   Ibid.

40   Evidence George Chesterton, Select Committee, 1831, cited Shore, *Artful Dodgers,* p. 205.

41   Miles, *Poverty, Mendacity and Crime,* p. 94.

42   Judge Coleridge, *Yorkshire Gazette,* (4 April 1840).

CHAPTER 4

1   *Tasmanian,* (25 November 1836).

2   Mayhew, Binny, p. 403.

3   *Tasmanian,* (25 November 1836).

4   Reynolds, George, *The Mysteries of London,* Vol. 3, (London: G. Vickers, 1844), p. 321.

5   Miles to Russell, p. 11.

6   Dickens, *Sketches by Boz, A Visit to Newgate,* (London: John Macrone, 1836).

7   Ibid, p. 13.

8   Miles, *Poverty, Mendacity,* p. 83.

9   Ibid, p. 44.

10   Miles to Russell, p. 10.

11   Ibid, p. 8.

12   Ibid, p. 12.

13   *Illustrated London News,* (7 January 1843).

14   Mayhew, Binny, p. 403.

15   Ibid, p. 407.

16   Ibid, p. 246.

17   *Morning Chronicle,* (14 July 1823).

18   Wontner, p. 360.

19   Dickens, *David Copperfield,* (London: Bradbury and Evans, 1849).

20   May, Margaret, *Innocence and Experience: The Evolution of the Concept of Juvenile Delinquency in the Mid-Nineteenth Century,* Victorian Studies Vol. 17- 1, (Bloomington: Indiana University Press, 1973), pp. 7-29.

21   Priestly, Philip, *Victorian Prison Lives: English Prison Biography,*

1830-1914, (New York: Methuen, 1985), p. 208

22   Ibid.

23   Dickens, *American Notes*, (London: Chapman and Hall, 1842).

24   Ibid.

25   Horn, p. 59.

26   Shore, Heather, *Transportation, Penal Ideology and the Experience of Juvenile Offenders in England and Australia in the early 19th century, Vol. 6-2*, (Geneva: Crime, History and Societies, 2002), p. 85.

27   Brenton, Jaheel, Sir, *Memoir of Captain Edward Pelham Brenton RN.*, (London: J.Nisbet and Co., 1842), p. 124

CHAPTER 5

1   Dickens, *Great Expectations*, (London: Chapman and Hall, 1861), p. 43.

2   Derricourt, William, *Old Convict Days*, (New York: The New Amsterdam Book Company, 1900) Ch. 8.

3   Vaux, James Hardy, *Autobiography, James Hardy Vaux*, (Covent Garden: Hunt and Clarke, 1827), p. 261.

4   Convict Prison Hulks: Registers and Letter Books, 1802-1849, Microfilm, HO9, National Archives (hereafter NA), Kew.

5   *London Illustrated News*, (21 February 1846).

6   Mayhew & Binny, p. 208.

7   Capper, John, *Superintendent of Ships and Vessels for the Confinement of Offenders Under Sentence of Transportation, Accounts and Papers*, (London: House of Commons, BPP, 1827), p. 139.

8   Ibid.

9   *London Illustrated News*, (21 February 1846).

10   Miles, *Poverty Mendacity*, p. 35.

11   *London Illustrated News*, (21 February 1846).

12   Miles, *Poverty Mendacity*, p. 36.

13   Reynolds, p. 123.

14   Miles, *Poverty Mendacity*, p. 37.

15   Brown, James Baldwin, *Memoirs of the Public and Private Life of John Howard, the Philanthropist*, (London: T. & G. Underwood, 1823), p. 232.

16   Wontner, p. 298.

17   Ibid.

18   Dexter, Thomas, *Report of the Select Committee on Gaols and Houses of Correction, Prisons Vol. 3*, (BPP, 1835), p. 323

19   Ibid, p. 321.

20   Ibid, p. 324.

21   Ibid, p. 323.

22   Ibid.

23   Bentham, Jeremy, *The Works of Jeremy Bentham*, (Edinburgh: William Tait, 1842), p. 120

24   Hughes, Robert, *The Fatal Shore: A History of the Transportation of Convicts to Australia 1787-1868*, (London: Collins Harvill, 1987), p. 265.

25   Bentham, p. 120.

26   Wontner, p. 360.

27   Select Committee, 1835, BPP, Series 4 & 5, Vol. 12, p. 508.

28   Brenton, Edward Pelham, *Observations on the training and education of children in Great Britain*, (London: C. Rice, 1834), p. 20

29   Holford, George, *The Convict's Complaint in 1815, and the Thanks of the Convict in 1825; Or, Sketches in Verse of a Hulk in the Former Year, and of the Millbank Penitentiary in the Latter*, (London: Holford, 1825), p. 18.

30   Capper, p. 572.

31   Brenton, *Observations*, p. 20

32   Brenton, *Memoir*, p. 124.

33 Davie, Neil, *Punishment, Reform or Expediency? Juvenile crime and the prison hulks, 1822-1843* (**Paris:** L'Harmattan, 2017), p. 17.

34 Horn, p. 59.

35 *Tasmanian*, (7 November 1834).

36 Home Office: *Convict Prison Hulks: Registers and Letter Books, 1802-1849.* NA.

37 Ibid.

38 Whatley, Richard, *Substance of a Speech on Transportation*, House of Lords, (London: B. Fellowes, 1840), p. 6.

39 Wilson, A.N., *The Victorians*, (London: Arrow Books, 2003), p. 28.

40 Russell to Glenelg, 1810-1841, BPP, C and P, T. Vol. 6, p. 739.

CHAPTER 6

1 *HT Courier*, (19 January 1841).

2 Humphrey, K., *Objects of Compassion, Young Male Convicts in Van Diemen's Land, 1834-50*, (London: Institute of Historical Research, 1992), p. 22.

3 Miles, *Poverty, Mendacity*, p. 35.

4 *Monthly Magazine* (1 March 1823).

5 PRO ADM 101/43/8 NA.

6 Ibid.

7 ADM/43/8 Medical Journal *Lord Goderich*, 1841 NA.

8 Surgeon Colin Browning, to William Burnett, Physician General of Admiralty, 13 December 1848, ADM 105/36, NA.

9 Brooke and Brandon, David, *Bound for Botany Bay: British Convict Voyages to Australia, (Kew:* Bloomsbury, National Archives, 2005), p.107.

10 Dickens, *The Posthumous Papers of the Pickwick Club*, (London: Chapman and Hall, 1838), p. 148.

11 House of Commons, *Report of the Commissioner of Inquiry on the Judicial Establishments of NSW and Van Diemen's Land*, (BPP, 1823), p. 37.

12 Stephen, Alfred, Letter August 1837, *Report to Parliament on the State of Prison Discipline in Van Diemen's Land, (London,* W. Clowes, 1838), p. 14.

13 Whatley, *Transportation*, p. 5.

14 *Edinburgh Review, Vol. 4*, (Edinburgh: Archibald Constable and Co. 1823), p. 104.

15 Bacon, Francis, *Bacon's Essays of Plantations*, (London: W.Baynes and Son, 1824), p. 335.

16 Whatley, Richard, *Thoughts on Secondary Punishment*, (London: B. Fellowes, 1832), p. 4.

17 Whatley, *Punishment*, p. 84.

18 Bathurst letter, *Report of the Commissioner into the State of the Colony of NSW 1819-1823*, (House of Commons, BPP, 1822), Enclosure 2.

19 *Report of the Commissioner into the State of the Colony of NSW 1819-1823*, House of Commons, 1822; *Report of the Commissioner of Inquiry on the Judicial Establishments of NSW and Van Diemen's Land*, House of Commons 1823; Project Gutenberg Molesworth TC 1837 Question 1061.

20 The Laws relating to the Government of His Majesty's Ships, Vessels, and Forces by Sea, *Articles of War*, Article 29, 1749.

21 Despatch, William Denison to Earl Grey, 9 September 1850, *BPP, Vol. 10*, (C & P, 1851), p. 54.

22 Lord Russell letter to James Stephen, 20 October 1836; Despatch, Lord Glenelg to Sir John Franklin, 28 October 1836, Appendix B, *Report from Select Committee on Transportation 1838*, Vol. 3, (BPP, 1837-61), pp. 214-5

23 Sir John Barrow, Lord Commissioner of Admiralty, to Treasury, 1 November 1839, cited Gilchrist, Catie, *Male Convict*

Sexuality in the Penal Colonies of Australia 1820-1850, (Sydney: University of Sydney, PhD thesis, 2006), p. 272.

24 *The Spectator,* (19 October 1833).

25 Lilburn, Edward, *A Complete Exposure of the Convict System: Its horrors, hardships and severities, including an account of the dreadful sufferings of the unhappy captives,* (Lincoln: Thomas Colmer, 1840), p. 6.

26 *Monthly Magazine* (1 March 1823).

27 Ibid.

28 Ibid.

29 Brooke and Brandon, p. 128.

30 Humphery, Kim, *A New Era of Existence: Convict Transportation and the Authority of the Colonial Surgeon in Colonial Australia,* (Labour History No. 59, November 1990), p. 63.

31 McMahon, Anne, *The Runnymede 1, 1839-40, Transporting Juvenile Prisoners,* (Hobart: Tasmanian Ancestry, September 2017).

32 Medical Journal of *Lord Goderich,* 1841, ADM/43/8 NA.

33 Medical Journal of *Hindostan,* 1840-41, ADM 101/34/NA.

34 Brooke & Brandon, p. 188.

35 Henderson, Andrew, *Scraps and Facts of Convict Ships,* (Devonport UK, 1845), p. 13.

36 *Launceston Courier,* (25 January 1841).

37 Thomas Logan, Surgeon-Superintendent, *Albion,* 1828, cited Brooke and Brandon, p. 216.

38 Ibid.

CHAPTER 7

1 *CT,* (26 January 1841).

2 *True Colonist and VDL Despatch* (Hereafter *True Colonist*), (21 January 1841).

3 *CT,* (23 November 1841).

4 *HT Courier,* (2 May 1829).

5 *True Colonist,* (21 January 1841), *HT Courier,* (19 January 1841).

6 *CT,* (23 November 1841).

7 Bathurst letter, 6 January 1819, *Historical Records of Australia,* Series 1, Vol. 10.

8 *Launceston Courier,* (17 May 1841).

9 Syme, Joseph, *Nine years in Van Diemen's Land,* (London: W. Middleton, 1848), pp. 12-13.

10 *HT Courier,* (2 May 1829).

11 Arthur to Goderich 1 December 1827, *HRA,* Series 3, Vol. 6, p. 369.

12 Arthur to Under Secretary Stanley, 12 August 1828, *HRA,* Series 3, Vol. 7, p. 470.

13 *HT Courier,* (2 May 1829).

14 Ibid.

15 West, John, *History of Tasmania,* (Launceston (AUS): Henry Dowling, 1852; reprinted Cambridge: Cambridge University Press, 2011).

16 *HT Courier,* (2 May 1829).

17 Ibid.

18 Ibid.

19 Clarke, Marcus, *For the Term of His Natural Life, Short Stories, Critical Essays and Journalism,* (Brisbane: University Queensland Press, 1976), p. 483.

20 Horne, Benjamin, *Report on Point Puer Boys' Prison, to Governor of Van Diemen's Land,* 7 March 1843, C0280/157/520 TAHO.

21 Arthur to Robert Hay, 8 February 1834, GO33/16 TAHO, p. 277-280.

22 Hooper, F. C., *Prison Boys of Port Arthur: A Study of the Point Puer Boy's Establishment, Van Diemen's Land, 1834-1850,* (Melbourne: University of Melbourne, 1967), p. 9.

23 *The Colonist,* (19 November 1833).

24 *Austral-Asiatic Review,* (24 December 1833).

25 *CT,* (18 August 1835).

26 *Austral-Asiatic Review,* (24 December 1833).

27   Ibid.

28   Shaw A.G.L., *Arthur, Sir George (1784-1854)*, (Melbourne: Melbourne University Press, 1966), pp. 32-38.

29   Samson, Jane (ed.), *The British Empire*, (Oxford: Oxford University Press, 2001), p. 58.

30   Arthur to Bathurst, 21 April 1826, *HRA* III, v p. 152.

31   Levy, Michael Charles Ivan, *Governor George Arthur: A Colonial Benevolent Despot*, (London: Georgian House Melbourne, 1953), p. 127.

32   Arthur to Bathurst, 22 May 1827, cited Richmond, p. 66.

33   *CT*, (18 August 1835).

34   *CT*, (8 October 1839).

35   Melville, Henry, *History of Van Diemen's Land*, (London: Smith and Elder, 1835), p. 127.

36   Evidence, *Select Committee on Transportation, Parliamentary Papers, House of Commons*, (London: BPP, 1837-8), p. 518, p. 669.

37   West, p. 451.

38   Newlin, George, *Everything in Dickens*, (London: Greenwood Press, 1996), p. 528.

39   Shaw, *Arthur*, cited *Australian Dictionary of Biography*, Melbourne University Press, Melbourne, 1979.

40   Arthur to Bathurst, 3 July 1825, No. 10, GO 33/1, TAHO.

41   *HT Courier*, (7 August 1835).

42   *HT Gazette*, (21 September 1816).

43   *Colonist*, (6 May 1834).

44   *Tasmanian*, (21 November 1834).

45   *HT Almanack*, (Hobart: James Ross, 1831), p. 7.

46   Booth, Charles O'Hara, *The Journal of Charles O'Hara Booth, Commandant of the Port Arthur Penal Settlement*, Heard, Dora (ed.)., (Hobart: Tasmanian Historical Research Association (hereafter THRA), 1981), CSO 1/483/10748.

47   CSO1-1-690 TAHO.

48   Ibid.

49   Ibid.

50   Heard, Dora (ed.), *The Journal of Charles O'Hara Booth*, (Hobart: THRA, 1981), p. 165.

51   *Moniteur*, (3 January 1803).

52   Booth, 24 December 1833, CSO1-1-690 TAHO, p. 151.

53   Ibid., p. 147-8.

54   Ibid.

55   Ibid.

56   Ibid., p. 167.

57   Spode, 7 January 1834, CSO1-1-690 TAHO, p. 151.

58   Ibid., (24 December 1833), p.151.

59   *Tasmanian*, (17 January 1834).

CHAPTER 8

1   CON 18/1/28 TAHO.

2   CON 33/1/4 TAHO.

3   CON 18/1/28 TAHO.

4   *CT*, (26 January 1841).

5   Ibid., (23 November 1841).

6   Molesworth, Sir William, *Report of Select Committee of the House of Commons on Transportation*, (London: Henry Hooper, 1838), p. 50; Molesworth, *Speech, House of Commons, 5 May 1840*, (London: Henry Hooper, 1840), p. 21.

7   Hogg, G. *D'Entrecasteaux, An Account of his Life, his Expedition and his Officers*, (Hobart: Royal Society Tasmania, 1937), p. 58.

8   *Tasmanian*, (7 November 1834).

9   *HT Courier*, (21 August 1835).

10   *Fraser's Magazine*, (September 1842), p. 41.

11   Leakey, Caroline, letter, cited Leakey, Emily, *Clear Shining Light: A memoir of Caroline Woolmer*, (London: J.F Shaw, 1882), p. 41.

12   *HT Courier*, (7 August 1835).

13 CSO, (14 February 1833); *CT*, (19 February 1833).

14 Arthur to Hay, 8 February 1834, GO33/16 TAHO, p. 277-280.

15 Arthur to Colonial Secretary Burnett, 5 May 1834, CSO 1-716-15655 TAHO.

16 *Booth Journal*, p. 168.

17 *Tasmanian*, (17 January 1834).

18 *HT Courier*, (15 April 1836).

19 Ibid., (16 December 1836).

20 *HT Almanack*, (1837), p.94.

21 Burn, p. 10.

22 Sir John Franklin to Lord Glenelg, 8 April 1837, *BPP, Vol. 22*, (1838), Appendix B #37.

23 *CT*, (23 November 1841).

24 *Booth Journal*, p. 167.

25 Booth Letter, AOT GO33/16 TAHO, p. 281.

26 *Booth Journal*, p. 158.

27 Ibid.

28 Ibid., p. 222.

29 CON 31-35 TAHO.

30 CON 32-1-1 TAHO.

31 Ibid.

32 Booth to Adam Turnbull, Secretary to Governor Arthur, 6 February 1834, GO33/16 TAHO, p. 281.

33 Arthur to Hay, 8 February 1834, GO33-16 TAHO, pp. 277-280.

34 Hooper, *Prison Boys*, p. 3.

35 **Arthur,** p. 36.

36 Arthur to Stanley, 16 May 1834, cited Levy, pp. 175-6.

37 Booth Journal, p. 51.

38 SC Transportation, *BPP, Vol. 22*, No. 38, (1838), Appendix B, p. 220.

39 Ibid.

40 Miles, *Poverty, Mendacity*, p. 92.

41 West, p. 247.

42 Franklin to Lord Glenelg, 8 April 1837, *BPP, Vol. 22*, p. 215.

43 Ives, George, *History of Penal Methods: Criminals, Witches, Lunatics*, (London: S. Paul and Co., 1914), p. 126.

44 *Booth Journal*, pp. 256-257.

45 Montgomery, J., *Letter to W.A. Miles, 21 December 1834*; Miles, *Poverty, Mendacity*, p. 159.

46 *Booth Journal*, p. 173.

47 *Booth Journal*, p. 33.

48 *Booth Journal*, p. 50.

49 *Booth Journal*, p. 33.

50 Booth, *Select Committee on Transportation*, 24 July 1837, Appendix B, Encl. 2, p. 219.

51 THRA Vol. 32/6, 1971.

52 CSO 5/236/6021 TAHO.

53 Horne, p. 3.

54 Ibid., p. 7

55 *Booth Journal*, p. 222.

56 Buddee, Paul, *Fate of the Artful Dodger*, (Perth: St George Books, 1984) p. 17.

57 Giblin, R.W., *Notes on the Journal of Captain Charles O'Hara Booth*, (Hobart: Royal Society of Tasmania, 1926), p. 158.

58 *Booth Journal*, p. 48.

59 Burn, 1842, p. 19.

60 Booth Journal, p. 48.

61 Arthur to Colonial Secretary Burnett, 5 May 1834, CSO 1-716-15655 TAHO,

62 Lempriere, p. 61.

CHAPTER 9

1 Blake, William, *A Little Boy Lost, Songs of Innocence and of Experience*, (London: William Blake, 1794).

2 Dickens, *Oliver Twist, p. 97*

3 *HT Courier*, (7 August 1835).

4 Booth to Montagu, 24 July 1837, *Booth Journal*, p. 75.

5 Ibid.

6 Horne, p. 15.

7 Booth, 13 January 1834, CSO1-1-690 TAHO, p. 154.

8   Dr James Scott, 5 April 1834, CSO1-1-690 TAHO, p. 168.

9   Booth, *SC Transportation 1838 report, BPP, Vol. 22*, p. 220.

10 Symons, J.C., *The Reformation of Young Offenders*, (London: Routledge, 1855), p. 2.

11 SC Transportation, *BPP, Vol. 22-38*, (1838), Appendix B #38, p. 220.

12 Ibid.

13 Prettyman, p. 14.

14 Dickens, *Lying Awake,* Essay, 1846.

15 Ullathorne, William Bernard, *The Horrors of Transportation Briefly Unfolded to the People*, (Birmingham: R. P. Stone, 1838), p. 14.

16 *VDL Commercial and Agricultural Advertiser*, (7 January 1834).

17 Commandants Report, *Tasmanian Papers 129*, (1 June 1836), reel 1383 ML; SC Transportation, *BPP. Vol. 22*, (1838), Appendix B #38, p. 220.

18 MacFie, Peter, & Hargraves, Nigel, *The Empire's First Stolen Generation: The first intake at Point Puer 1834-39, Vol. 6-2*, (Hobart: THRA, 1999), p. 143.

19 *Empire*, (16 October 1867).

20 CON 31-1-21; CON18-1-13 TAHO.

21 CON 32-1-2; CON 32-1-3 TAHO.

22 Frost, John, *The Horrors of Convict Life*, (London: Holyoake, 1856), p. 25.

23 Hughes, p. 402.

24 Frost, p. 28.

25 *Voice*, (14 October 1933).

26 *Booth Journal*, p. 52.

27 Crawford, William, *Report of William Crawford, Esq., On the Penitentiaries of the United States*, (London: House of Commons, 1834), p. 15.

28 Maxwell-Stewart, Hamish & Hood, Susan, *Pack of Thieves: 52 Port Arthur lives*, (Port Arthur: Port Arthur Historic Site Management Authority, 2002), p. 11.

29 SC Transportation, *BPP, Vol. 22* (1838), Appendix B #38, p. 220.

30 *Booth Journal*, p. 51.

31 Commandants Report, *Tasmanian Papers 129*, (1 June 1836), reel 1383 ML.

32 Lempriere, p. 95.

33 Backhouse, James and Walker, George, *Report of Visit to the Settlements of Tasman Peninsula*, (Hobart: Royal Society Tasmania, 1834), CSO/1/807/17244 TAHO, p. 55.

34 Alexander, Alison, *The Ambitions of Jane Franklin, Victorian Lady Adventurer*, (Sydney: Allen and Unwin, 2013), p. 93.

35 *Booth Journal*, p. 51.

36 *Tasmanian*, (7 November 1834).

CHAPTER 10

1   Whatley, *Speech on Transportation*, p. 30.

2   *Spectator, (*28 April 1838).

3   *HT Courier*, (8 January 1841).

4   *Booth Journal*, p. 51.

5   Horne, p. 26.

6   Ibid.

7   Ibid., p. 25.

8   Ibid., p. 26.

9   *Notes of an Officer of the Convict Department, Point Puer,* (Hobart: J. W. Beattie, 1913).

10 Burn, p. 28.

11 Horne, p. 26.

12 Lempriere, p. 94.

13 Horne, p. 26.

14 Ibid.

15 Miles, p. 11.

16 Lempriere, p. 94.

17 Horne, p. 20.

18 *Booth Journal*, p. 50.

19 *Booth Journal*, p. 52.

20 Dickens, *Oliver Twist,* p. 30.

21 Ross, James, *Excursion to Port Arthur*, (Hobart: HT Almanack, 1837), p. 59.

22 *Booth Journal*, p. 204.

23 Prettyman, E.R., *Some Notes on the Penal Settlement at Port Arthur*, (Hobart: Tasmanian Museum and Art Gallery, 1966), p. 77.

24 *Illustrated Australian News*, (1 January 1890).

25 Lempriere, p. 91.

26 Ibid., p. 101.

27 Lempriere, p. 97.

28 Hughes, p. 403.

29 Dickens, *Oliver Twist.* p. 388.

30 Horne, p. 6.

31 Ibid., p. 19.

32 CON 33-1-4 TAHO.

33 Ibid.

34 *Booth Journal*, p. 202.

35 Frost, p. 16.

36 Executive Council, EC 4-5 TAHO, (28 September 1837).

37 Booth Letter, (25 September 1837), CSO 5-81-1752 TAHO.

38 Ibid.

39 Frost, p. 16.

40 Horne, p. 7.

41 Ibid.

42 Ibid, p. 4.

43 CON 37-1-6 TAHO.

CHAPTER 11

1 *HT Advertiser*, (28 July 1843).

2 Horne, p. 25.

3 *VDL Gazette*, (11 June 1841).

4 *HT Courier*, (11 June 1841).

5 *CT*, (7 December 1843).

6 Ibid., (7 December 1844).

7 Coultman Smith, *Shadow over Tasmania*, (Hobart: J. Walch and Sons, 1941), p. 74.

8 Horne, p. 25

9 Ibid., p. 9.

10 Ibid.

11 Ibid., p. 4.

12 Ibid., p. 7.

13 Ibid., p. 10.

14 Lempriere, p. 95.

15 *HT Courier*, (8 December 1847).

16 *Notes of an Officer*, p. 43.

17 Ibid.

18 Horne, p. 25.

19 *CT*, 1 August 1843.

20 CON 33-1-22 TAHO.

21 Ibid.

22 Ibid.

23 *HT Advertiser*, (28 July 1843).

24 Ibid., (21 November 1843).

25 *CT*, (8 December 1835).

26 *HT Advertiser*, (28 July 1843).

27 Ibid.

28 Ibid., (23 August 1843).

29 Ibid.

30 Ibid.

31 Ibid., (28 July 1843).

32 Ibid., (23 August 1843).

33 *CT*, (1 August 1843).

34 Ibid.

35 CON 33-1-22 TAHO.

36 SC 1/11 195/908 TAHO.

37 SC 1/11 195/908 TAHO.

38 Letters from Colonial Secretary's Office to Captain Booth, (1836-18).

39 *Booth Journal*, p. 198.

40 *Austral-Asiatic Review*, (17 February 1843).

41 Booth to Franklin, 1 July 1843, CSO22-1-79 TAHO.

42 Ibid.

43 Ibid.

44 Ibid.

45 Ibid.

46 Ibid.

47 *CT*, (18 July 1843).

48 Whatley, p. 25.

49   *CT,* (11 April 1843).

50   *HT Advertiser,* (11 April 1843).

51   *Austral-Asiatic Review,* (28 April 1843).

52   Maconochie, Alexander, *Report Prison Discipline in Van Diemen's Land, British Parliament,* (London: W. Clowes, 1838), p. 3.

53   *Cornwall Chronicle,* (4 February 1843); *Launceston Courier,* (6 February 1843), *Cornwall Chronicle,* (6 May 1843); *CT,* (14 March 1843).

54   *Examiner,* (19 July 1843).

55   Ibid.

CHAPTER 12

1   Crime, Police and Convicts, *BPP, Vol. 42,* 1843, Encl. 3-1, p. 82.

2   Ibid.

3   Carpenter, Mary, *Reformatory Schools, for the Children of the Perishing and Dangerous Classes, and for Juvenile Offenders,* (London: C. Gilpin, 1851).

4   McConville, Sean, *A History of English Prison Administration,* 1750-1877, (Abingdon: Routledge, 1981), p. 205.

5   Sir James Graham, *House of Commons, Vol. 42,* (1842), p. 447.

6   Ibid.

7   Ibid.

8   *Southern Cross,* (24 November 1843).

9   Hill, Miciah & Cornwallis, C.F., *Two Prize Essays on Juvenile Delinquency,* (London: Smith, Elder and Co, 1853), p. 324.

10   McGoogan, Ken, *Lady Franklin's Revenge, A True Story of Ambition, Obsession and the Remaking of Arctic History,* (London: Bantam Books, 2007), p. 268.

11   Colonial Secretary letter to Booth, Jan 12, 1841, *Booth Diary,* (Hobart: THRA, 1981).

12   Maconochie, p. 5.

13   Ibid., p. 6

14   Maconochie report, (Hobart: William Gore Elliston, 1838), p. 9.

15   *VDL Chronicle,* (10 December 1841).

16   Horne, p. 1.

17   Ibid., p. 39.

18   Ibid., p. 4.

19   Ibid., p. 15.

20   Ibid., p. 15.

21   Ibid., p. 3.

22   Ibid., p. 24.

23   Ibid.

24   Ibid.

25   Ibid., p. 22.

26   Ibid.

27   Ibid., p. 23.

28   Ibid., p. 25.

29   Ibid., p. 7.

30   Ibid., p. 4.

31   Ibid., p. 19.

32   Ibid.

33   Ibid.

34   Ibid., p. 31.

35   Ibid., p. 25.

36   Ibid., p. 25.

37   Ibid., p. 26.

38   Ibid., p. 26.

39   Ibid., p. 26.

40   Ibid.

41   *Austral-Asiatic Review,* (10 February 1843).

CHAPTER 13

1   *Launceston Examiner,* (19 July 1843).

2   *Sydney Herald,* (1 May 1841).

3   *CT,* (13 August 1830).

4   Ibid.

5   Ibid., (3 May 1842).

6   Ibid., (13 August 1830).

7   *True Colonist,* (29 April 1836).

8   Dickens, *Sketches by Boz,* (London: John Macrone, 1836), Ch. 24, p. 1.

9   *Launceston Examiner,* (19 July 1843).

10 *CT,* (25 July 1843); *Austral-Asiatic Review,* (28 July 1843).

11 *Launceston Examiner,* (19 July 1843); *Courier,* (4 August 1843).

12 Hobart Town Advertiser, (25 July 1843).

13 Ibid.

14 *Courier,* (25 July 1843), *CT,* (1 August 1843).

15 *CT,* (25 July 1843).

16 Ibid.

17 *Austral-Asiatic Review,* (15 September 1843).

18 Miles, *Poverty, Mendacity,* p. 69.

19 *Launceston Advertiser,* (13 July 1843).

20 *Courier,* (21 July 1843).

21 *CT,* (21 July 1843).

22 Ibid., (3 January 1843).

23 Ibid., (24 July 1829).

24 Bennett, *Pedder,* p. 104.

25 Miller, Morris, *Pressmen and Governors,* (Sydney: Sydney University Press, 1973), p. 167.

26 *Courier,* (28 August 1854).

27 Calder Papers, ML A594.

28 Howell, P.A., *Pedder, Sir John Lewes (1793–1859),* (Melboune: Melbourne University Press, 1967).

29 *CT,* (24 May 1842).

30 Ibid., (3 January 1843).

31 Ibid., (3 January 1843).

32 *Mercury,* (27 August 1843).

33 Ibid., (28 August 1873).

34 *Launceston Courier,* (11 April 1842).

35 *Cornwall Chronicle,* (9 April 1842).

36 Bennett, John Michael, *Sir John Pedder, First Chief Justice of Tasmania, 1824-1854,* (Sydney: Federation Press, 2003), p. 65.

37 *Launceston Advertiser,* (13 July 1843).

38 *Austral-Asiatic Review,* (16 June 1843).

39 *CT,* (26 June 1829).

40 Bennett, John Michael, *Sir Alfred Stephen, Third Chief Justice of New South Wales,* (Sydney: Federation Press, 2009), p. 229.

41 *Courier,* (4 August 1843).

42 *Launceston Examiner,* (19 July 1843).

43 *Courier,* (4 August 1843).

44 *True Colonist,* (22 March 1844).

45 *CT,* (21 July 1848).

46 Ibid.

47 Ibid.

48 *Austral-Asiatic Review,* (17 February 1843).

49 *Sydney Herald,* (1 May 1841).

50 *CT,* (1 August 1843).

51 *Courier,* (4 August 1843).

52 *CT,* (1 August 1843).

53 Ibid.

54 Ibid.

55 Ibid.

56 Ibid.

CHAPTER 14

1   *HT Advertiser,* (28 July 1843).

2   Ibid.

3   Ibid.

4   *CT,* (1 August 1843).

5   *HT Advertiser,* (28 July 1843).

6   *Courier,* (4 August 1843).

7   *HT Advertiser,* (28 July 1843).

8   *CT,* (1 August 1843), *HT Advertiser,* (28 July 1843).

9   Ibid.

10 *CT,* (1 August 1843).

11 *HT Advertiser,* (28 July 1843).

12 *HT Advertiser,* (28 July 1843); *Courier,* (4 August 1843).

13 *HT Advertiser*, (28 July 1843).

14 Ibid.

15 *CT*, (1 August 1843).

16 *CT*, (1 August 1843).

17 *HT Advertiser*, (28 July 1843); *Courier* (4 August 1843); *CT* (1 August 1843).

18 Dickens, *Sketches by Boz*, (London: John Macrone, 1836), Ch. 24.

19 *HT Advertiser*, (28 July 1843).

20 *CT*, (1 August 1843).

21 *CT*, (1 August 1843); *Courier*, (4 August 1843); *HT Advertiser* (28 July 1843).

22 *HT Advertiser*, (28 July 1843).

23 *HT Advertiser*, (28 July 1843), *Courier*, (4 August 1843).

24 *CT*, (1 August 1843).

25 *Courier*, (4 August 1843).

26 *HT Advertiser*, (28 July 1843).

27 *Courier*, (4 August 1843).

28 *HT Advertiser*, (28 July 1843).

29 Ibid.

30 Ibid.

31 *Courier*, (4 August 1843).

32 Ibid.

33 *HT Advertiser*, (28 July 1843).

34 *Courier*, (4 August 1843).

35 *HT Advertiser*, (28 July 1843).

36 Ibid.

37 Ibid.

38 *Courier*, (4 August 1843).

39 Ibid.

40 Ibid.

41 Ibid.

42 Ibid.

43 Ibid.

44 *CT*, (21 July 1848).

45 *Courier*, (4 August 1843).

46 Ibid.

47 Ibid.

48 *HT Advertiser*, (28 July 1843).

49 *Courier*, (4 August 1843); *CT*, (1 August 1843); *HT Advertiser*, (28 July 1843).

50 *Courier*, (4 August 1843); *HT Advertiser*, (23 August 1843).

51 *Courier*, (4 August 1843).

52 *HT Advertiser*, (28 July 1843).

53 *CT*, (1 August 1843).

54 *Courier*, (4 August 1843).

55 *HT Advertiser*, (28 July 1843).

56 *Courier*, (4 August 1843).

57 *HT Advertiser*, (28 July 1843); *CT*, (1 August 1843).

58 *Courier*, (4 August 1843); *HT Advertiser*, (28 July 1843).

59 *Courier*, (4 August 1843).

60 Ibid.

61 *CT*, (1 August 1843).

62 Ibid.

63 Ibid.

64 *Courier*, (4 August 1843).

65 *Courier*, (4 August 1843); *HT Advertiser*, (28 July 1843).

66 *Courier*, (4 August 1843).

67 *HT Advertiser*, (28 July 1843).

68 *HT Advertiser*, (28 July 1843); *Courier*, (4 August 1843).

69 *Courier*, (4 August 1843).

70 *HT Advertiser*, (28 July 1843).

71 *CT*, (1 August 1843); *Courier*, (4 August 1843).

72 *HT Advertiser*, (28 July 1843); *Courier*, (4 August 1843).

73 *HT Advertiser*, (28 July 1843).

74 *Courier*, (4 August 1843).

75 *HT Advertiser*, (28 July 1843).

76 Ibid.

77 *Courier*, (4 August 1843); *CT*, (1 August 1843).

78 *Courier*, (4 August 1843).

79 Ibid.

80 Ibid.

81 Ibid.

82 *Courier*, (4 August 1843).

83 *HT Advertiser*, (28 July 1843); *CT*, (1 August 1843).

84 *CT*, (1 August 1843); *Courier*, (4 August 1843).

85 *Courier,* (4 August 1843).

86 *HT Advertiser,* (28 July 1843).

87 *Courier,* (4 August 1843).

88 Ibid.

89 Ibid.

90 Ibid.

91 Ibid.

92 Ibid.

93 Ibid.

94 Ibid.

95 *HT Advertiser,* (28 August 1843).

96 *Courier,* (4 August 1843).

97 *Courier,* (4 August 1843); *HT Advertiser,* (28 July 1843).

98 *HT Advertiser,* (28 July 1843).

99 Ibid.

100 *Courier,* (4 August 1843).

101 Ibid.

102 Ibid.

CHAPTER 15

1 *Courier,* (4 August 1843).

2 Ibid.

3 *CT,* (1 August 1843).

4 *Courier,* (4 August 1843).

5 Ibid.

6 Ibid.

7 Ibid.

8 Ibid.

9 Ibid.

10 Ibid.

11 Ibid.

12 *CT,* (1 August 1843).

13 Ibid.

14 Ibid.

15 Ibid.

16 *Courier,* (4 August 1843).

17 Ibid.

18 Ibid.

19 Ibid.

20 Ibid.

21 Ibid.

22 Ibid.

23 *CT,* (1 August 1843).

24 Courier, (4 August 1843).

25 Ibid.

26 Ibid.

27 *HT Advertiser,* (28 July 1843).

28 *Courier,* (4 August 1843).

29 Ibid.

30 *HT Advertiser,* (28 July 1843).

31 Ibid.

32 Ibid.

33 *Courier,* (4 August 1843).

34 Ibid.

35 *CT,* (10 July 1829).

36 *HT Gazette,* (26 June 1824).

37 *Tasmanian,* (26 May, 8 June 1832).

38 Ibid.

39 *Launceston Examiner,* (12 July 1843).

40 Whitman, James Q, *The Origins of Reasonable Doubt, Theological Roots of the Criminal Trial,* (New Haven: Yale University Press, 2008), p. 193.

41 *Courier,* (4 August 1843).

42 Dickens, *Sketches by Boz,* (London: John Macrone, 1836), Ch. 24.

43 *CT,* (1 August 1843).

44 *Sydney Herald,* (1 May 1841).

POSTSCRIPT

1 *Courier,* (4 August 1843).

2 Ibid.

3 Ibid.

4 *Cornwall Chronicle,* (22 November 1843).

5 CON 37-1-6 TAHO.

6 *Cornwall Chronicle,* (18 September 1850).

7 Hughes, *Fatal Shore,* p. 365; Brisbane to Under-Secretary Horton, 24 March 1825, *HRA, Series I: Vol. 11,* p. 553.

8   Burton, W. W., *The State of Religion and Education in NSW*, (London: J. Cross, 1840).

9   *Launceston Examiner*, (6 January 1847).

10   CON 37-1-16 TAHO.

11   *Colonial Times*, (20 April 1852).

12   *Freeman's Journal*, (20 May 1852).

13   Hoare, Merval, *Norfolk Island – An Outline of its History 1774-1968*, (Brisbane: University of Queensland Press, 1969), pp. 61-2.

14   *HT Gazette*, (15 January 1856).

15   *Daily Telegraph*, (12 September 1895).

16   *Mercury*, (16 September 1895).

17   *North West Advocate*, (15, 16 October 1908).

18   www.unesco.org.

19   Faulkner, William, *Intruder in the Dust*, (New York: Penguin, 1975), p. 49.

20   Jackman, Greg, *Get Thee to Church: Hard work, Godliness and Tourism at Australia's First Rural Reformatory*, (Parramatta: Australasian Historical Archaeology No. 19, 2001), p. 10.

21   *Leeds Times*, (18 October 1856).

22   Watkins, Emma Dr, *Life-Courses of Young Convicts Transported to Van Diemen's Land*, (Liverpool: University of Liverpool, PhD thesis, 2018), pp. 223-262.

23   Nichols, M (ed.), *Traveller Under Concern, the Journal of Frederick Mackie*, (Hobart: University of Tasmania, 1973).

24   *Huon and Derwent Times*, (17 August 1939).

25   *The Empire, (*16 October 1867).

26   *Courier, (*7 February 1847)

27   *Tasmanian Weekly Dispatch*, (24 July 1840).

28   *Bell's Life in Sydney, (*28 November 1846).

29   Champ letter, 29 July 1844, Tasmanian Papers 60 A1089 ML.

30   *Launceston Examiner*, (23 December 1846).

31   Ibid.

32   *Courier, (*12 December 1846).

33   Ibid., (10 March 1849).

34   West, p. 395.

35   Hooper, *The Point Puer Experiment*, (Melbourne: University of Melbourne, 1955).

36   Faulkner, William, *Requiem for a Nun*, (New York: Random House, 1950).

37   *Courier, (*4 August 1843).

INDEX

ACKNOWLEDGEMENTS

Firstly a salute to Charles Dickens, whose newspaper and literary pursuit of truth and justice remains as readable and relevant as when he first put pen to paper, and to those editors and reporters of early newspapers in Van Diemen's Land who courageously built foundations of press freedom within a hostile and repressive political environment.

I thank all the subsequent writers, academics, librarians, researchers, historians, historic societies, genealogists, archivists and museums who appreciate that 'the past is never dead, not even past'. It means our understanding of history, the story of us, becomes ever richer and more relevant, more truthful and more nuanced.

I salute all those authors and researchers who continue to enrich the historical narrative of Tasmania, such as Hamish Maxwell-Stuart, Alison Alexander, James Boyce, Stefan Petrow, Dianne Snowdon, Lucy Frost, Trudy Cowley and Simon Barnard.

I am grateful to all those staff and their supporting contributors and volunteers who collect, curate and cross-fertilise pages of written history into digital databases for the world to freely access, including Google, Gale Cengage, the Gutenberg Project, UK National Archives, British Library, British Newspaper Archive, the Old Bailey, Gale Cengage, National Library of Australia, Trove, Tasmanian Archive and Heritage Office, the international Digital Panopticon Project, VDL Founders and Survivors Project, Port Arthur Historic Site Management Authority, Female Convicts Research Centre, the Digital Reconstruction of Point Puer Boys' Prison project.

I particularly thank some of the many individuals and organisations who went beyond the normal call of duty to help in this project: Professor Heather Shore, of Leeds Beckett University and co-convenor of History UK, for her enthusiasm and assistance on crime and penal history; Dr Emma Watkins, of Middlesex University, for sharing her own research on 19th century juvenile offenders; the National Archives staff in Kew; National Records of Scotland search supervisor Jessica Evershed, and research assistant Peter Hammond; Nottinghamshire Archives archivist Mrs Jaime McMurtrie; Dr Tim Causer of the Bentham Project at University College London; policy analyst Renee Menart at the Center on Juvenile and Criminal Justice (US); Catherine Pearce and Anthony Black at the State Library of Tasmania and Tasmanian Archives and Heritage Office; Heather Excell at the University of Tasmania's Special and Rare Collections library; Port Arthur Historic Site Management Authority heritage programs officer James Westcott and resources officer Fiona Gleadow; Allport Library and Museum of Fine Arts archivist Caitlin Sutton; John Bryson QC, Dr Greg Woods QC and Dr Eugene Schofield-Georgeson and Professor Shaunnagh Dorsett at University Technology Sydney for colonial law guidance; Dr Jacqueline Fox, of University of Tasmania, for sharing her research on Judge Pedder; Professor Mark Finnane and his Prosecution Project at Griffith University; University of Tasmania research associate the late Dr Bruce Rosen for sharing his Puer research; Kevin Curtis at Damosels Printers Block for advice on typesetting; Lord Navnit Dholakia for advice on UK juvenile criminal law.

More personally, I thank David Tenenbaum and his team at Melbourne Books for their enthusiasm, editing, proof-reading and ideas; Robert Drewe, Ray Henderson, Meg Keneally, Muriel Reddy, Geoffrey Blainey, Alison Alexander, Andrew Rule, Peter Denmead and Michael Gawenda for their for timely friendship and encouragement; my beloved mother for showing that age is no barrier to discovery; my wife Maureen and Shannan, Elise and Clayton for their love; and those who are nameless but remain a very golden link in the chain of my 'fluctuations of life'.

THE AUTHOR

Steve Harris is a former editor, editor-in-chief and publisher at *The Age, Sunday Age* and *Herald Sun*. He is a fourth generation Tasmanian, life member of the Melbourne Press Club, and a John S. Knight Fellow at Stanford University. He is the author of *Solomon's Noose*, the true story of a young Van Diemen's Land convict who became Queen Victoria's longest serving hangman, published in 2015, and *The Prince and the Assassin*, the true story of Australia's first royal tour and the nation's first portent of world terror, published in 2017.